2/04

D1571810

This Is Rebel Music

A
volume
in the

Series

Series co-editors:

DAVID FARBER,
History, University of New Mexico

BETH L. BAILEY,
American Studies, University of New Mexico

Also available in the CounterCulture Series:

New Buffalo: Journals from a Taos Commune
by Arthur Kopecky

This Is Rebel Music

The Harvey Kubernik InnerViews

Harvey Kubernik

UNIVERSITY OF NEW MEXICO PRESS | ALBUQUERQUE

Library of Congress Cataloging-in-Publication Data

Kubernik, Harvey, 1951–
  This is rebel music : the Harvey Kubernik innerviews /
Harvey Kubernik.—1st ed.
      p. cm. — (CounterCulture series)
  ISBN 0-8263-3104-1 (alk. paper)
  1. Rock musicians—Interviews.   2. Rock music—Social aspects.
I. Title.   II. Series.
  ML385 .K924 2003
  781.66'092'2—dc22

                          2003018070

Design and composition: Melissa Tandysh

For Morris and Sonia Jairow

Table of Contents

Illustrations

Prologue

I partially owe this book's title to the influence of both Bob Marley and Phil Spector. But a vital acknowledgment depends on a riff from a moving tribute I was asked to attend several years ago, when friends and family gathered in Hollywood on Sunset Blvd. at the Directors Guild of America to remember film director and producer Stanley Kramer. I was invited by his daughter Casey Kramer to the memorial service. Sidney Poitier, in a eulogy for his dear friend and mentor, spoke in slow, deliberate, and penetrating single adjectives.

He gave an incantation that in just a few lines brought a man's life into focus. Afterwards, I talked briefly to Poitier and complimented him on the power of his carefully chosen words. He asked my occupation. "Writer, music journalist, poet, record producer, musical archivist." Poitier motioned me a little closer to continue our conversation. "Young man," he reminded me, extending his hand, "Stanley Kramer, rebel."

This Is Rebel Music: The Harvey Kubernik InnerViews is a document of the moment involving two people creating oral history. My interview subjects are involved in a question and answer forum akin to that used by writer Stanley R. Greenberg, who inaugurated the genre of docudrama for television in the early 1970s, and who liked to call the form the "theater of fact." Most of the pieces are built around a long, deep, unmediated Q and A; a one-on-one with a dozen or so men and women I've come to know.

Most everyone interviewed for this book is over thirty—not thirty years of age, but thirty years or more of knowledge and experience. What they tell us about their lives and their careers will change how you think about the relationship between music and the music industry and how you hear the sounds that these men and women created, played, produced, promoted, and made an integral part of the culture.

This collection includes people who have sold millions of records. It includes people who built the music industry. And it includes a special few men and women who influenced the artists who made the music.

The decades I've toiled in the recording studio, as both a player and producer of over fifty albums, inform the materials you'll be reading. My interview methods and style have developed over decades, based on hundreds and hundreds of taping sessions and hangs with musicians, poets, authors, DJs, professional basketball players, and writing for rock-'n'-roll-themed television assignments. My techniques have also been shaped by childhood exposure to national TV shows hosted by Ed Sullivan, Nat King Cole, Steve Allen, Dick Clark, Oscar Levant, Jack Parr, and Soupy Sales, as well as "Shrimpenstein," viewed on KHJ-TV (Channel 9) in the Los Angeles area.

For me as a teenager, hearing Alan Watts and Krishnamurti speak over the Pacifica Radio airwaves was a monumental soul-stirring signal of communication and life path direction.

In addition, I'd like to volunteer that my stints as a drummer and studio percussionist have fused a little bit of beat and tension to the conversations collected in *This Is Rebel Music*. You'll feel it.

The subsequent work I've done as a spoken word producer for jazz arranger and activist Buddy Collette, The Doors' Ray Manzarek, Jefferson Airplane's Paul Kantner, legendary Basketball Hall of Fame coach and player John Robert Wooden, and another Basketball Hall of Famer, now TV broadcaster, Bill Walton, in addition to other recording sessions, meals, performances, lectures, brief meetings, and interviews over the years with arrangers and producers like Herb Alpert, Gene Page, Barry White, Lou Adler, Terry Melcher, Jan Berry, Nik Venet, Jimmy Webb, Henry Mancini, Ray Manzarek, Bob Crewe, Willie Mitchell, Chris Darrow, Jimmy Bowen, Rick Henn, Jerry Wexler, Tom Dowd, Denny Bruce, David Carr, Jim Latham, Jill Fraser, Tony Visconti, Jack Nitzsche, Quincy Jones, Kim Fowley, Leon Russell, Snuff Garrett, Andrew Loog Oldham, Elmer Bernstein, Andre Previn, Paul A. Rothchild, Jimmy Miller, Sonny Bono, Norman Whitfield, Burt Bacharach, Stevie Wonder, Phil Spector, Brian Wilson, and Sir George Martin have definitely enhanced my own chord book. And I've learned it's all in the wrists.

Then add hearing Carmen Dragon lead the Hollywood Bowl Orchestra and the Glendale Symphony Orchestra; Gordon Jenkins, Nelson Riddle, and Don Costa conduct for Frank Sinatra; Lee Hazelwood's charts and haunting neo-classical arrangements on those Nancy Sinatra sides; Al DeLory's sharp production and arrangements on the classic 1960s Glen Campbell records; Marty Paich's orchestrations on the Mamas & the Papas' albums and his terrific string additions to the telling songs of Spirit; Paul Buckmaster's jagged symphonic strings behind Elton John on those early albums; Curtis Mayfield with Johnny Pate during his collaborations with the Impressions, and later as a solo artist. That's not even counting the impact and education I received from devouring Chess, Philles, Vee-Jay, Motown, and Stax Records that I know slightly informed my sense of timing and structure that underscores *This Is Rebel Music*.

In addition, the musical scores and atmospheric cues from the black and white episodic television series, "The Twilight Zone," "Mr. Lucky," "77 Sunset Strip," "Route 66," "Naked City," "The Outer Limits," and "The Fugitive," as well as regional Los Angeles and Hollywood-based music shows "Hometown Jamboree," "Town Hall Party," "Wink Martindale's Dance Party," "Stars of Jazz," "Frankly Jazz," "Make Believe Ballroom," "The Johnny Otis Show," "Lloyd Thaxton," "9th Street West," "Hollywood A Go Go," "Groovy," "Shindig," "Where the Action Is," "Shivaree," and reflections beamed in color from "Hullabaloo," "Hollywood Palace," and "The Johnny Cash Show" fortify the subsequent pace and rhythm revue guiding *This Is Rebel Music*.

On reflection, this book might have had its physical birth one night after one of the countless "Midnight Special" TV tapings I went to in Burbank in the mid-'70s, or from what I gleaned a few years later by producing and hosting my own talk and music TV program, "50/50," in 1978.

Since 1972, when my work was first published in the *Los Angeles Times Sunday Calendar* section, I've always believed my recorded journalistic experiences and artist dialogues could live within the pages of a book.

I'll also cop to the fact that the cinnamon-flavored iced tea at any Good Earth restaurant has magic properties.

One of my goals in constructing *This Is Rebel Music* was to serve the gathering while maintaining a free agent independent posture. That's why my fieldwork and first-hand endeavors make some of these reads, I hope, vital and alluring. I hope it's valuable to you as well.

The Rolling Stones are a recurring theme in the program. I was listening to a lot of Stones music the last few years, and went to a bunch of their last Hollywood recording sessions at Ocean Way Studios in 1997 and a slew of their 2002 concerts. I hope you're receptive to Marianne Faithfull, Andrew Loog Oldham, Keith Richards, and Jack Nitzsche helping tilt the table towards Jagger and Co. You're gonna get some Beatles, too. Ravi Shankar with George Harrison, and Jim Keltner's warm soulful chat with me on his friend George. Allen Ginsberg discussing working with Paul McCartney.

I know one thing: I went to places and spaces where I'd never been.

My vision of the book continued to emerge in the process and I am thankful every moment. I am so grateful for my life.

The majority of the talks and interviews in these pages were executed throughout the last half of the '90s and the early part of this century. In a mid-'90s meeting with Ram Dass in North Hollywood, he gave me instruction to "Honor the incarnation."

A handful of these interviews like Berry Gordy, Jr., Marianne Faithfull, Keith Richards, Ravi Shankar, Allen Ginsberg, and Chrissie Hynde were assigned to me, some after comical negotiation, by Roy Trakin, editor at *HITS* magazine, a music and radio trade weekly. Trakin has been receptive to a lot of things I've hurled at him. We both wrote for *Melody Maker* in the U.K., shortly after college in the 1970s. One of the published sessions with Ray Manzarek came by way of *Goldmine*, the record collecting publication, and another was initiated from the U.K. music magazine, *MOJO*. My conversation with Andrew Loog Oldham had its origin as a *discoveries* cover story. One of my late '80s interviews with Jack Nitzsche was used in *Goldmine* as well, and *New Times* was the source for another Nitzsche expedition. Allen Ginsberg suggested that I "go talk to Marianne Faithfull." There were also choices and voices I wanted to fuse into the rhythm room, like Grace Slick, Little Steven, and reggae music scholar and author, Roger Steffens.

Overall inspiration for this book comes from Bob Marley, whose image is displayed in a place of honor in my residence. I saw him and the Wailers many times. "This is rebel music" is a line combo culled from his songs, "Roots, Rock, Reggae" and "Rebel Music (3 O'clock Road Block)," and I thank him for the title (which is also a nod to Phil Spector's production of the Gene Pitney composition, "He's a Rebel").

I think this book represents a spectrum of personalities, talents, and different approaches to all these different artists that very few people would actually be able to gather into a single collection. I wanted to cover issues that some writers aren't even aware of, how these things relate, and how I bring the action to the forefront. You may have read a whole lot about Keith Richards and the Rolling Stones or Ray Manzarek and the Doors, but I'll bet you haven't heard them talk about some of the musical topics that I've asked them to detail.

Sometimes I bring a captainship to my role. Like with Marianne Faithfull, I knew what kind of cigarettes she smoked and what she drank. It was a move I got from renaissance man and Yogananda follower, Chris Darrow, who always said the best way to know a woman is to know her smoke and drink requirements. I obtained a better and longer interview with Marianne by arriving with her menthols.

Feel the exploration that permeates *This Is Rebel Music*. Sacred movements and executed rhythm shots for your eyes. Go with the know flow. The participants are now members of a thematic print lineup combining components of dance floor and the Hollywood Ranch Market that imbued the book contents one late evening, after I heard on my radio the command of Charles

Wright & the Watts 103rd Street Rhythm Band, demanding in their song to "Express Yourself."

I eventually produced the word-salad collaborators and their individual chapters like a huge Slauson Line movement, reminding myself I was once on the corner of Fountain and Vine in Hollywood, dancing on the TV shows "American Bandstand" and "Shebang." Their language, observations, and melodic creations drive my passionate rock-'n'-roll drum circle. Audio analog interview meetings that initially began between us have now grown through faith and destiny into a gift expanding our consumer audience demographic. I had a lot of fun, too.

I hope that there are times and moments when my encounters with these wonderful artists make you receive knowledge, bliss, and reinforcement that you may blend into your daily life and ritual.

This Is Rebel Music is a spiritual design, and it's reminiscent of Tibetan monks making a mandala out of sand.

I've had many interactions and been in the recording studio with Brian Wilson of the Beach Boys over the years. I was recently invited to his sixtieth birthday party on the evening I finished the manuscript of *This Is Rebel Music*. Brian opened my gift to him and said, "Music is in your soul." I know the same comment can apply to everyone in the following pages.

This anthology breathes because it is the exact document of a moment, and involves quest and disclosure, thus making a very pure oral history. There's nothing that is manipulated in terms of text and tone. In today's short attention society, people are revealed here because of what they are saying, not because of what someone is saying about them.

This Is Rebel Music involves surf and turf wisdom, and it doesn't involve illusion and delusion. It involves the actuality of the people. It's a whole era I'm bringing for examination. It's a big basketball court and everyone is on my team. Besides producing and directing *This Is Rebel Music*, maybe my supplemental role in the book is as tour guide, influenced by the now sorely missed voice of the Los Angeles Lakers professional basketball team, radio and TV broadcaster, Chick Hearn, who delivered a "word's-eye-view" to his audience. Chick didn't just call the game—he brought you into the game. So, in *Rebel Music*, you're now on the floor with me in our triangle offense. I'm in the center and the ball handler constantly. I have a very personal interest in who is on the roster. The people are *alive* inside the raw questions and responses.

And by the way, this is a real-deal Hollywood-based presentation, shaped and defined by the geographical fact that I was born on the border of Hollywood and Los Angeles. So, naturally, I absorbed and mirrored everyone's projections, and felt very comfortable stocking the squad and my debut book with music and literary veterans.

Open your heart and rock with me on this one. Nothing needs to be justified.

This Is Rebel Music, a cast of characters who wear no masks for protection and deflection. A book where the heard word and found sound reflect a territory of inclusion, not exclusion.

The talented voices you read in *This Is Rebel Music* really extended their schedules to speak to me. We all benefit from their honesty and the journeys depicted in the various interludes.

Here's a dozen men and women who are true rebels. *This Is Rebel Music: The Harvey Kubernik InnerViews*, an intentional community, a collective for all.

"Somebody Up There Likes Me."
Harvey Kubernik,
Los Angeles, California

Ray Manzarek:

"Bloody Red Sun of Fantastic L.A."

For keyboardist and Doors co-founder Ray Manzarek, it's always been about words and music. When a young poet-turned-songwriter first read him some of his words on the beach in Venice, California, some four decades ago, Manzarek was already hearing the sound of the Doors in his head. "Those are the best lyrics I've ever heard," he told Jim Morrison. You know what happened next.

That commitment hasn't changed. Morrison, of course, has been gone over thirty years. But the music of the Doors, the words of Jim Morrison, and the vision of Ray Manzarek, are more powerful—and more pervasive—than ever.

No less than five Doors songs found their way into the mega-hit film, "Forrest Gump"—one, "Soul Kitchen," appears on the soundtrack album. Prior to that, Manzarek directed three films featuring his former band, "The Doors: Live At The Hollywood Bowl," "The Doors: Dance On Fire," and "The Doors: The Soft Parade."

Ray Manzarek was born in Chicago on February 12, 1939. Before he attended UCLA and earned an M.A. in Cinematography from the film school, he graduated from DePaul University with a B.A. in Economics.

Of course, Manzarek has not spent the last twenty-five years living off his memories. His post-Doors creative endeavors have been many and diverse. He has recorded a number of solo albums, including an electronic adaptation, with Philip Glass, of Carl Orff's "Carmina Burana." He produced the first four albums by Los Angeles punk-rock band X.

More recently, Manzarek released a CD and video—both titled "Love Lion"—featuring his collaboration with renowned poet Michael McClure.

Photo by Todd Gray, courtesy of Ray Manzarek.

Manzarek also contributed musical coloring to numerous other spoken word recordings that I arranged, and recently added his piano and organ parts to "Men Are Made in the Paint," a double CD audio instructional guide to the world of basketball, featuring Basketball Hall of Famer Bill Walton. I later produced Manzarek's own audio biography, "The Doors: Myth and Reality."

I saw the Doors in concert at the Inglewood Forum in 1968 and have known Ray since 1973, conducting my first interview with him in 1974 for the influential U.K. music weekly, *Melody Maker*.

In the early '70s at San Diego State University, I was involved with an accredited literary course and had Jim Morrison's *Lords & New Creatures* on the required book list, with some Doors albums as mandatory items as well. Manzarek heard about the class, and was very complimentary to me

The Doors 1968 L.A. Forum concert advertisement, from the collection of Kirk Silsbee.

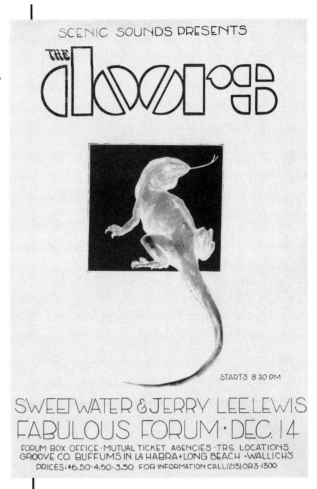

and about the students studying his collaborator Jim as a writer. We've been friends ever since.

In 1990, I was the project coordinator of the "Jack Kerouac Collection" CD box set and asked Manzarek to contribute one of the liner notes to that package.

It seems every five years we do a lengthy interview. I thought the last couple of conversations of the mid-'90s and a new 2002 dialogue really addressed some new Doors-related areas not often chronicled in the band's literature.

This is one case where actually knowing someone is an asset when reporting on him. I've been quoted in several books on the Doors as well, and feel part of the extended family.

Around the 1995 interview, some portions were utilized in both *HITS* and *Goldmine*. Ray and I had just watched on TV the UCLA Bruins win the NCAA basketball championship over at our pal Lanny Waggoner's house, along with my brother, Ken, and dad, Marshall. Ray exclaimed, "This is like the Sixties! The Doors are recording, and the Bruins won!"

In 1995, I produced and helped curate a music literary series at the MET Theater in Hollywood. The three remaining members of the Doors reunited and performed one evening. I read on stage as well.

That same year I went over to the Beverly Hills home Ray shares with his wife Dorothy, who went to Dorsey High and UCLA—now that's an L.A. woman.

It was time to talk to Raymond Daniel Manzarek. I let the tape catch our action.

Q: You've been touring the U.S., playing keyboard with writer/poet Michael McClure. And you recently participated in "The Beat Generation Legacy and Celebration" at New York University. I don't think a lot of readers realize that you and Jim Morrison were big Beat Generation fans. When I helped put together the "Jack Kerouac Collection" set, you contributed a note to the liner notes booklet, "If Jack Kerouac had never written *On the Road*, the Doors would never have existed." Long before the Doors were even formed, you actively followed the Beat Generation and saw some very early '60s readings of some of the poets with whom you are now actively playing and performing.

A: Dorothy and I went up to San Francisco in approximately 1963, during a spring break from UCLA. We tried to get up to San Francisco as much as possible. I always wanted UCLA's film school to be at Berkeley. San Francisco was really happening then, lots of stuff going on. L.A. was pretty square in 1962. Real Beach Boys country. Great if you were a surfer, but the West Coast jazz scene had passed by then.

So we went to San Francisco to feel the atmosphere and there was a poetry reading going on, featuring Lou Welch, who had just come out of the forest after being a hermit for the last three or four years. This was his return, reading the stuff he had written over the last five years. He was just charged and wired out of his mind. (Poet) Gary Snyder had just come back from Japan, wearing his Japanese schoolboy's outfit. He was mellow and tranquil. And Philip Whalen read. Whalen was just a house of fire. Words were coming out of his mouth so fast, you had to listen so closely. Somebody in the audience yelled, "Speak slower!" And Philip Whalen stopped for a second after he heard that and said, "Listen faster!" There were 2,000 people in the audience, man. This was probably 1963.

Q: Did that gig have an impact or fuel the co-creation of the Doors?
A: I did not think in terms of applying that form of spoken art to music, verbal art to music, because it was just words themselves that were so powerful that in that situation there was no need for music. Those guys had complete control of the stage, complete control of the audience. Anything added to what they were doing would have been superfluous. There's a point where you don't want to add anything to poetry, and that was certainly one of those moments. But it did reinforce for me just the power of the word on the stage. So maybe, subliminally, probably, it was the sheer force and power of the word, well delivered, that had an influence on the music and words I would be involved with later.

Q: In April, the first CD version of Jim Morrison's poetry album, "An American Prayer," is being released.
A: It's the first time the entire album will be out in the CD format. It's the original album plus two new pieces. Originally, four hours of Jim's poetry were recorded. "An American Prayer" has not been available for many years and is out of print. We've also included one bonus track that hopefully they can play on the radio, a three-and-a-half minute version of "The Ghost Song," that will have (drummer) John Densmore, (guitarist) Robby Krieger, and me uniting to polish up the tracks that are there and to make some segues to the cuts. Paul Rothchild and Bruce Botnick (the Doors' producer and engineer) are there, too. All the Doors.

Q: What attracted you to "An American Prayer?" I remember when it was first released around 1979 on LP vinyl and I was at a college radio convention in San Diego. The album was playing at the Elektra Records booth, and it scared some of the students and vendors. It was raw.
A: It was the first full-length rock-'n'-roll poetry record that's been released. Back in the '50s, we used to get spoken word records by everybody, Dylan Thomas, e.e. cummings, Kenneth Patchen. This is entirely different.

I don't think anybody has actually been ready for this record. I think the record was fifteen years ahead of its time. The subject matter was very different, very difficult. I would advise anybody under twenty-one not to buy this record [Laughs], certainly not let your parents see you in possession of this record.

Q: Let's discuss Jim Morrison's singing voice. You've been listening to his voice on the big speakers, preparing a future Doors release. As a singer, people rarely talk about his voice.

A: What did I like about Jim's voice? Well, the voice had a softness to it. I think people are going to be really surprised, because they think of Jim Morrison as this hell-bent-for-leather, screaming maniac, wild lizard king. When they hear him read his poetry, they're gonna know the side of Jim Morrison that I knew when I first started the Doors. A sensitive person. A very quiet guy. You can hear the vulnerability. I think that's what people are just gonna be shocked at. Jim is a very vulnerable human being, a poet putting his words out in complete nakedness for you to hear, to judge. And opening himself like a flower.

Q: Who is buying Doors records? I remember doing an interview with you in late 1976, or '77, when you had a solo LP out, and I had the feeling— and correct me if I'm wrong—that between 1971 and 1979 there was little grieving for Jim Morrison. His voice, and the Doors, seemed absent from the radio dial. And, in a way, a lot of people seemed glad Jim was out of the ballgame.

A: Yeah. True. True, man. Right after he died (in 1971), we as a trio made a couple of albums ("Other Voices" and "Full Circle") that didn't sell. There was a period, all through the 1970s practically, here in Los Angeles, where "the country-rock sound," like the Eagles, Jackson Browne, Linda Ronstadt, started to sweep America. Then David Bowie and "glitter rock" came. And the Doors sales were like, "Holy cow." It was almost time to go back to law school or something like that [Laughs]. Then, Danny Sugerman and I said, "Wait a minute man, we're not gonna allow this to disappear."

I don't care what you think about Jim, what you think about the Doors, but man, you are gonna listen to the Doors. So, little by little, we started beating the drum, saying, poet, poet/philosopher, Doors, jazz/rock, rock/jazz poetry, like beating the drum.

Q: Then the Doors' song, "The End," appeared in the film, "Apocalypse Now," and a book about the Doors, *No One Here Gets Out Alive*, hit the sales chart.

A: The film and the book really did it.

Bloody Red Sun of Fantastic L.A.

5

Q: The Doors have a song, "Soul Kitchen," on the soundtrack to "Forrest Gump," and pieces of five Doors songs appear in that movie. The Doors have always had a relationship with film and movies. I would imagine that the inclusion of "The End" in "Apocalypse Now" sort of revved up the Doors' soundtrack possibilities.

A: The original version of "The End," with the word "fuck" from the original four-track recording, was mixed in San Francisco for "Apocalypse Now." We went to UCLA film school with (director) Francis Ford Coppola. "Break on Through" was in "Gardens of Stone." "Light My Fire" was used in "Altered States." "Light My Fire" was used in "Taps." Original Doors recordings were the soundtrack to the film, "The Doors." "People Are Strange" by Echo & the Bunnymen was in "Lost Boys." "Hello, I Love You" was also in the Aykroyd and Belushi movie, "Neighbors." PBS has actually used a few songs over the years, especially with Vietnam documentaries.

Q: Besides the supplemental exposure a movie and subsequent soundtrack collection brings to one of your recordings, and the economic gain, what kind of feelings do you get when you hear and see one of your songs taken out of the original context it was written and recorded in?

A: Here's what it is from my perspective. This is my relationship to it. It always becomes the matter of the art. The art is the important thing. What is being communicated to the people who are listening to or watching and listening to the art form. You are taking the Doors' songs, and the Doors always tried to make those songs as artistic as they possibly could. It was never a commercial attempt, it was an artistic attempt.

Now, if you take that artistic attempt by the Doors and couple it, the synchronization, if you can synchronize that with an artistic vision of images on the screen, that's the best of all possible worlds. When it works, like in "Apocalypse Now," at the beginning, it works like a champ. And it's absolutely delightful. To sit back in an audience and hear "The End" come on in the beginning of "Apocalypse Now," and see the jungle go up in napalm where Jim says, "This is the end," it's absolutely thrilling from an artistic standpoint.

Film school guys founded the Doors. When we made the music, each song had to have a dramatic structure. Each song, whether it was two-and-a-half minutes or an epic like "The End" or "When the Music's Over," you had to have dramatic peaks and valleys, and that's the sense of drama within the Doors songs which comes right from the theater. The point of art is to blow minds.

Q: Let's talk about the film, "Forrest Gump." Were you aware of the movie being made and that some of the Doors tunes were going to end up on the screen and soundtrack compilation? Excerpts of "Soul Kitchen" are on the soundtrack double-CD. "Break on Through," "Hello, I Love You," "People Are Strange," "Love Her Madly" are in the movie along with "Soul Kitchen."

A: We got the initial request from the production company that wanted to use five Doors songs in the movie, "Forrest Gump." And immediately everyone said, "Time out, what do you mean, five Doors songs? We don't give five Doors songs to anybody." Maybe one, or two, if you have a really good movie. Like Francis could have used a couple more songs if he wanted to. That would have been fine with us, it's a great film.

"Five songs? 'Forrest Gump?' Impossible, man." Then they said, "Look, come down, see the film. We'll show you a preview of the film, of what we want to do." We went to see it, and I saw the movie, and I thought the use was so tasty, so tastefully done, and as we used to say in the '60s, so "right on," that we said, "Hey, five songs, man." It's just little excerpts and little bits and pieces that are just so skillfully used in the source of the film, we gave them the okay to use all five of them.

Robert Zemeckis, the director of the film, did such a wonderful job. And there's a sequence where Tom Hanks, Forrest Gump, is playing ping-pong, and becomes a ping-pong expert, and the click-click-click of the ping-pong ball against the paddle and the table corresponds with the drumbeats of "Break on Through," the fast Bossa Nova. So John Densmore is playing the sidestick on his snare and the click-click of the ping-pong balls is working as a counterpoint to what Densmore is doing. I saw that and said, "Brilliant! This is good. That's the use of music and picture. That's art." So we gave them the okay for all five songs.

Q: I asked you to be involved in playing the organ and piano segments to the spoken word audio guide I produced on basketball player, now TV basketball broadcaster/analyst, Bill Walton, on his "Men Are Made in the Paint." Music and hoop are big factors in your life.

A: Morrison was a swimmer at UCLA. I was the basketball guy at school. Later, during the Doors tours, before a gig, I'd be watching UCLA playing on television or during tournament time backstage. When it was time to perform, I'd only get to see the first half of the basketball game, and find out what the score was after the show. "What do you mean, we have to go on stage? UCLA is on a run . . ."

Q: There are a lot of similarities between basketball and music, especially the hoop and jazz relationship. I recall you running down the basketball and jazz relationship to (now professional) basketball player, Baron Davis, at a party.

A: Basketball is an improvisational sport. Jazz is improvisational music, especially in a jazz group: two horns, tenor, trumpet, piano, drums and bass. That's the Charlie Parker Quintet, which is a basketball team. Charlie Parker is the center, ya know? And you have all these guys around him.

Jazz/rock, jazz groups, rock-'n'-roll bands, are exactly the same thing. You've got the lead singer and a four-piece. Most of the time you have a four-piece support band behind him and everybody works together. You throw the ball around, you throw the music around. You do exactly the same thing with the ball that you do with the music. You have your set play, and then you have your set variations on the play. You have your set tunes and you run variations on the tunes. You have your set list, you run variations on your set list.

First quarter, second quarter, save something for the third, you know you have to kill 'em in the fourth quarter. You gotta be strong for the fourth quarter. Same way with a rock-'n'-roll or jazz set. You better have your hot numbers saved and be ready to blast that audience right at the end of the set. You pace yourself. You don't blow it all at the beginning. The same way in a basketball game. The similarities are amazing.

Q: I really enjoyed the fact that Bill Walton has always been a big Doors fan and obviously a well-known Deadhead, and that you followed his game as an All-American player at UCLA and as a pro athlete.

A: I was a big fan of Bill Walton on and off the court. As a player he was a brilliant passer, always got the rebound, and I never had the sense that Bill banged to get in position. He used his grace, his inner Zen-like strength, to get into position. Basketball is a real Zen sport. You and the hoop. Do you have the grace and ability to leap into the air, hit the circle, the hoop, the symbol of holiness? Putting the globe of the earth into the circle of the universe? Sometimes, when I'm playing basketball, or at the gym, or playing music, I'm "in the zone." It's all working. As Joseph Campbell calls it, "a peak experience."

I'm really happy with the way that recording turned out. After hearing it, you are in control of the action on the court. What I liked about the audio that you and Bill did, and the teaching and feeding off basketball from a performer like Bill, was that you get into the mind of the narrator. I grew up playing basketball in Chicago and I wish I would have had something like this when I was fourteen.

When I play this music, I really feel like I am playing basketball.

Q: Let's talk about the Doors movie, directed by Oliver Stone, who took some liberties, especially around the facts about Jim Morrison's life at the UCLA film school.

A: (Actor) Val Kilmer did a wonderful job. Ray Manzarek goes on record as saying Val Kilmer did a wonderful job as Jim Morrison. The rock-'n'-roll scenes were real good, and maybe the first half-hour of the movie was very good. But the rest of it just sucked. The problem with the movie is that Oliver Stone doesn't know what psychedelics are.

Q: Was it awkward to see yourself being portrayed on the big screen?

A: Well, yes. The fellow who played me, I felt was rather stiff and wooden [Laughs]. And I would highly recommend a serious session with some hemp. I think some hemp would have loosened him up very, very nicely and he would have been a lot more spontaneous.

In 2002 I went back to Ray's Beverly Hills home for a meeting and a new interview session.

At his house we primarily talked about his autobiography, *Light My Fire: My Life with the Doors*; his recent debut novel, *The Poet in Exile*; Jim Morrison; and our joint concerns about planet earth in the post 9/11 world.

I was deeply touched when I was listed on the dedication page of Ray's *Light My Fire: My Life with the Doors* book. He signed a copy of the autobiography to me: "To Harvey: It's all your fault! You, my good & hip friend, are the cause of this tome."

Q: When you wrote your book, *Light My Fire: My Life with the Doors*, did you have any initial concerns you really wanted to address and bring forward?

A: Well, the reason I wrote *Light My Fire* was to tell my side of the story, and to be the antidote to Oliver Stone's poison film, "The Doors."

Q: Do you feel that all of the documentation on the Doors has been correct?

A: All of the written documentation on the Doors, except for John Densmore's book, has been written by people who weren't there. All they've done is to take articles, and compile articles, do a few interviews, but for the most part, compiling articles that were probably wrong to begin with, or were sycophantic kind of "girls who were in love with Jim Morrison" articles, and others who had a bone to pick or something to grind about. So those compilation stories that are based on articles are invariably flawed and faulty. The Sugerman and Hopkins book is pretty good, and Densmore's book is not necessarily about the Doors.

What I tried to do was to be an antidote to Oliver Stone. I thought the movie was just awful, and what he did to Jim Morrison was just a travesty, reducing him to "sex, drugs and rock-'n'-roll."

Q: Just having the guy proclaiming, "I quit!" in the film school was not the truth. I know Jim Morrison graduated college. Jim's parents wouldn't have paid the rent on his Westwood apartment without that UCLA degree!

A: Exactly.

Q: That's actually a non-truth. Let's set the tone of the outsider, non-participant, by walking out at film school, when there is documentation of a degree. Make him a rebel.

A: The man's a college graduate. "I quit!" Why would Jim quit? First I thought, "What a wussy! He quits! They criticize his student film, and he quits!" Jim would never quit; he's got the balls to stand up and say, "You don't like my movie, well, I don't like yours either!"

Q: There's such an extensive video catalogue on the Doors, and you're involved in the promotion and accuracy of these. It pushes people to go the other way sometimes and there's a sense of . . .

A: Of course, yeah. "What's Manzarek's role in the Doors? Maybe it was nothing?" Somebody read my book. Somebody said, "Boy, you had nothing to do with the Doors." But you know, whatever, who cares? To clear the record and to tell the story of where the Doors came from, who are these four guys, what is psychedelic? You certainly didn't find out what psychedelic was from Oliver Stone. It's a crazed white powder version of his mysticism, and I wanted to write a book about who the Doors were, what's psychedelic, what happened at UCLA, what are the Doors into. What's the spirituality of the Doors, what's the cinematic background of the Doors, bringing in Beat literature, politics? The Doors existing is a political statement, an anti-establishment statement. So Oliver Stone was afraid to go anti-establishment, and he is beholden to the establishment. He wanted to find the internal conflict within the Doors, which really didn't exist any more than it exists in any other four guys. There was never "fighting" amongst the Doors. There was like, "Where's Jim? Jim's not around, and we'll have to work without him until he shows up." But nobody fought in the Doors. We fought the establishment. It's a "wrong thing" for a white civilization to do, to play for white men and young women, to play rock-'n'-roll is against the Judeo, Christian, and Islamic tradition.

Q: Your experience in the 1960s is a little different, in that you served in the military.

A: I did a little time. I did my time in hell. I was in Fort Ord for basic training, and then I went to signal school as a darkroom man, and then they sent me off to Okinawa, and then to Thailand.

Q: Also the book allowed you to present spirituality, politics, and numerology. You have to say that you got to do your thing in this book.
A: Oh, absolutely. There was no one saying, "You can't do this or that." I just wrote the book, and the company edited it ever so slightly. I had 500 pages in there, and we got it down to 300. The idea of talking about marijuana and LSD was not expunged.

Q: By the way, your writing procedure? I remember you writing longhand on a tablet. This is a world pre-computer for you? No co-writer. You did the whole thing yourself.
A: I did it all myself. The reason I did the book, interestingly, is because of the double CD called "Myth and Reality," that you produced.

Q: I've always said, if you really want to know the stories behind the music or a band, try to ask the keyboardists, the arrangers, or even the drummers, not just the lead singers.
A: And when you, Harvey, had the transcription made from our series of studio interviews, I said, "My god, there's a book here." And I read it and thought, "Maybe I can put this into a book form." The script wouldn't work as a book, because it was talking, it wasn't writing. And talking and speaking doesn't read as well as writing reads. So that was my inspiration, doing "Myth and Reality." If you hadn't done that, I wouldn't have the book out. So I sat down and said, "Lemme write the book." I sat down and wrote it down on legal pads, longhand. If it was good enough for Shakespeare and Goethe, it's good enough for Manzarek.

Q: Your creative process? I remember you get up early in the morning and write.
A: Early in the morning, yes. You get up and you're in the REM state and you're just coming out of sleep, and maybe the sun hasn't come up yet.

Q: Do you eat before you write?
A: No. I go on an empty stomach and work for three to four hours. I get up early, maybe 5:30, 6:00 in the morning. I sit at a little Chinese table, a writing table, sitting on the floor, leaning back on a couch up there, and I've got my pencils and my legal pad. Pencils, I use the Blackfoot Indian cedar pencils. They're just the best pencils made.

Q: Editing and revisions?

A: No, I just write and write and write as fast as I can, and as much as I can. I envision the scenes taking place. What I'm doing is I'm watching a movie or watching the events take place, and I'm trying to transcribe the events for you, the reader, as quickly and succinctly and interestingly written as I possibly can. Then, after I have it all done, all those pages, or in the process as I'm going along, I have someone type up the hand-writing into the computer; then I finish it off in the computer. That's where I edit and polish and word-process.

Q: Does your film school experience help in translating observations into narrative text?

A: You know where that comes from? It comes from script writing. So what I'm doing is elaborating on script writing. If I were to write a script on the Doors, it would be very much like what I wrote in *Light My Fire*. That's basically what I'm doing; my training comes from script writing. So now, writing a novel or an autobiography is really fun, because it's an expanded script. You don't have to do punchy shorthand, you can actually write a literary sentence.

Q: What about the pre-conceived ideas and "baggage" that exists around the Doors, and yourself, especially Jim, too, because the band has been chronicled by so many people. From the people who bought the records, to available literature and books. Do you feel like you're carrying Morrison into literature, too?

A: Oh absolutely, yeah. It's my job to give Jim voice, and my job to explain Jim Morrison, and the guy who put the band together on the beach in Venice before John and Robby joined up a couple of weeks later. The two of us assembled, and met on the beach in Venice. Jim sang some songs to me and I said, "That's it. We're going to get a rock-'n'-roll band together, we're going to make a million dollars, we're going all the way to the top." He said, "That's exactly what we're going to do. We're going to fit in somewhere between the Beatles and the Stones," and "We're gonna do psychedelic music; it's going to be strange and eerie and LSD-infused with (my) Slavic organ and (his) Tennessee Williams and Carson McCullers Southern Gothic words." And I knew we were gonna go all of the way with it.

It's my job now to explain that Jim Morrison to people, 'cause that's the artist, that's the poet that I put the band together with in the first place. Rock-'n'-roll and poetry? That was the whole point of it, just like the Beatniks did with poetry and jazz, we were going to do poetry and rock-'n'-roll. And of course today, Jim Morrison metamorphoses into the "Lizard King." You know, my god, I'm dealing with people out there who think of Jim Morrison as the Oliver Stone movie. "Lizard King?" Wait a minute; the guy may have worn leather, but that movie isn't true, he's not the "Lizard King," he's portraying a part, he's acting. When he says, "I am the Lizard King, I can do anything," he's not saying that, "I, Jim Morrison, am the 'Lizard King.'" It's that part in "The Celebration of the Lizard" that he's playing.

Q: Getting back to writing, don't you think that film school coupled with your extensive background as a keyboard player helps the writing?

A: Well, keyboard is all linear, music is all linear. You can only play one section at a time, one note at a time, or a cluster of notes at a time. On wind instruments and brass instruments, you can only play one note at a time. You play that note, then you play the next note and you play the next note after that. So it's all linear, it's all laid out, and writing is linear, so I'm doing exactly the same thing.

Q: There was always an inherent political undercurrent in the Doors' music. "Five to One," "Unknown Soldier." I seem to recall that the Doors participated in a local "No War Toys" rally. I mean the concept, "No War Toys," lending your name to that. That's a pretty radical thing to do. Did that cost you or gain the band bookings?

A: Not in the '60s. Not in that period when it was all anti-war. All of the young people in America. Well, not all. But anybody who had read the book was against the war, and it was a ridiculous thing to be doing. Nobody believed in the Domino Theory, that's been proven incorrect. Nobody went Communist. Vietnam went Communist, nobody else went Communist. As a matter of fact, Vietnam may be that sort of strange, Oriental, Capitalist, Communist kind of thing. Certainly a Capitalist country, as China will eventually become, too. So, being against the war and "No War Toys" and "Anti-Speed," "Don't do Speed. Speed kills." We did that, too. But the times were so radical and the people were in the streets protesting to stop the war and stop bad drugs and stay strictly psychedelic, what a joke today that it's become a heroin, crack cocaine, crystal meth-infused society, and psychedelics don't hardly enter the equation at all! [laughter] I'm completely shocked that we are at this point today, instead of where we were back in 1965.

Q: Water elements are a re-occurring theme in the music of the Doors.

A: Yeah, the water element is always there: the Manzareks living in Redondo Beach, the Doors in Venice, California.

Bloody Red Sun of Fantastic L.A.

Q: "Horse Latitudes."

A: Always the water. The water is the unconscious, and that's what the Doors dove into. That's where LSD takes you: it takes you into the sun, into the light. The fire is the sun, our father in the sky. The watery element is our mother, returning into the womb, diving into the unconscious, swimming around down there to find out what's lurking below our regular level of consciousness. That's what opening the doors of perception does.

Q: Your book reinforced the durability of the songs.

A: It's all about the songs, and unlimitedly they have to be strong songs to transcend the handsome guy with the shirt off. It's always been for me about the music, and for John and Robby. Just listen to the words. That's what Jim was saying: "Just listen to my words." The songs must be there. All the rest of this is peripheral. But unfortunately his images become so dominant, that his image becomes more dominant than the songs are. The songs are peripheral, the songs and the art of Jim Morrison are peripheral to the image of Jim Morrison.

The Doors under the pier in Venice, California, during a photo shoot for "Morrison Hotel." Photo by Henry Diltz.

Q: I know that every picture is worth a thousand words, but it also showed you his photogenic

Jim Morrison at
the Shrine Auditorium,
Los Angeles, California,
1967. Photo by
Heather Harris.

abilities. There are some people who really can't even get deep into the music of the Doors 'cause they're in heat over the visuals.

A: Can't get past his image; the Lizard King, and the wildest man in rock-'n'-roll. What it is, that unconscious, diving into the waters of the unconscious no matter where we are today as Judeo-Christian society, beneath us are still those archetypal leanings, and Morrison is the archetype of the wild man that clicks with people, that connects with them. That whole serpentine thing. I mean, Jim represents the serpent out of the Garden of Eden, for God's sake!

Q: The Doors' Miami concert of 1969, in which rock-'n'-roll later went on trial when Jim Morrison was arrested for public exposure, and although nothing was proved, and posthumously all charges were dropped, *you*, my man, scored and "composed" the spontaneous incidental music to that Miami show. Isn't that interesting, that in the state of Morrison's birth (Florida), where the arrest happened, previewed in the exact same county (Dade) as the chaotic results of the voting tabulations in the 2000 U.S. Presidential election . . .

A: Yes, and the trial of Jim Morrison was a trumped-up, absurd trial with absurd charges, where Jim Morrison was alleged to have exposed himself. But not one photo, out of hundreds of photos offered in evidence? Not one photo showed Jim Morrison's "ivory shaft."

Q: But there has always been a history of free speech infringement on stage, from Lenny Bruce being arrested for doing his club act, to Canadian authorities considering arresting Madonna around her repertoire documented in the "Truth or Dare" film. Come on, man, I checked out Tina Turner's stage act in 1969, and have seen performance art, punk rock, rap and the sex beat all over the stage, and available in the record stores today—as well as the likes of MTV's "Spring Break" TV stuff—and some rappers on that channel really detailing physical geography in songs and videos. What James Douglas Morrison was accused of, and ultimately not proven guilty of, was really pretty mild.

A: It's pretty mild, (even) at that time. So the trial was trumped-up, money was exchanged, the judge, not in our trial, had taken bribes from child molesters, and had let child molesters get off easy. Then, thirty years later, 2000, Bush and the election concerns went on in Florida. I'm watching, and the whole thing's going on in Florida. In Miami! We were in Dade County!

Q: What albums do you sign at your book promotion tours? Besides the *Light My Fire: My Life with the Doors* autobiography?

A: Well, everybody loves the first album, "The Doors," and "L.A. Woman," those are our best-selling albums. But invariably, I'm signing "Strange Days." A lot of people come with their CDs, but a lot of the old-timers come with their albums. So, I'm invariably signing the inside of "L.A. Woman," and the inside of "Morrison Hotel," while we're sitting in the bar. They love "Morrison Hotel" and "Strange Days."

It is a collective journey, that's a good way of putting it. It's of course Jim Morrison as the charismatic lead singer, and I've got to address Jim Morrison, but it's Densmore, Krieger, and Manzarek (too). It's a journey of these four guys, the Four Horsemen of the Apocalypse, the diamond-shaped, no bass player that made a five-point pentagram the shape of the diamond. It's the inverted pyramid, it's an archetypal journey of four young men into the unconscious, and coming out of that and creating a musical art form.

Q: There's always light at the end of the darkness.

A: That's the point of "Light My Fire," the organ solo into the guitar solo, and it's five minutes of building and building to an orgasmic release. So sex enters into it, but it's a great infusion into the sun; if you listen to it, you'll find that the light is always infusing everything that we do. And Morrison was always filled with the light, although he was not afraid to talk about the darkness within him. And when he would talk about the darkness, the Doors would invariably balance that darkness with a joyous music, and that's the music. It's a balanced music.

Q: And one thing I get in hearing the Doors now is how vital engineer (later producer) Bruce Botnick, and Paul Rothchild, your producer, were.

A: Six guys made those records, it was not the "four Doors," it was the "six Doors." It was Bruce Botnick as the ultimate engineer/techie/knob-twister, and Paul Rothchild guiding the whole sound. Paul Rothchild is the only guy who is older than I am. It was wonderful to have him there, so I didn't have to assume the role of the father when I was tired of that role. "Paul, you're the father, I'm tired of that role!" [laughter] "I just wanna be a crazy keyboard player; you just make sure that it sounds right." So Paul always set an atmosphere in the recording studio, and he always allowed and encouraged us to experiment in the studio, as did Elektra Records. Elektra Records always allowed us to experiment.

I introduced you to Bruce at my house a couple of years ago. "Kubernik, meet Botnick." You two boys went to Fairfax High.

Q: And one of the reasons for the success of the band economically with stable reissue programs, at least to me, it seems that there weren't a whole lot of "greed heads" in the Doors camp. I've seen so much craziness in today's bands. You guys have always had a four-way publishing split. Not a Lennon/McCartney scene, where two people out of four basically wrote the bulk of the material and the publishing agreements were not inclusive of the other two members, due to the writing dynamic established early in the Beatles. Was that by design, and was it a sort of hippie ethic, sharing the pot?

A: Well, here's what's so great about Morrison. It got to the point where we were going to sign to Elektra Records and it was like, "Uh-oh, we'd better get our songs published; we gotta publish the songs." It fell to me to actually write out the music. I don't think you could send a tape of it. Today, you can just send a tape in (to get a copyright). You had to have a lead sheet, with the chord changes and a one-line melody with the lyrics underneath it. So I had to do the whole damn song, [hums] "da-da, dum, dum" and write "you know that it would be untrue" underneath. That took a long time. So it got to that, and I said, "Okay, I got these damn things finished," and I said to Jim and John, "Now we've got to figure out who wrote what. Okay, Robby, you did 'Light My Fire,' but then I did the introductions and the solo, that whole thing. Jim wrote the second verse and John put in this . . . well, we've all sort of written the songs. Okay, let's get started, let's break these things down, song by song, who wrote what . . ." And Jim said, "Wait a minute, man. We've all written the songs. Ya know what? I've written a lot of lyrics, but so has Robby. Who cares who wrote what? Here's what we're gonna do to solve all of that problem . . ." This is Alexander the Great cutting through the Gordian Knot. How do you untie the Gordian Knot? And Alexander the Great just pulls out his sword and slashes through that. Jim Morrison slashed through all of the complexities and said, "We're gonna make it a four-way split. There's only four of us, we'll split the royalties four ways, we'll split the publishing four ways, we'll split the songwriting four ways. Everybody gets an equal share. What could be easier?" And I went, "My god, this guy is so generous," because he wrote the initial batch of songs.

Q: Was he really generous or was it lack of business acumen?
A: He was generous! Because he knew that we'd have to go through who did what on every song, and divide it that way. "You did this, you get fifty percent Jim, but I get twenty-five percent, now Robby and John, a third here, a third there." And Jim said, "Forget it man, we're not gonna do that."

Q: That's why I'm always puzzled when the media says, "Jim Morrison and the Doors." People, follow the money; it's a four-way split! I think that's one of the reasons, sales, exposure, karma-wise, this band still continues a third of a century later, because there weren't dollar signs or an initial greed cow scene evident. The Doors' stability in the marketplace might be traced to the democratic split on monies and roles within and around the band.
A: There was no greed. And how easy it was. It was a group effort. The surrendering of ego. The Doors were surrendering ego, the music was surrendering ego. I surrender my ego every time I play a song. The

music is the only thing that matters. I mean, back to the question about the money, the publishing being split equally, Doors Music Company, and not like most bands with one or two principal writers, or different publishing companies within the band, I mean, wait a minute! There should be a five-way split, [Laughs] 'cause "Lefty" here is playing the bass. I was playing the bass and keyboards, so make it a five-way split. And that would have been insane, because after all, we were all psychedelic. We were pot-heads and acid-heads. The whole point in opening the "Doors of Perception" and ingesting psychedelics is to put you into a new world of harmony, peace, love, and sharing. "Make Love Not War." "Save the Environment." Give everybody a decent break. A decent day's salary for a decent day's work. How simple it all is.

Q: Another factor in the Doors' artistic and commercial success and influence on so many bands and people might also, ironically, be linked to the military components that impacted the band. Jim Morrison being the son of a military family, and you starting to complete your service obligation by serving in Asia, even before the Doors. And the fact that the government, via the G.I. Bill, partially paid for your UCLA Film School education. Two of the four principals in the Doors had military ties. And songs like "Unknown Soldier" were informed by this fact. That's not even counting that the video of the song was partially filmed at the Westwood Cemetery amongst soldiers' marked graves next to UCLA . . .
I mean, really, who else asks these questions?
A: No one, man . . . The military background gives us a sense of discipline. No matter how much you've rebelled against it, you still have the sense of discipline. And the discipline with writing songs is that you get the work done. In the Doors, we got the work done. "Let's do the work." No matter how Jim was out there, gone, later on after the fourth album, "Morrison Hotel," Morrison completely drunk and out there, he was still disciplined enough to get the work done. To write the songs, rehearse the songs, record the songs. He had the discipline. That's where the military comes in.

Q: And your own keyboard, your primary organ sound, combined military and improvisational elements simultaneously. And in the Doors, your keyboard work was a lead instrument, not the traditional background or supplemental keyboard that helped flesh out a group sound.
A: The whole Doors organ sound, what makes that work, that's my whole Slavic upbringing. That's being a "Polish Pianist." That's

that dark Slavic Stravinsky, Chopin, that great mournful Bartok type thing. Dark, mournful Slavic soul married so perfectly with the Southern Gothic–American Florida "Tennessee Williams' boy poetry," that the two of us went "Crunch!" and the whole thing came right together perfectly.

Q: Why is it that some other legacy band members and music people, even occasionally in our hometown local media outlets, feel compelled to always take a shot at Jim Morrison and question the Doors' influence constantly? Are they mad that your catalogue still sells? Is it also the fact that, unlike many of these musicians, who weren't born or raised in L.A.—basically interlopers, who moved out West after not charting in New York—you and Jim were byproducts of UCLA, and John and Robby went to University High School in L.A. Like Love, L.A. guys making L.A. music. Too real for a lot of these folkies who came to L.A. to make it in the business.

A: [Laughs] What difference does it make? The thing about the Doors always being slammed a bit in the media. We were never part of the team. The Doors were never part of the folk-rock, country-rock, laid back, "Peaceful Easy Feeling" of Los Angeles. The Doors were part of Raymond Chandler, John Fante, Dalton Trumbo. It was the dark streets and *The Day of the Locust,* ya know. *Miss Lonely Hearts.* That's where the Doors come from. What are you gonna do, man? We always looked down upon the folk-rockers. And I think they innately understood that. "I don't like the Doors . . ." Look, it's not a white band. It's a black and white band. It's white guys infused with jazz. You see, nobody came here to make it. Jim and I came to go to the UCLA film school, and John and Robby are natives. Westside boys who surfed, for God's sake. The Doors are L.A., the beach, and downtown L.A.

Q: And, adding to the music made, where did your ability for total recall and memory come from? I know you were a great student in school, and I feel it helped the music being created. I know you have an Economics degree from DePaul University.

A: That's the 5:30 A.M. wake-up. That's that REM state, sitting up in a little room facing the east where the sun is going to rise and watching it go through its arc from the winter solstice to the summer solstice, and I know right where it rises. I'd watch that thing—on December twenty-first it's way to the south, and on June twenty-first it's way to the north—and I'd see that sun coming up. And you're in that REM state. And it's just opening up the doors of unconsciousness. There's a big latch and you unlock that thing and open those two doors up and out it comes. And the images just come out and you have to be there to catch them. And anybody can do it. And I think the hard part, and this might be the military again, is catching it, and the discipline of writing the damn things down. That's the hard part. The discipline was there and we had to do it.

Q: And you recently directed your first film, "Love Her Madly." You've done audio, print, and celluloid.

A: It was great, and the film was the hardest thing I'd ever done since being in basic training. I'm not sure whether or not the creation of a movie, the actual shooting of a movie is an art form. I think it's more like a war. A small D-Day. A small invasion of Normandy. Writing a movie is art. Editing a movie is art. Scoring a movie and mixing all the elements together is art. Working with the actors is fabulous. Shooting a movie is a war. But actually shooting on location and to get everything happening in the right place at the right time. To get the caterer there and the camera working . . . Every medium is different. Making music is the easiest. I've been doing it since I was eight years old. Playing with Jim, Robby, and John was like falling off a log. Writing those songs and inventing things. That was such a fecund time, as Jim said, in that year we had a great visitation of energy. That year with the Doors lasted from 1965 to 1971. We were just composing fools. So that was the easiest thing I've ever done. Writing a book is a long, slow process, and making a film is complete chaos. Total madness.

Q: But you were helped or nourished by all the previous directing and producing work you had done with the Doors on film and video.

A: Yes. And on the Doors DVD you can see my UCLA student film, "Evergreen," an homage to Evergreen Press and the Beatniks. It was one of the twenty best UCLA films by students shown at Royce Hall to the public in 1965. Everybody dug it. I had a class with Josef Von Sternberg, the great director of Marlene Dietrich, who did "The Blue Angel," "Morocco," "Shanghai Express." He came up to me afterwards and said, "Very good, Manzarek. Very good." One of the greatest moments of my life. And Jim had him too. So he's the guy who really kind of gave a real sense of darkness to the Doors, not that we wouldn't have been there anyway. But having Von Sternberg, seeing the deep psychology of his movies, and the pace at which he paced his films, really influenced Doors songs and Doors music. The sheer psychological weight of his movies on what we tried to do with our music.

Q: And in 2001 you wrote and published your debut novel, *The Poet in Exile*. What is the difference in writing an autobiography and a novel?

A: The only difference is you are making up the scenes. In an autobiography, the scenes have already played themselves out. You call them back and view them, and write them down. Writing a novel, you've got your story together and hopefully an outline. You know where you will be going. *The Poet in Exile* came from everybody wanting Jim Morrison to be alive. This is what I get at my book signings. I'm always asked if he is alive. They want a resurrection. They want Morrison to come back. They want Elvis to come back. "We need his inspiration. We need his power." "We need his poetry." "We need the assurance that he would bring to his performances."

We need to search for something beyond ourselves, something higher than ourselves. Rather then being catered to. Today we are being catered to by all the media and what do we know, man? We're just a bunch of consumers. We will take anything they will give us. We're reacting to the crap they will give us. We'd like somebody to say, "Hey, there's a higher reason and a higher message and a better way of being. Come on, let's go there." That's what Morrison represents. So I wrote this book to give him his life. To say, yes, he is not dead. He is alive. I'm putting all my philosophy into Jim Morrison's words. It's a work of fiction.

Q: And there is a sense of patriotism that permeates the book.

A: Absolutely. We are Americans. We love this country. If you are born here you are a Native American. We are all the tribe. My patriotism is for the hope that America ultimately is the great Aquarian country. Let's do it. Let's live it. Let's make it a beacon of liberty and light and under the eye at the top of the pyramid shining down on us all.

Q: But it's hard to have a vision of a new America in a post-9/11 world. Or even before then.

A: Isn't it? Isn't that the truth? It's really hard right now because we've slipped way back. The idea of spirituality is virtually gone from our society. There's not a hippie or a psychedelic soul left. And the war against terrorism? What's it going to do to our internal security? We're afraid and scared, and it's a time of war, and the powers that be want to keep it on that war footing because that allows them to drill for oil anywhere they want to. Because we need all the oil we can possibly get to power the country, and we're gonna make millions and millions of dollars. Billions of dollars.

And oddly enough, they don't care. The conservatives don't conserve the nation. They don't conserve America, the Native American soil. They're not conserving it. They will spoil it and ruin it. Melting glaciers, global warming. I mean, Jim says in one of our songs ("When the Music's Over"), "What have they done to the earth? What have they done to our fair sister?"

We worship the dollar. Wealth is the whole ball game. And showing your wealth. So we're worshipping the dollar. *The Poet in Exile* shows that you as the individual are never going to be happy with all the money. The poet is saying he had everything. The fame. The women. The drugs, drink, and money. And he was empty on the inside. Then he had an epiphany in the ocean and went on his journey to the East. He found the fact that we are all one, we're all God. God is us. The planet is God. You as a human being can either spoil it or make it thrive. And right now we're spoiling it because we've gone totally mad.

In writing *The Poet in Exile*, I didn't concern myself with the reader at all. I concerned myself with writing a good story. Taking the poet on his journey to enlightenment, having the keyboard player become all excited about the idea of bringing the poet back to civilization and a new vision of America that is possible for humanity, and incorporating that into a new kind of jazz Indian Raga rock-'n'-roll, and the keyboard player's excitement with that possibility, and then of course that tragic ending where the poet finds out he has six months to live, and the keyboard player leaves to let the man live out his life with his wife and two children.

My concern was to give the reader a good trip, a good journey, a good voyage, a good story, with each sentence being a well written sentence. What they would bring to it with their interpretation was not my concern at all.

Q: But Jim Morrison was a guy who also wrote and sang, in "When the Music's Over," the lyric, "Cancel my subscription to the Resurrection."
A: I never even thought of that. That's great.

Q: The Aquarian age is just in front of us.
A: Well you know, the Aquarian age hasn't really started yet. It really begins to get started in 2012. Which is also when the Mayan calendar, the calendar of the Maya, the Aztecs and the Maya, the calendar comes to an end. 2012 is the very bare bones beginning of stepping off into the new age. So we're convulsing with the Judeo Christian Islamic big three, the big three of Jerusalem. The Jewish bible, the Christian bible, and the Islamic bible called *The Koran*. We will move beyond the books into the Aquarian age, when the character of a man will be

judged in his heart. That's what is going to happen. Martin Luther King, Jr. said, "We will judge a man by the character of his heart." It's got to, man. It's gotta come. It will come. It will happen but we will have to go through a decade of shit before we start to even see the light at the end of the tunnel . . . India and Pakistan having nuclear stuff is horrifying. The artist will take over again. As Thomas Jefferson said, "I'm a fighter so that my son can be a farmer, and his son can be a poet, an artist." It's coming.

Q: What about the Internet? I participated in a web chat interaction with you and an audience of Doors fans a few years back. The Doors have an official web site, and now an Internet-driven record label, Bright Midnight Records, has issued some really interesting never-heard official recordings of the band.

A: Bright Midnight shows you about building the structure. The outtakes we've got, the concerts we recorded, 8-track and little cassette recordings. There's interviews with Jim Morrison, the Doors Live at the Aquarius Theater, one of our very first San Francisco appearances at Marty Balin's Matrix club. We did two nights there. Doors in Detroit, Doors in Boston, Doors in Vancouver. The Doors all over the place. Basically, it's for Doors fans.

Q: You like the accuracy of the documentation, don't you?

A: Well of course! I mean, that's a Doors concert in its entirety. No concert was ever the same. We never played the same. That was the whole point of it. You pretty much play a lot of the same songs. If you go to a Doors concert, and the Doors don't play "Light My Fire," you get your money back. So Bright Midnight Music is about building that wall, that structure, that house, and showing you the Doors in all their permutations, their facets, and their flaws, and the brilliance of their diamond. The diamond is not a perfect diamond, it has a few flaws in it.

Our ninety minutes went by so quick. I got plenty on tape.

A few years back, Ray and I drove to downtown L.A., to the Sports Arena, to see the Clippers play basketball against the Utah Jazz. At the game, Manzarek pointed out that Utah's coach, Jerry Sloan, looked like director/actor John Cassavetes. Hoop and film. The following week, Ray and I went over to UCLA in Westwood and the Pauley Pavilion arena. Then-current UCLA Basketball Coach Steve Lavin had invited me to the Bruins' afternoon practice and Manzarek came along to check out the team. It's a yearly ritual. We later stayed for a Pac-10 game, and Hall of Fame player and former UCLA coach John Robert Wooden at halftime waved me over for a hello, and I introduced him to Ray, who had been a student at UCLA when Wooden won his first NCAA championship title. As we prepared to go back to our seats, Wooden leaned over the guard-rail and whispered to me, "Nice to see you music fellows still tuck in your shirts."

Berry Gordy, Jr:

Motown Records' Main Man

When you speak of Motown Records, you sometimes forget the miracle that so many great artists came together at one small, independently owned company. Diana Ross and the Supremes, Stevie Wonder, Marvin Gaye, the Temptations, the Four Tops, Martha Reeves and the Vandellas, the Marvelettes, Michael Jackson and the Jackson Five, Smokey Robinson and the Miracles, Brenda Holloway, Kim Weston, Mary Wells, Junior Walker and the All-Stars, Edwin Starr, the Commodores. Also think about the fine Motown staff songwriters, session musicians, arrangers, and record producers who helped put the label's sound in your ears.

Due to television jingles and commercials, soundtrack albums, and the plethora of "cover records" that seem to still be done on a daily basis, the sound of Motown Records is in front of our ears all the time. Hundreds of recording artists have picked at the classic catalogs of Motown Records and Jobete Music Company over the last forty years. Thousands of amateur and professional music makers, performers, and club and concert artists still do the material on a nightly basis. Isn't it about time we knew a little bit about the person who put together the potent melodic brew that everyone is still sipping from?

Berry Gordy, Jr. was born November 28, 1929, in Detroit, Michigan. A former boxer and assembly line worker, and a veteran of the Korean War, Gordy, in 1955, ran a jazz record store, his first foray into the music business. Although the shop failed, he didn't give up. He wrote songs and got his first break when Jackie Wilson cut some of his

Berry Gordy, Jr. at Marvin Gaye's "Star on Hollywood Boulevard" ceremony, 1990. Photo by Harold Sherrick.

compositions, including "Reet Petite," "That's Why (I Love You So)," and "Lonely Teardrops."

Gordy's sisters, Anna and Gwen, along with Billy Davis, started the Anna label, which scored a major success with Barrett Strong's "Money (That's What I Want)" in early 1959. The Beatles and the Rolling Stones both later covered the tune in the U.K. Gordy, who was involved with the Anna label, then launched the Tamla label. Motown itself, with Berry Gordy at the helm, soon followed.

Although many factors and many individuals came together within the Motown family framework, Berry Gordy, Jr. was the enterprising genius that put all of the elements together into place.

Gordy ran a tight ship. Unlike most other labels, he didn't see only as far as the next hit. He built talent from the bottom up, using the artists' raw materials and his own expertise—and that of his team—to train his roster of artists in not only the nuances of singing and performing on stage, but in how to walk, dress, and speak while in public. To be a Motown act meant being part of a well-oiled hit-making machine.

By the early '60s, Motown dominated the black music scene. One after another, the great artists of Motown turned out hit after hit. Although each was fundamentally unique, they were all part of a larger world, that of the "Motown Sound," or "The Sound of Young America," as Gordy named it.

By the early '70s, having outgrown its "Hitsville U.S.A." outpost in Detroit, Gordy moved the Motown operation, now a true entertainment complex and the largest black-owned corporation in the country, to Los Angeles, California.

How many British bands then, and even today, include Motown songs in their live repertoire and recording efforts?

The Rolling Stones on their global 2002/2003 tour are still inserting a couple of Motown covers in the show some nights, and their latest batch of CD reissues incorporates several famous Motown-birthed (Jobete Music) publishing copyrights.

And in America, the impact of the historic music of Motown is also not lost on Bay City, Michigan-born Madonna. Still a top music video product seller, long after she earned and attained multi-platinum status as a recording artist, her "Ciao Italia: Live From Italy" home video pays psychic and geographic homage in a full dance and vocal troupe rendition of the Four Tops' "I Can't Help Myself (Sugar Pie Honey Bunch)," while a more recent available concert video, "The Girlie Show—Live Down Under," gives appropriate and licensed lip service to the Temptations' "Just My Imagination," and she also performs an excerpt of Marvin Gaye's "After the Dance."

It is to the credit of the Motown legacy and the potent Jobete Music copyrights that popular arena and stadium artists like the Rolling Stones and

Madonna have the musical literature in their repertoires for years at a time, and Jobete Music shares in ancillary income generated from these classic offerings. Look, I've been around the block plenty in the music business, and I know one thing for sure: Bands and performer/singers don't give any slots away, especially if they write songs themselves, whether it be a BMI or ASCAP performance fee, or in a live show set list, let alone inclusion in subsequent and guaranteed released CD recordings or video/DVD products, unless they really have an almost spiritual bond or appreciation of those tunes. Plus, the big fees that will eventually be paid must in some manner reflect the Stones' and Madonna's longstanding relationships with Motown Records, the Motown songwriters, and the original artists who first introduced the compositions to their young ears. Man, talk about giving at the office . . .

Gordy eventually withdrew from the day-to-day operations, and finally, in 1988, he sold his brainchild to a major corporation, MCA. More recently, the Motown empire shifted ownership to the PolyGram group of companies, now called Universal Music Group. Gordy himself was by that time no longer a key player in its future. He's still involved with Jobete Music, the publishing company that houses the widely utilized and still influential copyrights that have impacted the radio and sound waves all over the world.

In 1994, Warner Books published Gordy's autobiography, *To Be Loved*. The book's title is taken from a song Gordy penned for "Mr. Excitement," Jackie Wilson.

After talking to Gordy's book publicist about conducting an interview with the Motown Records founder, and then having conversations with the legendary Ewart Abner of Vee-Jay Records fame, a former president of Motown Records himself, and now running The Gordy Company, arrangements were made for a formal talk in the mid '90s, and I was given directions to Gordy's Bel Air mansion in Southern California.

Cruising through the gate to his hillside home, past the tennis court, I dropped my car off to valet parking and was quickly ushered into a waiting room den area, filled with photos and memorabilia of Gordy's groundbreaking melodic life. I glanced at a note from President Clinton, I fondled Gordy's statue from the Rock and Roll Hall of Fame. He is also the recipient of the Songwriters Hall of Fame Abe Olman Publisher Award. There are pictures of Gordy with Muhammad Ali, and black and white framed shots of Gordy's children with the Beatles from a 1964 U.S. tour.

I was originally on assignment for *HITS*, a weekly U.S. trade magazine. I was waiting five years for Gordy to get his book out, and every six months I'd be on the phone with my editor, Roy Trakin, as well as various people in Gordy's orbit giving me the progress report on when he'd be ready to talk. In addition to preparing a piece for *Goldmine* magazine, a national collector's journal, which was planning a special Motown issue, former Detroit resident Bill Holdship of *BAM* magazine called, after *HITS* was printed, and asked for an excerpt for his readership. "They need to know about Berry Gordy and Motown." I replied, "Take what you want and pay me later." After the *BAM* edition was published, a delighted Ewart Abner called me two different times requesting extra copies of the magazine to use in the ongoing Gordy *To Be Loved* promotional campaign.

I had covered the Motown Records label and their touring acts for years when I worked for *Melody Maker* in the '70s.

I wasn't in the room today to discuss the passing of Marvin Gaye, record industry rumors about the label, or to probe further into the chaos and pain of Tammi Terrell's tragic life. Berry had a book to promote, and I offered a forum to discuss his *To Be Loved*, and garner some reflections on his life before and after his Motown crusade. The interview arrangements were helped out by some old school Motown employees who were fans of my work, and remembered I had done stories on former Temptation David Ruffin, and I did conduct the first U.S. interview with the Commodores. I went to their "Brick House" recording session in Hollywood. It's my "party piece."

Ewart Abner, Gordy's right-hand man and mentor, and before that, a historic music executive working with Nolan Strong, Dee Clark, and the Impressions, greets me and instructs me to set up my tape recorder.

Abner tells me I'm on the clock for ninety minutes, and Gordy arrives looking healthy. The house cook is preparing a sliced sashimi lunch.

Berry Gordy then introduces me to some of his family, including his brother Robert, of Jobete Music Company, Inc., who is sitting in on the interview with his wife. Gordy's assistants set up their equipment to film and record us, and I tell Berry that he can relax, "I'm here just to talk music."

We had met briefly a few times over the years, and today I was just a writer and fan. During our exchange, he answered everything I asked, was charming, and often became animated with hand gestures when describing entertainers like Jackie Wilson and Michael Jackson.

Berry Gordy, Jr. has your attention at all times. I didn't even drink my glass of imported water during my audience with him.

Q: Why did you write *To Be Loved*?

A: Several reasons: The history and the legacy. As a general thing I wrote it to, of course, set the record straight, which had long been misunderstood. I wrote it because there were many unsung heroes in my company that were part of this operation, you know, who were not known and who taught the artists how to walk, sing, dance, talk, and even eat, and stuff like that. And they've been with me twenty-five, thirty years, these people. The chaperones who went on the road so much of their time and their life, really being very strict on these artists, and working with these artists.

The artists are famous, and they will always be famous. And the Motown artists are still working today, you know, (in) clubs, going on television, and doing a lot of stuff. So, the unsung heroes were another reason I wrote the book.

And then, I wanted to tell my own story in my own words. Because so often, I have wanted to read about my heroes: Dr. King, Jackie Robinson, J.F.K., Sugar Ray Robinson, Joe Louis. I would have loved to have read their story in their own words. Because when others write about you, they write about what you did or what they think you did, and how they think you did it. And it's nothing like writing your own story about not only what you did but how you felt doing it and, more importantly, why you did what you did at that particular time. And that's what I tried to do.

Then, in setting the record straight, I wanted to set the young minds at ease, put the young minds at ease. Not only the young minds, but the old minds, the people who have been following me for thirty-five years, who believed in me and Motown no matter what they had heard or read in the papers. I felt I owed it to them to do that.

And, whether I like it or not, I'm a role model, you know? So I wanted young people to know that a company like Motown could never have been built as beautiful and as big and as strong as it has become, and the music created like it was, through devious means. Being in the Mafia, cheating artists and all that garbage, you know? And that's why I wrote it.

Why it took so long to write it was because I didn't have the time. I was busy. I mean, I was busy building my dream, going for my vision, trying to focus on what we were doing.

Q: Did you work off a general outline? Can you describe the process of putting this book together?

A: It was the hardest five years of my life. I worked with so many professional people. David Ritz [author of books on Marvin Gaye, Smokey Robinson, Jerry Wexler, Ray Charles, and Etta James] was one. He did a great outline. I mentioned him and I thanked him for that, because only I knew the depth. I wrote it on computer. Tapes, notes, recorded meetings from thirty years ago. I've got so many tapes of those meetings.

Q: Were you always so archive-oriented early on?

A: Yes, without knowing it, I was archive-oriented. I just wanted it for memories, records of things, so I would make tapes of the meetings and stuff like that. I never heard that word before, "archive-oriented." It was before I knew what the word meant. [Laughs] So yes.

Q: You are still involved in Jobete Music, the publishing house and music company. In a recent issue of *Daily Variety*, you discussed the catalog and areas for songs including TV, CD-ROM, commercials, learning outlets. You said, "Everything needs songs. Only five percent of the songs (in the catalog) are making ninety-five percent of the money. We haven't touched the surface of this diamond."

A: Jobete is busily dealing with Motown and we are aware of the ninety-five percent written by the same writers and how we're having a plan for developing that. Already we're probably the most (active) publishing company in movies, and in sampling by others, even rap artists, and so we'll be in whatever it is.

Q: You are meeting people at signings and doing radio station visits and interviews. It seemed you were always more comfortable staying out of the public eye. What kind of experience has touring been for you?

A: Brand new. A totally different experience. When I started it, it was meant to be work and to get the book out, promotion. Because you got to do it. The publisher says, "You got to go for a signing." And they said, "We'll make it as light on you as possible." So I've increased it. They're shocked. Because I've increased it!

I went to Philadelphia and they had all this stuff set up for me. I asked about Georgie Woods [a former DJ at WDAS who broke the Miracles' "Way Over There"]. And they said, "He's not on your schedule, because you are hitting all the top places." He wasn't on the schedule. I said, "He's not in radio anymore?" "Well, yes, he's on a very small station. A talk station somewhere, and it doesn't have that many listeners."

So I said, "Well, I'll tell you what. I don't know where he is, but I want him to be the first. I'm going to see him first." And they said, "That will mess up this . . ." I said, "Rearrange what you have to, but I'm not going to Philadelphia unless I can see Georgie Woods first, because he played 'Way Over There' when I went to him first."

It was the first record I went national with, and Georgie Woods played it, and he didn't have to. He had a whole stack of records and he played mine. And I was just a guy sitting in there (at this station) that didn't know anybody and didn't know how to promote records. I was just a nice guy sitting there waiting, and he played it.

So we ended up going to see him. They changed the schedule, Ewart Abner understood. He was with me and knew exactly what I was talking about, because he was in radio. So he worked it out and we went to see Georgie.

It was the most emotional thing of the whole trip. He actually cried. He was on the air. He knew I was coming and still he was nervous and so thankful. He was thanking me on the air for coming by there and I was busy thanking him for . . . We've been friends throughout the years. We know each other. But on this promotion tour he knew how tight my schedule was. Up at five A.M. to twelve or one o'clock at night. So that's the fun that you get, going to the other radio stations. Some are new, some I didn't know, but their respect . . . and what I had heard about what Motown had done for their lives, when they got married, when they had kids. I heard so much stuff, I had no idea.

So it was a new experience for me. I have always been behind the scenes, so after thirty-five years I was getting out there, and I would be talking, like spewing out all these great feelings I was having. And they looked at me and expected me to be cool and for them to tell me, so I was telling them and so I was like a babe in the woods out there, you know, really the first time. So I realized something. If anything had been missed in those thirty-five years, that was it. Being out there with the people who were really the foundation of the company.

Q: What's it like hearing the songs on the radio now? I know you still get a sense of pride, hearing the sounds, but is it different not being in ownership? What's the feeling like?

A: The feeling is one of great relief. Great relief because the business has changed a lot. And for me, my style of entrepreneurship, it wasn't fun anymore. Because I was too involved, too immersed in it, and it was a major relief because I wanted Motown to live on. I wanted the legacy to go forward.

I made them know they had valuable masters, they had valuable contracts, valuable things going on.

And once they got the deal (the sale), I was thrilled when they were able to see the real value of it and pay the kind of money for it. Because it justified the legacy and what it was.

Because money has never been the main thing for me. It's the legacy that was important. Sure, you try and make as much money as you can but at the risk . . . I could have done a lot of things with Motown.

Q: Piece it out. Go territorial.

A: Piece it out . . . That would have been very bad for the legacy, for the whole thing. Ideas came to me, like auctioning off some of the master tapes at Sotheby's, because we had so many of them. People would love, around the world, to own a master by Diana Ross and the Supremes, Stevie Wonder, the rights to that master, one at a time. I would have made five times the money. So it wasn't about "the money." It was about the legacy.

When Motown was bought by PolyGram, I was very happy, because I knew it had a home then, and I had given my masters and my legacy a home. And that would keep the Motown artists still in the limelight. And they're continuing to work. The Four Tops, the Temptations, Martha and the Vandellas; they are traveling around the world.

Q: But is it a different listening experience for you now?

A: Much different. Much different. In fact, I just did a radio interview on Stevie Wonder's station, KGLH. When I do the radio interviews, I always use the headphones. When I give an interview I want to hear the music, hear the voices, hear things. I have a ball. I'm rediscovering some of these things. There are hundreds and hundreds of records.

Every time I hear those great Motown songs . . . I mean, I'll hear Marvin Gaye's "What's Goin' On" album. He had three voices: Marvin on top of Marvin on top of Marvin. Just incredible. Now I'm appreciating it a lot more, because there we were going for perfection. Now it's there, and I can listen to it without having to worry about a follow-up, or another record by another artist on this and that. It's great.

Q: Motown began with 45 rpm records. Then the album format, eventually 8-track cartridges, cassettes, and now compact discs. Were you personally impacted by the growth of the LP market?

A: Not very much. We were about producing songs that were great. And so a lot of the producers who would be coming to our Friday morning meetings, they would say when the song wasn't that great, "Oh, that's an album tune. That's just going on the album." I'd say, "No. No. There are no album tunes. Every tune has to stand on its own." We didn't look at album tunes as such. We would pick tunes that were hits and that's why they would go on albums and pull out a hit here, a hit there, you know? So it didn't impact us that there were albums and we had departments and all that stuff. But as far as recording, unless there was a concept album and things like that, we would say there are no album tunes. We'd say that all the time.

Actually, we made money on every new format that came out, because it was a new configuration. So they'd buy all over again, whatever it was. Then you have software, that's what it is now. That's why Jobete is so important to us, because of the songs and its software. Whatever it is, a great song is a great song. That's all it is. And whatever configuration comes, we don't worry about the configuration. We worry about if we have the product. And that's what we're doing, going into Jobete saying, "Hey, before we do anything else, let's make sure we have great songs. Make sure these songs are still great. Let's look at all the other ninety-five percent of our songs."

'Cause there's great songs that were great, but they were produced wrong, or maybe the wrong singer, or maybe this or maybe that. But the quality is still there. So let's look at all that. So that's what we're doing now, and that's fun. Because I started as a songwriter. I love songs, so you know, that's a hobby.

Q: I love the descriptions and the anecdotes in your book about the junkmen you met in your childhood. I gleaned that they explained many things to you that impacted your life, personally, and in how to do business.

A: With the junkmen, they sat down with me as a little kid in the neighborhood, and they had wit, wisdom, and told me some stuff for my own good. And the fact they owned most of our buildings around us, I thought they were brilliant. And I said, "I want to learn what they are doing." They taught me about supply and demand! And that's what the book is supposed to do for inner city kids, to understand if they want to build something like Motown, see, it's not built by devious means, the Mafia, cheating artists out of their stuff. You understand it very well.

Life is not nearly as complicated as people make it. See, it's basic. We got to get back to basic values and basic communication. Two and two is four. And all people want the same things, I constantly say. Each one of us is different though, and I tell artists to bring out their own uniqueness. That's why you'll get a Stevie Wonder, a Marvin Gaye, a Smokey Robinson. You've got to nurture that. That's what we try to do. Nurture their difference.

And so it wasn't me that was the genius. If I was a genius of anything, it was bringing out the genius of others, because if they reached their potential then I had felt that maybe I could reach mine. So in bringing out the genius in others and finding it, sure, it was hard and tough, but your clues will tell you. And then, stopping them from focusing on other things other than what they're doing.

And there's still ninety-nine percent of the people, in my opinion, running around there now with this great talent, great art, great ideas like that, but they will never make it through. The idea is that when you make it through the fame, fortune and riches and power, and you are not the same person you were when you started out, then you have been a failure. I don't care how much money you got, fame or fortune you got. You got to be the same person that you started out with. And when you are, then you can consider yourself a success.

Q: What have been some of the artist reactions to *To Be Loved*?

A: Diana (Ross) called. Martha (Reeves) called. The people who were in the book. They just love it. "We never knew what you went through." "You were so busy thinking about us, ourselves, our stardom, but what you went through—we appreciate it." The five years writing it were so well worth it. And I'm getting nothing but accolades from the people in the street. The radio stations and my own artists. And my own family. My own family is saying, "Wow!" No one hardly knows anybody, and I wish more people could write their own story the way it is.

Q: I know, but I bet a lot of people reading this conversation might not be aware that you had a life, from age 18 to 29, before Motown began. You talk about it in the book. Auto plant, the 3D Record Mart, writing songs. A ten-year period where being in the real world probably paid dividends later.

A: The real world. I learned a lot. If I hadn't worked in the factory at Lincoln-Mercury, I wouldn't have had the assembly line idea. I wouldn't have written a lot of songs. I wouldn't have been locked into a place where I had to write a lot of thoughts I had. I saw what the real world was like and I saw what I wanted and what I didn't want.

Q: After you were discharged from the Korean War, you opened a record shop, 3D Mart—House of Jazz, that stocked exclusively jazz records in 1953.

A: Yes. That's all we stocked. I did know a lot about the blues. I did hear the old people playing it on the weekends. They'd have these parties, these house parties on the weekends, drink beer, and the blues was wailing in the bars on Hastings Street. B.B. King, you know? I was aware of it, but it was beneath us, my little group. We (liked) "The Bird," Charlie Parker. If you weren't hip to "The Bird," man . . . or Miles Davis could soothe you to death. I can still hear it today. I really did love jazz.

So, when I went in the record business, I opened up a jazz record store. The people in our neighborhood were factory workers and things like that and they did not know jazz, nor care about it. They were older, and I said, "I've got a major job to do. I'm gonna help these people with their life. I'm gonna teach them about jazz. These people are ignorant about jazz." And so I started telling them about Charlie Parker, and they kept saying, "You got Muddy Waters? Jimmy Reed?" I said, "No. If you want that stuff, you'll have to go down Hastings Street."

And I'd say, "Here's jazz, let me explain it to you." They did not want to hear it. They wanted the blues. And so, anyway, when we started going out of business, started losing money, I decided maybe I'd better listen to some of this blues stuff, and then just get some stock around.

So that's when I met the Mad Russian, who was a card, who was great, and I had to communicate. But see, there again, it was communication. I communicated with him. And I started buying boxes of records that I thought would hit. He was a one-stop. He went to distributors and he could buy 'em from Chicago before they ever got here (Detroit), or he'd buy them all out from the distributors. He only charged a nickel more, but he was this crazy guy that walked around there, but he was crazy like a fox, all of a sudden he wasn't crazy no more. "You want two? You want three? What do you want?" And then you'd say, "I want a box of so-and-so." "Okay." Then he was kind of sane.

Q: I was always impressed that you later had a spoken word label at Motown, the Black Forum, where the voices of Dr. Martin Luther King, Jr., Stokely Carmichael, Elaine Brown, and Imamu Amiri Baraka, among others, were recorded.

A: I put out several things by Dr. King, including "The Great March To Freedom" in Washington, probably the biggest, "I Have A Dream." One of the things in those days, in the '6os, there was a civil unrest and the various people who had things to say. I was very closely connected to Dr. King and liked his philosophy, and he taught me the wisdom of non-violence. As I said in *To Be Loved*, I was never like a "turn the other cheek kind of guy," you know? I wasn't brought up that way. In the inner city you don't do that.

But he taught me the wisdom of non-violence. While we were victims, others were victims, too. White people were victims when they let their prejudices hold them back. He was more with my philosophy of communicating with people around the world. Understanding. I think we all want the same kind of thing. We all want peace, we all want love, we all want togetherness. And I think one thing that music has done is brought people together with the same ideas. We had a family of people that were dealing with that fundamental thing about communicating love.

Q: What was your first impression of Smokey Robinson?

A: Well, Smokey Robinson, my first impression was he was great, a great poet, but he didn't know how to really write songs, or put songs together. When he learned how to put stuff together and he really understood, Smokey was incredible. When I turned down his first 100

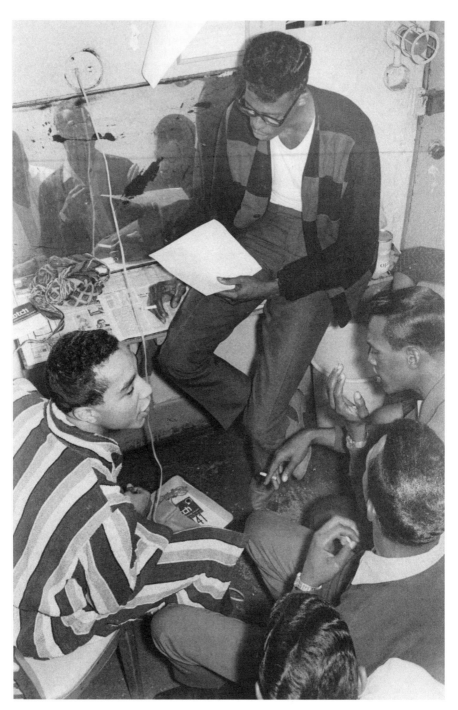

Smokey Robinson teaching the Temptations the song "My Girl" backstage at the Apollo Theatre, New York City, 1964. Photo by Don Paulsen.

songs, he got more excited with every song. I said, "This guy has to be either crazy or one of the most special people I'll ever meet." He was incredible. He turned out to be one of the most special people I ever met.

Q: And that angelic voice.

A: Oh, yes. Pure. And then, he got it and understood it. So now Smokey has succeeded at the cycle of success. It takes a lot of character, because you are tempted along the way. The cycle of success is a vicious cycle. It takes you into places. People offer you things never offered before. To succeed and be successful is tough, so it takes a lot of character. You got to keep your same values. So Smokey has done that. The Four Tops have done that. And most of the Motown artists have it drilled into them and they were all very tight.

Q: The Temptations?

A: Legends. They've managed to keep their look and their style all these years and they've changed members constantly, but Otis and Melvin have done just an amazing job of finding one major talent after another. Because they are legends, people want to be with the Temptations, and they have proven that the group is stronger than any of its parts. I don't care how great that part was, the Temptations are an institution.

Q: The Four Tops?

A: The epitome of loyalty, integrity, class. They've been together for forty years, the same members. That is unheard of, impossible, and I just admire them so much. I admire them the most of any of the artists.

Q: Diana Ross?

A: Diana . . . Special, magic, sensitive. When she does a song like "Somewhere" in front of an audience, she still cries. I mean, I've never seen her do "Somewhere" without crying. In fact, we used to stop her from doing it every night in the week. The Bernstein song from "West Side Story." She was so dramatic, and then she did the second ending and it was too much emotionally. She's so emotional and she gives all to her audience and she is sincere about it and serious about it.

Q: Marvin Gaye?

A: The truest artist I've ever known. Whatever he was going through in his life, he put on records. So if you want to know Marvin just listen to one of his records.

Q: Stevie Wonder?

A: Innovative. The most innovative person that I've ever known. But also unique with his tones and his voice quality and all that. He was as close to genius, and I don't like to use the word genius, you know—Marvin could have been a genius—I don't like to throw it around, but Stevie is one of those kind of special, special, special people that had a sound, and he's quick. He's creative and he can make up something very quick.

Q: And he is involved in technological developments.

A: That's what I'm saying. Contraptions. He would take technology. He was the first in technology. He's an innovator.

Q: Michael Jackson?

A: Greatest entertainer in the world and one of the smartest people and businessmen in the world. He conducted his own career, basically. He knew what he wanted. And, from nine years old, he was a thinker. And I called him "Little Spongy," because he was like a sponge and he learned from everybody. He not only studied me, but he studied James Brown, Jackie Wilson, Marcel Marceau, Fred Astaire, Walt Disney . . . And he bought the Beatles' catalog. Michael is nobody's fool. Very bright. Very smart.

Q: Jackie Wilson. People are rediscovering Jackie due to some of the repackages.

A: The most natural artist I've ever seen in terms of dancing, vocals. His voice was the strongest. He could do opera, he could do rock, he could do blues and he created, the most creative singer that I'd known. As I said in the book, he never sang a bad note. Maybe a bad song, but never a bad note . . . One of the most talented artists I've ever seen. Of course, I'm talking about all great people here. So when I say talented, in another way, I mean he was the most natural.

Q: Was he more dynamic live than on record?

A: Yes, of course! He was more dynamic live than on record. And he could dance, and could do flips and splits. Different than Michael. Michael studied a lot of people who did a lot of things. Jackie did not study anybody but Jackie. Jackie was Jackie, the most natural, innate performer, probably that I've ever seen. He had nobody to study that I know of. Jackie was an original. Probably the most original artist that I've ever seen. And he should be rediscovered. Because he created stuff and he could wink on cue. I said it in the book. He could do things, do a spin, and then wink at the girls.

Q: In *To Be Loved*, you discuss the Motown session musicians, some who played with Dizzy Gillespie and had jazz backgrounds, and potential musical conflicts that emerged when you first put the group together.

A: Absolutely. We had a big story in there (the book) about me and (bassist) James Jamerson, when I threatened him and gave him an ultimatum, and I was praying he would . . . I could have put him out. I wanted control of all the guys 'cause I was the boss, and I wanted to make sure they knew that, because otherwise I couldn't have any order. And Jamerson, I mean, he came very close to me having a confrontation, but neither of us . . . He loved what he was doin' and I loved him being there. But I still wanted him to have freedom in the restriction and he took it and was great.

Q: I need to ask you about the Holland, Dozier and Holland production and songwriting team . . .

A: H-D-H was phenomenal. They came up with hit after hit. They started a thing. They had a lock on the Supremes and they took them, and did stuff on Marvin. H-D-H was absolutely brilliant. The three of them were different and they all complemented each other.

Eddie (Holland) did mostly vocals, Brian (Holland), I thought, was the most talented, creative person. He was my protégé for many years. I thought Lamont (Dozier) was also a good writer, and he was good on backgrounds and this and that and so forth. But Brian would do something like he would play and sing and create something and all he would give 'em was, like, "sugar pie honey bunch," and pass it on. So they had their own assembly line. And they were tremendous.

Q: The producer and songwriter, Norman Whitfield?

A: Norman to me was probably the most underrated of all the producers, because he was producing by himself. And he would deal with different sounds, different beats, change with the times and write his stuff, and also Barrett Strong would work with him as a writer on many of his things. Norman was innovative and he had fire. And he had a different kind of style. His beat was different and could go from "Cloud Nine," "Psychedelic Shack," "Papa Was a Rolling Stone," to "Just My Imagination." He was sensitive and I think he could do so many different types of things. Then he'd come right back with "War," and then "Ain't Too Proud to Beg."

He could take one chord, like on "Papa Was a Rolling Stone," and play the same chord and do all these different beautiful melodies and things that many people could not really imagine this guy doin'. And

I would watch him, and he did it all by himself as a producer. He would work with five guys in the Temps and he would change leads on each one. He would pick the right lead for the right song, ya know, and he'd utilize all five of those leads in a song, that was just incredible. When I listen to 'em today, now that I have time to listen to 'em, I'm saying, "Wow! This guy was probably the most underrated producer we had."

Ewart Abner politely signaled that our interview was over. At the end of our rap, I requested a signed Motown CD for my friend, Rosemarie Patronette, the baddest white woman in Los Angeles. I then mentioned to Berry that my favorite Motown and Jobete song and current Northern Soul dance floor disc was the Supremes' "Up the Ladder to the Roof." Diana Ross didn't even sing on it. "That was Jean Terrell," he answers. "Frank Wilson was the producer! That's one of those ninety-five percent," responds Berry Gordy, Jr.

Afterwards, Gordy autographed my *To Be Loved* book, he embraced me as the valet pulled up with the keys to my ride, and then I drove home down the hill to Sunset Blvd. Turned on my car radio and KRTH-FM was having a "Motown Monday." "My Girl" was in rotation.

"Can I Get a Witness?" Indeed.

Driving through Bel Air, I flashed on a "Letter of Employment" that Berry Gordy, Jr. had sent to music industry veteran Kim Fowley in 1960 that still hangs in Fowley's office. Just before I left for BG's residence, I told Fowley I was interviewing his old boss. Fowley was Motown's first West Coast promo man for a month in 1960, handling several records, including the Miracles' "Way Over There," their single after "Bad Girl," and just before "Shop Around" went Top Ten. In 1960, Fowley had just co-produced and co-published "Alley Oop" by the Hollywood Argyles, a big hit record, and was on six months' active duty in the Air Force National Guard, while waiting for his royalty statement from the national "Alley Oop" chart sales.

"I was also working five records a week as a promo man after working for DJ Alan Freed," Fowley recalls, "and making $250 a week in U.S. dollars. I got the Motown job after seeing their ad in *Cash Box*. Berry Gordy's sister Loucye took my phone call, in Detroit, that I placed from Happy's Gas Station on Hollywood Boulevard, which I also used as an office. She was gracious, focused, heard my *spiel* about how I could help the label out in California. Berry then got on the line, we talked about singer Marv Johnson who he'd just cut, and he quickly sent me a letter with a check. You could be on the street then, based out of a gas station, and get a label head on the phone in those days."

Kim Fowley has nothing but admiration for Berry Gordy's contributions to the music business and his impact on earth. "Berry Gordy. Pioneer, military strategist, musical genius, and business icon. The role model of every record company that followed him," Fowley offers. "What he did, helping to bring forward so many talented artists, musicians, songwriters, and producers, was heroic, especially in the 1957–1960 period, before Martin Luther King, Jr. emerged from Selma, Alabama. An impossible fantasy," Kim concludes.

Grace Slick:

A Rock-'n'-Roll Memoir

This Grace Slick profile, conducted over the telephone, was originally intended for *HITS* magazine. Due to space limitations, it never made it to publication until now. Grace has lived to tell her rock-'n'-roll tale with Jefferson Airplane in her autobiography, *Somebody to Love?*

I've known Grace for years, and previously chatted on the record with her and Jefferson Airplane/Starship members for *Melody Maker* in the late 1970s. I stayed for the weekend at the 2400 Fulton Street "Airplane" house in San Francisco.

Her daughter with Paul Kanter, China, is married to my dentist buddy Jamie, who lived in a dormitory with me at San Diego State College. Grace's first husband, Jerry Slick, also briefly attended San Diego State College, and Grace would visit him on campus before she joined Jefferson Airplane. Jerry's brother Darby wrote the song "Somebody to Love."

A couple of years ago, China and I both took our moms for Mother's Day, to the Canon Theater in Beverly Hills for a production of the stage play, "Bill Graham Presents," starring Ron Silver, that author Robert Greenfield adapted from his book on music promoter Graham, who at one time managed Jefferson Airplane.

I play Jefferson Airplane's 1966–1970 albums religiously. I have a signed "Surrealistic Pillow" from Grace, and a signature from Paul on "Early Flight." I always groove on their unique blend of voices and instrumentation.

In the mid '90s I produced Paul Kantner's "A Guide through the Chaos (A Road to the Passion)—The Spoken Word History of the Jefferson Airplane & Beyond." Grace wrote a short liner note for the package.

Grace Slick, Bolinas, California, 1971. Photo by Henry Diltz.

Grace Slick is best known for her work and life as the lead singer of Rock-'n'-Roll Hall of Fame members, Jefferson Airplane. Slick has penned, with Andrea Cagan, *Somebody to Love?* (Warner Books), which chronicles her long journey from Bay Area socialite to counterculture goddess.

Grace recalls her drug-dazed and alcohol-soaked performances, as well as her friendships with music royalty like Janis Joplin, Jimi Hendrix, Paul Kantner, Bill Graham, Jim Morrison, and Jerry Garcia, and also provides an intimate look back at the legendary rock-'n'-roll festivals, Monterey Pop, Woodstock, and Altamont. Jefferson Airplane is the only band to have played at all three.

Advertisement from the L.A. Free Press, courtesy of the Harvey Kubernik Collection.

In reading her book, I was happy to learn that Grace lived locally in the Los Angeles area as a young girl, and shared some memories of meals at the Farmer's Market on 3rd and Fairfax. I think she had an uncle who worked at MGM, too. Grace has many links to Southern California. Do I even have to add that many of the classic and monumental Jefferson Airplane studio recordings of 1966–1969 were done at RCA Studios on Sunset Boulevard in Hollywood?

Today, the recorded music of Jefferson Airplane is heard on countless radio stations, and many of their songs continue to surface on numerous film soundtracks. "Platoon," "Forrest Gump," and the current "Without Limits" incorporate their impressive catalog of romance, love, and frantic possibilities that underscored their albums during the 1966–1970 period. Some people forget the impact and influence of Jefferson Airplane and the role model position Grace Slick was afforded as the powerful singer-lyricist with the band. She was last heard on Linda Perry's solo CD two years back.

Grace now lives a sober life in Malibu, California. Her book also reflects her efforts on behalf of animal welfare and her reconciliation with her adult daughter, China. The songs Grace Slick sang with Jefferson Airplane, and later Jefferson Starship, only hinted at the complex woman documented on the recordings of this Bay Area "group therapy experiment."

Grace Slick is a very opinionated subject around a tape recorder. What a delight for someone rolling and reporting. Which is exactly what we did in the spring of 1998 . . .

Q: Originally, when you first started writing your book with Andrea Cagan, she initially asked you questions about your life, then you would review the responses, but the results sounded disjointed. Then, you tried a method where she provided you with a foundation for each chapter, and a list of topics, and you would write down your recollections or interpretations of that aspect of your life. Can you discuss the actual collaboration and process of this book? And why did you even do a book?

A: Because a friend of mine, a lawyer, Brian Rohan, came over to my house and asked, "What are you doing?" And I said, "I'm drawing." I had done 150, 200 drawings, and he just passed over that like, "That's not doing anything, that's nice, why don't you write a book?" "Because I don't wanna write a book." And he said I should write a book, and he knew this great agent . . . "Will you just talk to her?" She (Maureen Regan) talked to me for about seven hours and I finally just sort of gave in as far as writing a book goes. Because I had no interest in it. But, once I got going, I enjoyed it. I had never written a book. I had written short form, which is lyrics, but that is very different from the long form. But I really enjoyed the process of writing a book. At first I thought, "O.K. They pay me money, and somebody else does the work." The publisher recommended some writers and I liked Andrea.

Q: By the way, I liked the photo of her in the book. A blonde in a bikini . . .
A: Yeah. I thought the guys would like that. And I liked Andrea as a person. She had done some previous books, written with Marianne Williamson and Diana Ross. What happened first of all was that she would come over to my house and say, "What do you think of . . .?"— whatever the topic was—when I was four years old, or my grandmother.

Q: And you have done hundreds of interviews over a third of a century. Is (or was) a "book" interview different than the traditional music interview?
A: No, not really. Interviews over the years had shorter questions and

shorter answers. So this was to elaborate, and she had a tape recorder. So I'd elaborate on some subject verbally, and she'd take it home, write it up on her computer and fax it back to me and say, "How does this look?" And it looked fine, and she writes well and everything, but it's not my voice. She's a very nice person. And I don't speak that way. So we changed it to where she would suggest to "give me some stuff about your grandmother" and I would write it and fax it back to her. She would say, "It's a little long here," or "your spelling needs some work." So it turned out to be me writing the book, which I sort of balked at in the beginning, and I thought, "Oh God, I just wanted a free ride here." But it turned out I enjoyed it, though I'd write about stuff, and I'd forget specific dates. Or, "Is this accurate?" "Where were we?" There's a section on Jim Morrison and, to this day, I still don't know what country we were in when I discuss it in the chapter, "Strawberry Fuck."

Q: Well, since you brought him up, I especially liked the description of your "involvement" with Morrison.

A: I had to call [author and Doors manager] Danny Sugerman and ask him, "Could you possibly figure out where we would have been when I fucked Jim [Morrison, during a 1968 Doors and Jefferson Airplane European tour]?" Danny was funny about it. To this day, I still don't know what country it was in. At least Danny had an idea by process of elimination. I don't think it was in Amsterdam, but it might have been. I do know that, one of the days both groups were in Amsterdam, Jim took more drugs than anybody I'd ever seen in my life. The two bands were walking down the street in Amsterdam and drugs were legal. And the kids knew the bands and they would come up to us and offer all sorts of drugs. And we'd either say, "Thank you" or put them in our pocket for later. Jim would take everything they would give him on the spot. He'd sit down at the curb and do it up. Whatever it was. I thought, "Jesus, we've got to play tonight. I wonder how that's gonna work?" Sure enough, he came on stage that night and looked like a pinwheel going around. Totally on some other planet. So they had to take him away and he landed up in a hospital. So, obviously, it wasn't that day we were together. Maybe it was the day before. Generally I can remember the country but not exactly. Like with Paul [Kantner] on a boat where we took some acid. It might have been Sweden. But I'm not sure.

Q: It almost appears by your description in the book like you had an out-of-body experience with him, or at least he was supplying an out-of-body experience.

A: Well, it felt like that. He can be with you and not with you at the same time. And it's not the same as someone being snobby and mean and being detached. It's more like he has two things going on. One, he's interacting with you and the world and whatever is going on around him. And two, you can see him enjoying what is also happening in his mind. Which may or may not have to do with what is going down at the moment. I'm not real good at one night stands. I generally have had sex with people that I know. And I'm fired up by people, and it takes more than appearance. So yes, I had sex with his mind, as well as his personality and every other thing I can think of.

On stage he didn't do the same thing that [Mick] Jagger did. But he did what he wanted. He would do what he wanted. Miles Davis used to play and would turn his back on the audience for the entire time he was playing. So that's kinda doing what you want, rather than being an entertainer. More than an entertainer, Morrison just did what he felt at the time and it may not have been what you wanted either. Or it may not have been what the band wanted. I'm sure, like me, when you can't count on what they're gonna do. That was kind of interesting. [Laughs] Time to time.

Q: Does the printed page capture the feelings of the moment you are trying to convey to the reader?

A: Yeah. You've got 390 pages or whatever and you do the best. That's the part that is fun about it, taking an event or a situation and doing it in a paragraph. Andrea's best attribute as someone who did the book with me was that she was good at organizing and had done it before. "Are we going to do it chronologically? Then let's do it this way. Let's start at the beginning. We can back-track." What I write is the situation, the idea. A remembrance of a specific individual, and then she's got to organize that so it has some continuity: "The third paragraph needs work." Then I'd do it.

Q: How did the editing process develop, and was it hard cutting down the pages?

A: There were a few places where I felt some things were more important than they did. Basically, in order to sell books you have to have sex, drugs, and rock-'n'-roll. As far as the book coming from me, there are other things that I'm interested in.

Q: You could have done 400 pages on biomedical research.

A: Exactly. But that's not what people are buying and I understand that. But it is a part of my life, so there's, "How much do we put in there?"

That would have been my focus. A lot of people have written about the sixties and I knew that was what they wanted and what they were paying me for. So that's what I did primarily. It took four months to write. Andrea lives in L.A. and she came over three times a week and we'd do it like, when she'd make suggestions, "We need some more on Woodstock." I'm not as interested in Woodstock as most people. So I had to draw that out. "What did you wear?" "How was it when you first got in?" That kind of stuff. As far as editing, Rick Horgan (editor) had suggestions, but for the most part was good. He let us fly. On the chapter titles, some are mine, some are Andrea's. The chapter titles are usually obvious by what you are writing about.

Q: And the illustrations in the book. Your own drawings are included with some key photos.

A: The illustrations were done within the last two years. A lot of them were specifically for the book. About a year and a half ago, I was drawing animals and my agent said, "Why don't you draw (Jim) Morrison, Jerry Garcia? So I did. I will draw anything people tell me to draw or I won't do it. But I won't draw how they tell me to draw it. In other words, the agent took copies of these things to an art gallery who said, "I like this style." I draw, and it looks like a different person every time. And I mean to keep it that way.

Q: Was selecting the photos an emotional experience?

A: It's not emotional. It's a big, tedious process. My house burned down in Northern California, and one of the parts of the house that did not burn down was the basement. I don't hang up gold records or pictures. I put it all in the basement. So I transferred all that junk down here and, basically, I had the agent, my co-writer, and my friend Vincent Marino, who knows a lot about the Jefferson Airplane, go through all the stuff and pull things out. It bores me to do this kind of stuff. I could care less. So it was, "This is wonderful!" and I'd say yes or no occasionally. But I didn't do all the hard work, which was going through all the boxes. When I did the book, I set up a time. Other people who do these kinds of books might be comfortable at night. Or without a co-writer. Other people might be too far apart to do it. You may live in L.A. and they may live in New York. It depends on the person.

Q: How have the in-store appearances and retail book signings been across the nation? Who are the fans? What do they bring for you to sign, or what do they like about the book? Or do they have favorite albums and songs?

A: It's not traumatic meeting the audience. I usually do a twenty-minute Q&A session and I'll get up with a microphone behind the lectern and people will ask any questions. I don't have any secrets, except my knees, which I keep covered at all times. Because they're kinda funny looking. Then I'll sign books. There are people I've known from the Grateful Dead to some people who had to be taken out by the police, to young people who don't know what's going on, but their parents were into the Jefferson Airplane. "Little Trudy wants you to sign a book," and she doesn't know who I am. Then the people who bought T-shirts in 1974, and it's a real mishmash.

Q: When I did the album with Paul Kantner, Jefferson Airplane bandleader, he made it a point to tell me that when you played venues like the Fillmore West or Fillmore East, your favorite place to be was on the stage, because it was the least crowded place at the party. And there's a new live Jefferson Airplane CD recorded from 1968 Fillmore gigs.

A: Exactly. The audience and the bands were not that separate. In other words, a large amount of the audience was the other bands at the time. There were lots of bands that were working in San Francisco and we played with each other on the stage sometimes. Somebody would walk up from the audience and play guitar for a while with somebody. Another band. So it was casual, and not that separated. Also as Paul said, and it's true, there's more room on the stage. And I don't like a whole room of people talking. It's not organized and it makes me nervous. So I prefer music, where everyone is playing pretty much in the same key. They are being unique, expressing themselves, but they are playing in the same key. So I enjoyed going to parties and playing music for quite a bit of the time. Because I loved that. It's a lot better than just going into a room with a bunch of people blowing smoke up each other's asses and talking. And everyone talking. Different conversations, different people, I find that confusing.

Q: And obviously in the book you discuss Bill Graham of the Fillmores, who at one time managed the Jefferson Airplane. What was he like? I interviewed him once at his house and he could work a phone!

A: As a rock-'n'-roll force, I mostly liked his energy. Both physical and mental. He was able to keep an awful lot of balls in the air. He could organize, and do business, whereas most of us were on the artistic side, which is a positive thing, but also we would not have been able to deal effectively, I don't think, with the business end of it. Which he did. And without that, we would not have had what we did. A venue to express ourselves.

On the stage at
Woodstock, August
1969. (Sitting, l to r)
Jack Casady, Grace
Slick, Sally Mann,
Michael Casady, Spencer
Dryden. (Standing, l to r)
Musician Country Joe
McDonald, rock music
promoter Bill Graham.
Photo by Henry Diltz.

Q: How do you feel about some of the Jefferson Airplane's songs being utilized in films and subsequent soundtrack albums? "Comin' Back to Me" from "Surrealistic Pillow" is a major cue in the current Robert Towne film, "Without Limits."

A: I like it when the songs are in films. It hasn't been misused. There was some jerky thing on television, "Go Ask Alice," that was kinda dumb. But most of them are used appropriately. To either represent the era, or a feeling, or a situation. And God knows it pays well! Personally I love music from movies. And it's the only venue where we can hear people who write for orchestra. Modern music. Like the soundtrack from "Zorro," or "The Mission." I want to get the soundtrack from "Wag the Dog," which is by Mark Knopfler. I love soundtracks. Not the ones where they bunch singles together. People who actually write music like an opera. They write for the story.

Q: Was it hard creating and editing the profiles of the Jefferson Airplane band members for the book? Everyone is still alive and you've known these guys, and were intimate with just about all the lot for decades.

Your first solo album was called "Manhole." What constitutes the paragraphs to describe your feelings and reflections on band members?

A: I couldn't do whole chapters, because you only have a limited amount of space. It makes it a little easier having written lyrics, which are short form. And you have an idea and you better make it concise. So there's a little practice in that area of bringing a large subject, a human being is so complex, but they do have characteristics that stand out, making them individuals. That's where you pull it into a paragraph.

Q: Based on feedback and audience interaction at these book promotional appearances, and the TV and radio interviews you've done in conjunction with *Somebody to Love?*, what album and what song has emerged as the record or tune that seems to be their favorite song?

A: Hmmm. Well, "Surrealistic Pillow" is the one most people know of or have. As a song, I was surprised doing the book tour signings and talking to people, "Lather" apparently is very popular. People were very interested in "Lather." And then there are people who know all the albums and have specific things that they really like. And more people knew my solo albums than I thought would know them, because they didn't sell all that well. Either they weren't that good, or we didn't promote them. I didn't go on the road with any of them. And that's a very important thing as far as selling solo albums. But I was amazed at the amount of people who had the solo albums and actually knew them. I don't pay attention to royalty statements. I send all that stuff to an accountant. I have never spent more than I have. And I have a vague idea of how much I have. I don't have managers and lawyers because I haven't been in this business for a while. And when I did the book with Andrea, we didn't go back and play the albums. Because I really didn't dive heavily into the music. Talking about music doesn't do a lot and doesn't blow my skirt up.

Q: You've always loved the Miles Davis "Sketches of Spain" CD. Why?

A: It was both classical and orchestrated, and jazz. And Spanish and very well constructed by Gil Evans. I listened to it about fifty times without stopping and wrote "White Rabbit." "Sketches of Spain" was beautifully played upon and danced over and through by Miles Davis. I appreciate jazz and classical music and the construction, and how the orchestra was utilized. It's just an amazing album.

Q: Was there a difference in listening to that album thirty to thirty-five years ago stoned or not under any influence? Is there a difference in the absorption of that record, or any recording, when high?

A: Yeah. Tones sound different depending upon how your chemistry is any one day or another. Tones will be different, how the speed feels will be different. Which area of the record is profound will vary from chemical to chemical and from straight, which is still a chemical construction when you're straight, it's your own chemistry working. So it does vary. When I wrote songs, I read them over on a variety of different chemicals and straight, to make sure it worked all ways instead of just one way.

Q: These days you are really a Gipsy Kings fan. What attracts you to their music and sound?

A: Because on stage they don't do a lot of silly business. They don't have exploding chickens and act silly. They just stand there and do their music. And they do it well. It is the mass of guitars which creates undertones, overtones, and side tones that you can't get with one or five instruments. The two major guys who sing have beautiful voices and really they know how to play. They know how to produce a record.

Q: I know "La Bamba" by Ritchie Valens was the first song that brought you into a record shop, and simultaneously you noticed an album cover on that visit by Lenny Bruce, which directed you towards his comedy albums. Subsequently, when you were in the Great Society, you wrote a song, "Father Bruce," about him.

A: Most people, if they look at their lives, have some things that are consistent. Reoccurring attractions. Spanish music for me has been a consistent, continuous attraction. Like "La Bamba" to "Sketches of Spain" to the Gipsy Kings.

I saw Lenny Bruce a couple of times. And he was fabulous. After he got into the trial segment of his life. The legal thing. He got so attached to that and it was tedious for other people because they weren't as strung out, literally and figuratively, with the legal system. It wasn't as interesting to people. So his performances during that time got somewhat tedious. But before that, the guy would hit all different kinds of subjects. He was just amazing. When I saw his album cover at a record store, where he was having a picnic in a graveyard, I had never seen any bashing of so-called sacred cows. Having a picnic in a graveyard. We are talking about the fifties. They just didn't do stuff like that. It was "Leave It to Beaver" time. And "Father Bruce" came out of that experience. Comedians very often are letting us know about morality through humor. That's why I called him Father Bruce. They are preachers telling you what it's like in society without being particularly dogmatic. It's an easier way to swallow morality, listening to a comedian.

Q: And I know both you and China rave about the Dave Matthews Band.

A: Oh yeah. I like everything about him and the band. When I listen to people, it's a combination of things. When you meet an individual, you like them for a combination of reasons. The way they carry themselves. The way the entire band sound together. The way they interact musically and physically on stage. What they are saying. How it's produced. How they act when they feel something has gone wrong. Do they fall apart, or get mad, or do it with humor? Do they derive their music from a bunch of different areas, which is very American to do because we have a lot of different cultures living here? All music that inspires me is a life force. It's like eating the right food. Only better.

Q: You know, the most amazing thing I found out about you from *Somebody to Love?*, and various band members have told me this over the years but somehow I couldn't believe it, was that really you didn't have a plan to be a lead singer in a band that eventually sold millions and millions of records. Jack Casady, the Airplane bassist, said, "What do you think about singing with Airplane?" "Yeah, that might work." I know you knew you were going to be on the varsity squad, but it always appeared you just did things as they were presented to you and you never had careerist aspirations, or even during college at University of Miami and Finch finishing school, this wasn't the academic way to enter the music world, let alone rock bands. And you've never struck me as a competitive individual with the selfish aspect almost required in today's music and rock-'n'-roll climate.

A: Well, now it's more corporate. And it's very hard to get away with it. Ani DiFranco is trying to retain some dignity and make records at the same time. Since the record companies know what they want now, they will say, "It's got to be this long. We will take pictures here." Back then, they really didn't know what to do with us. It was a lot easier to impose what we wanted to do on them, because it was so new to the record companies. All they knew is that the kids were showing up for this and maybe they could make a buck off it. "What is this?" They really didn't know. They were coming out of the organized New York, Philadelphia, L.A., Frankie Avalon, Fabian, Dinah Shore, whatever world. That's a whole different thing. We had a great deal of freedom that the kids don't have now.

Q: Your mother was a singer, and long before you joined Jefferson Airplane and even before you cut with the Great Society, you were doing marketing research involving aluminum foil. Then you answered an ad, "Singer wanted for new record label. No experience necessary." You picked out "Summertime" and it was an all-black record label. In the book you mention you rehearsed and dressed that song to the nines, but didn't get a callback from the men at the label's recording studio. What did you learn over the years and decades about recording and specifically recording your voice, or preparation for the studio?

A: It's fifty-fifty. You go into a recording studio and you know if you can more or less sing. But the part you learn is where your strengths and weaknesses are. My strength is volume and interpretation, and the weaknesses are range and quality of my vocal chords. I have to work around that. You learn, "I'm really good at that," or "Not too good over here." So . . .

Q: And in the book you acknowledge that the records by the Rolling Stones, and especially Mick Jagger's stage performance, influenced your own stage personality, or at least how you worked in concert.

A: Yes. More than any other individual, as far as being an entertainer within the rock-'n'-roll medium, he was amazing to me. I had never seen a singer challenge the audience to have a good time. Not, "Aren't we having a good time?" "How you feeling tonight?" That's so stupid. They came to see you perform. So he was just amazing and completely different. He just took charge of the stage. Most singers had a band, but to be able to front that volume of music, you can't just kinda stand there [Laughs]. Amazing entertainer. For rock-'n'-roll—these people are not opera singers, O.K.? It's not the business of how fine and pristine your voice is. It's about the entertainer enjoying himself. Not the audience. Hopefully the audience will. If the entertainer is enjoying himself and feels at home on a stage, that's fifty percent of it.

Q: When did you first get involved in biomedical research and animal welfare? I know on your 1989 Jefferson Airplane tour you did a song called, "A Panda."

A: I had no interest in animals before the middle of the '80s. They were just part of the scenery. I went into a hotel room and turned on CNN when we were on the road. I called up World Wildlife after they did a story on pandas. They told me it was because they were endangered. And I got interested in why they were endangered. What is going on here? That's how it got started.

As for biomedical research, and I talk about it in the book, it's fraudulent nature the fact that it's so pervasive and such terrible science. In other words, ninety percent they use rodents, not because they are like human beings, but because they are easy to handle and they reproduce fast. That is not science. That is simply easy to handle. And you wonder why we have so many diseases and why we aren't getting over them, and why more are coming up every day and why everybody is sick. It's because our approach to medicine is treating symptoms rather than prevention. It's just totally out of whack. So that fascinated me when I got into that.

Before I started the book, I had no interest in writing about my life in music. The only reason at the beginning I wanted to write this book was to get some of this fraud into this book. Because people have to know what's going on. The rest of this (book) everybody has talked about for thirty years.

Allen Ginsberg:

Verbal Herbal

I interviewed Allen Ginsberg just after he put out a rocking protest song, "The Ballad of the Skeletons," b/w "Amazing Grace," with the lyrics rewritten as an ode to the plight of the homeless.

"The Ballad of the Skeletons," as a word/rock merger excoriating the corporate-political establishment, was initially published in *The Nation* in November, 1995.

The recording was produced by Lenny Kaye and featured multi-instrumental support from Paul McCartney and pianist-composer Philip Glass.

At the time of the interview, Ginsberg had also just released *Selected Poems 1947–1995* through HarperCollins Publishers.

A distinguished Professor at Brooklyn College when he died at age seventy in 1997, Allen Ginsberg always had an audio relationship with musicians. Over the years he collaborated with Ornette Coleman, Bob Dylan, and the Clash, among others.

In 1994, a couple of years before his death, Rhino/WordBeat Records issued Ginsberg's four-CD box set entitled, "Holy Soul Jelly Roll, Poems and Songs (1949–1993)."

Born in 1926 in Newark, New Jersey, the son of Naomi Ginsberg and poet Louis Ginsberg, Allen Ginsberg is a direct literary descendent of American poets Walt Whitman and Hart Crane. He is a member of the American Academy of Arts and Letters, was awarded the medal of

Allen Ginsberg (left) and Paul McCartney performing on stage at the Royal Albert Hall, London, England, 1995. Photo by Linda McCartney, courtesy of MPL Communications, Ltd.

Chevalier de l'Ordre des Arts et Lettres by the French Minister of Culture in 1993, and is co-founder of the Jack Kerouac School of Disembodied Poetics at Naropa Institute in Boulder, Colorado, the first accredited Buddhist college in the West.

While Ginsberg's considerable literary reputation has been chronicled and discussed for years, the media has never really documented Ginsberg's links to music, and his recording process, the actual collision of melody and words.

Allen Ginsberg's life was lived over a variety of musical settings. Blues, jazz, folk, rock, punk, and rap have been melded with his voice and words. In the mid-1990s he did a live show that included Thurston Moore and Lee Renaldo, recorded with U2 in a studio in Ireland, and filmed a revealing video for "The Ballad of the Skeletons," directed by Gus Van Sant.

Ginsberg knew how to work product. In person or on stage, his voice remained gorgeous, rich, and full. The role toll never fatigued this "*yenta king documentarian.*"

His radio career actually began in Chicago, where the renowned Studs Terkel aired some of his poetry (which was censored at the time), and later Ginsberg was heard on the Pacifica Radio chain. He is still heard these days through radio interviews and college and National Public Radio airplay.

In 1970 I worked in Culver City at West L.A. Junior College in the campus library between classes. I used to stock and order as many Ginsberg and Jack Kerouac books as I could for the students.

In the 1980s I produced a live recording of Allen at The Unitarian Church in L.A. and also arranged for him to read at some music venues around Southern California over the years, including his debut McCabe's date in Santa Monica.

Allen was always supportive of my recording and literary projects and offered some valuable criticism about a few of my own poems over corned beef sandwiches at Canter's Deli in West Hollywood. Around 1976 we also performed some background vocals on the Phil Spector-produced Leonard Cohen album, "Death of a Ladies Man," recorded at Gold Star Studios.

I talked to Ginsberg one late afternoon in 1996 in Rhino Records' conference room in Westwood, California, where poet Gregory Corso sat in with us, and the following year we conducted another extensive interview by phone from his New York City apartment.

An abridged version of this interview appeared in 1996 in *HITS* magazine, and a shorter edited version appeared in the *Los Angeles Times Calendar Section* on April 7, 1997, when the newspaper asked me to pen one of several tributes at the time of his death. Still another excerpt of our tapings was published in the *Rolling Stone Book of the Beats* volume a few years ago.

Allen Ginsberg really enjoyed doing these long-form interviews that focused on his word/musical collaborations. He later called me, upon the first publication, and was pleased with the results and happy he got a chance to talk about topics he usually didn't address in his publicity and book promotion work.

In 2002 I was interviewed and later quoted in the liner notes by Mitch Meyers for the re-release of the Ginsberg album, "New York Blues: Rags, Ballads & Harmonium Songs," recorded by Harry Smith and produced by Ann Charters.

In early 2003, Paul McCartney's office called and invited me to a cast-and-crew screening of his "Back in the U.S." concert film in Hollywood. I had a very nice chat with Paul during the lobby reception at the ArcLight Theater on Sunset Blvd., and mentioned an interview I'd conducted with Allen would appear in my book. He gave me his address and I sent a copy of the original text to him in the UK.

A year earlier I had mailed McCartney my Ginsberg feature from the *Los Angeles Times* that contained a photo of Paul and Allen during their poetry and music performance at the Royal Albert Hall. "Allen was a very lovely man," Paul beamed. Subsequently, a few weeks later, he arranged for a picture of himself and Allen together, taken by Linda McCartney at that same event, to be sent to me for inclusion in *This Is Rebel Music*.

I'm confident "A.G." would want word-heads to read our complete music-driven discussions. Over the decades I had a series of encounters and conversations with him. Initially as a college student, later as his recording producer and concert promoter. When we sat down in person I could toss out a question to him like a friend, and he'd swing.

Q: What was the genesis and development of "The Ballad of the Skeletons" poem and printed context?

A: It was published in *The Nation.* I started it because of all that inflated bullshit about the right wing, and the family values, contract with America, Newt Gingrich, and all the loud mouth stuff on talk radio, and Rush Limbaugh and all those other guys. It seemed obnoxious and stupid and kind of sub-contradictory, so I figured I'd write a poem to knock it out of the ring.

Q: Unlike most of the things you write, were there any inherent music or melodic rhythms in the poem when it was first written?

A: Yes. I had a riff, "Dum. Dum. Dum." "The New York Times . . ." I first thought of singing it, but then I thought, better to speak it with that riff behind it. I had the riff. It got printed in *The Nation,* with illustrations by Eric Drooker, and it came out in a book I did, *Illuminated Poems.* The next stage was a benefit somewhere in a club at a reading I did with

Amiri Baraka in New York and I ran into guitarist Marc Ribot there. I had worked with him before on an album, "The Lion For Real."

Then I had a gig at Albert Hall in London. A reading. I had been talking quite a bit to (Paul) McCartney, visiting him and bringing him poetry and *haiku,* and looking at Linda McCartney's photographs and giving him some photos I'd taken of them. So, McCartney liked it and filmed me doing "Skeletons" in a little 8mm home thing. And then I had this reading at Albert Hall, and I asked McCartney if he could recommend a young guitarist who was a quick study. So he gave me a few names, but he said, "If you're not fixed up with a guitarist, why don't you try me? I love the poem." So I said, "It's a date." It was last November. We went to Paul's house and spent an afternoon rehearsing. He came to the sound check and we did a little rehearsal there, again. And then he went up to his box with his family. It was a benefit for literary things. There were fifteen other poets. We didn't tell anybody that McCartney was going to play. And we developed that riff really nicely. In fact, Linda made a little tape of our rehearsal. So then, we went on stage and knocked it out. There's a photo of us on the CD. It was very lively and he was into it.

Linda likes my photos and she likes Robert Frank, who is my mentor. And I had taken some photos of them in Long Island, where they have a place and were saying goodnight to me when I was going back to New York. Good photos of them. We traded some photos. Paul was into poetry, and publishing his poetry. So he asked me to look at his poetry and critique it. We got onto *haiku* and Linda liked the form, so she used those seventeen-syllable forms for her book of photos. Paul is also a painter and had published a little book of his paintings. I also wrote *haiku* to a book of watercolors. One hundred and eight of them, to which I had written a *haiku* for each one, describing the painting. I showed it to him in Long Island and he was knocked out, and liked the form, so he began working with that, also. So we had a rapport about technical things. I had done an album, recordings with (Bob) Dylan back in 1971, and the idea was that it was going to be put out by Apple (Records). But at that time, (John) Lennon had encouraged it and I paid for the thing, and they were going to pay me back, but it turned out, that I had made this album, paid for it myself, which was quite expensive. I had the money from poetry readings and actually it was a great idea because I had all the stuff with Dylan which later came out. In the late '60s or early '70s, I visited McCartney in London. I was on TV that day, a "Pro-Pot" rally in Hyde Park, and the cops had stopped me from playing a harmonium or talking on a microphone. So I came down from my ladder from where I was talking, and gave the cop a flower. That was kind of a knock-out for everybody in London at that time, rather than getting mad. And I was watching that on TV with Mick Jagger at McCartney's house. And McCartney was painting a satin shirt and he gave it to me as a "performance shirt." We talked a little. We met each other over the years and then we met again when he did "Saturday Night Live," and he greeted me like an old lost buddy.

Q: Didn't you see the Beatles play, and there's a poem you wrote about the event?

A: Yes! I saw them in Portland, Maine. I was up there with Gary Snyder, probably 1965, 1966. In my *Collected Poems,* it's dated by a poem describing the Beatles playing in Portland. I was with a couple of little children. I had gotten tickets and was sitting way out in the bleachers, and John Lennon came out and said, "We understand that Allen Ginsberg is in the audience. So three cheers. So now we'll have our show." He saluted me from the stage, which amazed me and made me feel very proud with all these young kids at my side. Then I knew Lennon and Yoko Ono lived in New York and visited on and off. I was involved in some political things with them occasionally.

Q: What did Paul McCartney add to your recording of "Skeletons?"

A: He reacts to the words in an intelligent way. You can hear it on the tape. Like if I say on the recording, "What's cooking," all of a sudden he brings in the maracas to get that really funny excitement. When I say, "Blow Nancy Blow," he blows on the Hammond organ. He added a lot of enthusiasm and a lot of interpretation. And sometimes when I made a flub, he covered it. He left his lead sheet in his guitar case, so we had to share my lead sheet (at the gig), which was fun. Then I did the poem at Carnegie Hall for the Tibet House; that followed the Albert Hall show . . .

McCartney had said, "If you record it, I'd like to work on it. It would be fun." So we did a 24-hour overnight mail to him, and he got it and listened to it after a few days. He spent a day on it. He put on maracas, drums, which was unexpected, which we needed, and organ, Hammond organ, trying to sound like Al Kooper. And a guitar which was very strong. Then the day it arrived, Philip Glass was in town and he volunteered because he thought it was my hit, so he wanted to do something with it. He added on piano, very much in his style, and fitting perfectly onto the rest of the tape. Then Hal Wilner wound up mixing it and brought out McCartney's role and the structure that McCartney had given to it, 'cause he gave it a very nice, dramatic structure. I had planned that after "Blow Nancy Blow" you would have four consecutive choruses of instrumentals. McCartney and I had planned the breaks the first time, and varied it a little. I'm understanding the recording process more.

I'm basically the poet. I have tunes I got up with. I have ideas but I still can't make a song with a bridge [Laughs].

Q: You also did a re-written version of "Amazing Grace" on the flip-side of "Skeletons?"

A: About three years ago, Ed Sanders asked all of his friends to write new verses of "Amazing Grace" for one evening of "Amazing Grace" in St. Mark's. A lot of people from the Naropa Institute wrote. Anne Waldman, Tuli Kupferberg, and I heard of a Zen master who was working with the homeless, who had a sitting meditation on The Bowery with a lot of his students, including Anne Waldman. And they reported in mid-winter that it was terrible finding cardboard boxes to sleep in. The worst thing was that people would pass them by and not acknowledge their existence. Shutting them out. The sense of alienation and helplessness, and being ignored. No eye contact. People were scared of them. And that's what turned me on. Acknowledge them. That was the inspiration. Keep them in human contact. The verses I wrote seem to be full of heart, to the point, compassion.

Q: And now something you began as a poem, "Skeletons," has evolved into a recording collaborative. Do you consider the projected expanded audience?

A: Yeah, but when you write a poem like that, you run through in your mind, who is going to listen to it? President Clinton is going to hear this. I'll send it to Stephanopoulos, who I know. Dole will probably hear of it, or someone around Dole will hear it. Rush Limbaugh will probably hear it, because it's me and it's nasty to him. Young college kids will hear it. I wonder what (Bob) Dylan will think? I wonder what McCartney will think? So all those people are present in my mind, inevitably, 'cause I know them. My father. My mother. My brother. What is Robert Creeley gonna think? What is Gary Snyder going to think? What is *People Magazine* gonna think? What is God gonna think? What's Buddha gonna think? But literally, what will my Tibetan Llama teacher think? Is this too aggressive, or is this helpful? Things like that. I was fed up with the inflation of the right wing "contract with America" double-cross hypocrisy, basically. And it didn't seem to me that anybody was responding. *The Nation* asked me for the poem. I waited about a half a year and completed it. I originally called it "Skeleton Keys." Poet Carl Rakosi made some suggestions for me to edit and add "Ballad."

Q: Is there a reason you used skeleton as a metaphor throughout the poem?

A: I'm Buddhist, and you look at these issues through the grave, and also setting them up as skeleton puppets, setting up the military people, the advertising people, the network people, the talk show junkies, Big Brother. Setting them up as skeletons, as puppets. Setting them up as transparent phantoms, and looking at the issues out of the grave. The idea of putting all the present factions and seeing them from the grave as walking skeletons.

Q: What about poetry readings and performances? Is it different reading with a musician next to you or now a bunch of people sharing the stage?

A: I have to focus on my text. I'm still pointing toward the tornado.

Q: You still read from text on stage, from a book, or typewritten. Do you ever read from memory?

A: I rarely read from memory. I sing from "Father Death Blues," and can sing "Amazing Grace" from memory, but I don't know what lines are coming, so I have to refresh myself. I'm not particularly interested in memorizing perfectly, 'cause I think it's distracting from interpreting the text differently each time. I think you have to have all the dimensions at once, the book thing, the poetry thing, plus the performance, plus the musical accompaniment, and if you have all of them, and they're all in a good place, that's fine. But the reason I don't try to memorize, I guess I could, but I'm too busy, and I like to re-interpret the poem each time. Certain cadences are recurrent and certain intonations are recurrent, but on the other hand, if I don't memorize it, there's always the chance that somebody noticing something, and empathizing puts it a little differently, and bringing out meaning that I didn't realize before. So I prefer to have the score in front of me and interpret it new each time.

Q: Artists from new generations, alternative rock bands, still keep discovering your work and acknowledging your influence.

A: It's fun. You always learn from younger people. I learned a lot from William Carlos Williams, and the elders of my generation. People who were much older than me when I was young. And that inter-generational amity is really important, because it spreads myths from one generation to another of what you know, and all the techniques and the history. At the same time, Williams learned connection with Corso and myself and (Peter) Orlovsky. Renewed his lease, so to speak. And the advent of the Black Mountain Beat Generation Poetry Renaissance, San Francisco, really renewed his poetic life, in a sense, brought him out to the public and his mood of poetry as the mainstream, rather than as the eccentric jerk from New Jersey. All of a sudden, with the phalanx of younger people following his lead, he became the sage that he was. And I think it gave him a lot of gratification to realize he had been on the right track, and that it wasn't in vain. And I get the same thing whenever I get to work with younger people. And I learn from them.

I don't think I would have been singing if it wasn't for younger Dylan. I mean he turned me on to actually singing. I remember the moment it was. It was a concert with Happy Traum that I went to and saw in Greenwich Village. I suddenly started to write my own lyrics, instead of Blake. Dylan's words were so beautiful. The first time I heard them, I wept. I had come back from India, and Charlie Plymell, a poet I liked a lot in Bolinas, at a welcome home party played me Dylan singing "Masters of War" from "The Freewheelin' Bob Dylan," and I actually burst into tears. It was a sense that the torch had been passed to another generation. And somebody had the self-empowerment of saying, "But I'll know my song well before I start singin'."

Q: Are you aware there's sort of a re-evaluation of Dylan's film, "Renaldo and Clara"? I mean, I first didn't understand a lot of it when I saw a rough cut before release, and now it's garnering new acclaim in the U.S. and around the world with both movie fans and Dylan collectors.

A: Dylan delivers. It's going to be a marvelous picture when people begin appreciating it. Well, first of all, it's Dylan extending himself to the extreme, and including all his friends and all his inspirers, and all his workable companions in a big circus going through America. A musical circus. His mother was along at one point. His kids were along at one point. His wife was along. Joan Baez's kid was along. So it was this great family outing trying to hit all the small towns, originally, like in Kafka's *America*. The traveling circus in Kafka's *America*. For me it was great, and to hear Dylan so often, I was able to hear backstage, in the audience, from the side, in the wings, and go out to the furthest seats with a pass. He was at a peak of musicality and energy and inspiration. Like "One More Cup of Coffee" and "Idiot Wind," which is one of my favorite lyrics. A national lyric with its great "Circles around your skull . . ." Really quite manic. It was great to see a band on a rock-'n-'roll tour. Rolling Thunder Review on a grand tour, and see all the work that went into it.

"Renaldo and Clara" was a great artistic film that was mocked when it first came out, although it was a hit in Europe, or it was very much appreciated in Europe. Now, when people see it now, I think people will realize it was a great treasure. At first people were screaming "Four Hours!" "What a big egotist." But actually it's four hours of Dylan exploring the nature of identity of self, and pointing out there is no fixed identity. It was making a huge movie in an interesting way. I did an interview with Dylan for the *Telegraph*. Dylan requested me to do it, and he explained the technique and construction and structure of the film. Specifically that they went through all of the footage and isolated everything that seemed to astound them. Then they divided it up into various topics, like marriage, rock and roll, children, God, poetry, politics, war, peace, and all that. Then they made card files with those topics, and the primary colors, and the hooks in between, he composed it like a tapestry, not a linear composition, but a composition by artistic elements. You'll find the rose travels from hand to hand, throughout the film, along with the hat.

Q: Why has there been a Beat Generation literary renaissance and '80s/'90s new appreciation now of audio/video "Beat" writing and performance activities?

A: Audiences now are really interesting. It's about a quarter young kids from the ages of fourteen to eighteen, due to the retro renaissance of Beat interest. Maybe it's the actual expression of emotion that interests people who have been deprived of emotion, and not really been able to express their erotic joy or grief for a long time, under the Reagan and Bush repression era. Also, in the '80s, the renaissance might have been a reaction against the mid-'70s disco music, which was totally mechanical, and characteristic of that retreat from feeling. The later generation now feels a sense of alienation, voidoid, Generation X, grunge, Kurt Cobain, enemy, so what is really needed is another shot of emotion, or a renaissance of people being able to express their emotions in music or in poetry. And, that's one thing that I think my new recording collection is really useful for, musically as well as verbally. So I'm glad to show my heart. People now want to say what they really think, because they are faced in every direction by plastic, corporate protrusion of fear, and the substitution of violence, kitsch, stereotype, discontinuity, and no sense of ground. But there is a real ground in everybody, and there is longing and desire. Desire for affection, desire for tenderness, desire for love, desire for security and safety, desire to be cuddled. And that was mocked for so many years by the Malthusian idea of "I'm all right," "Dog eat dog," "I got mine, Jack," cut-throat, ya know, the Darwinian competition as the keynote, until that collapses under its own weight of both moral and economic bankruptcy. And debt. Trillions of dollars in debt that we will never climb out of. Spending, S&L's, the military wasting the money to show off.

People are now more receptive to candor, cheerfulness, and some kind of openness and reality against the pessimistic, negative FBI in the closet, J. Edgar Hoover secrecy then, when we were proposing a better world. In fact, I remember when (Jack) Kerouac was asked on the William F. Buckley TV Show in the '60s what "Beat Generation" meant, Kerouac said, "Sympathetic."

Q: With the release of your box set, the vinyl-to-CD reissues, new audio recordings by local and national writers, my own spoken word productions, as well as TV product advertising, utilizing Beat slogans and phrasing(s), is this further proof of the literature living and breathing, and the era for once being displayed correctly, or at least an influence in commercial view?

A: The actual texts, however, have not been re-written, and are now coming up to more public notice like Burroughs' "Naked Lunch," and Kerouac's new, unpublished poems, and for the first time, my actual voice available on a bunch of CDs, going all the way back to 1949 and stretching up to 1993, with the very first original reading of "Howl," which is sort of a standard anthology piece, that has never been heard, or a poem like "Sunflower Sutra" or "America," which was standard in the Norton anthologies in high school.

Q: On a recent radio interview on KPCC-FM, National Public Radio, you again stressed that the Beat writers were always candid in feelings and observations.

A: The renewed interest stems from the fact that we were being more candid and truthful than most other public figures or writers at the time. We were switched over to writing a spoken idiomatic vernacular, actual American English, which turned on many generations later. Dylan said that Kerouac's "Mexico City Blues" had inspired him to be a poet. That was his poetic inspiration.

Q: I know that Burroughs introduced you to some key books in the mid 1940s that were influential to your thoughts and writing, and Kerouac, around the same time, when you were attending Columbia University, maybe around 1950, had been into some form of Buddhism and spontaneous prose, but an older generation of writers had an impact on your eventual voice. I once joked to you that as far as New Jersey goes, it's you, Bruce Springsteen and Frank Sinatra, but you added, "William Carlos Williams," whom you met around age twenty.

A: I knew him from my hometown of Patterson, New Jersey. I'd seen him in 1948. He actually innovated the idea of listening to the way people talked and writing in that way. Using the tones of their voice and using the rhythmical sequences of actual talk instead of dat dat dat dot dot dot. "This is the forest . . ." Instead of a straight, square, metronomic, arithmetic beat, there's the infinitely more musical and varied rhythmic sequences of conversation, as well as the tones. 'Cause if you notice, most academic poetry is spoken in a single solitary moan tone that maybe doesn't have the variety of when you are talking to your grandmother or baby.

Allen Ginsberg and Harvey Kubernik at a live poetry recording session, Unitarian Church, Los Angeles, 1981. Photo by Suzan Carson!

It happens every 100 or 150 years. It did in the days of Wordsworth, who in his preface to lyrical ballads, suggested that poets begin writing in the words and diction of men of intelligence, or talk to each other intelligently, instead of imitating another century's literary style. So, I think what happened is that we followed an older tradition, a lineage, of the modernists of the turn of the century, continued their work into idiomatic talk and musical cadences and returned poetry back to its original sources and actual communication between people. That was picked up generation after generation, up to people like U2, who are very much influenced by Burroughs in their presentation of visual material, or Sonic Youth.

Q: "Holy Soul Jelly Roll" is a very comprehensive survey of your recorded (audio) life. Poems, songs, musical collaborations.

A: It includes about a half hour of music with Bob Dylan, and songs of

William Blake that I've set to music, some of it is uproarious and funny, and very hilarious, joyful yodeling involved in that, and a live cut with the Clash.

Q: You worked with the Clash on "Combat Rock." How did "Capitol Air" come together, incorporated in this box set? I debuted it on KLOS-FM when I did a radio interview two years ago on Frank Sontag's "Impact" shift, and every phone line at the station lit up.

A: Well, it's an accident. I wandered into a place called Bonds, which at that time was a big (couple of thousand people) club in New York. The Clash at the time had a seventeen-night run, and I knew the sound engineer, who brought me backstage to introduce me, and Joe Strummer took one look at me and said, "Ginsberg, when are you going to run for President?" And then he said there was some guy "that we've had trying to talk to the kids about Sandinistas and about Latin American policy and politics, but they're not listening. They are throwing eggs or tomatoes at him. Can you go out and talk?" I said, "Speech, no, but I have a little punk song that I wrote that begins, 'I don't like the government where I live.'" So, we rehearsed it for about five minutes during their intermission break, and then they took me out on stage. "Allen Ginsberg is going to sing." And so we improvised it. I gave them the chord changes. It gets kind of Clash-like, good anthem-like music about the middle, but they trail off again. The guy who was my friend at the soundboard, mixed my voice real loud so the kids could hear, and so there was a nice reaction, because they could hear common sense being said in the song. You can hear the cheers on the record. I wrote "Capitol Air" in 1980, recorded with the Clash live, in 1981 or '82. "Capitol Air" was written coming back from Yugoslavia, oddly enough from a tour of Eastern Europe, realizing that the police bureaucracies in America and in Eastern Europe were the same, mirror images of each other finally. The climactic stanza:

> No hope Communism no hope Capitalism Yeah
> Everybody's lying on both sides . . .

We didn't play the whole cut because we didn't have enough time, but they built up to a kind of crescendo, which was nice when the whole band came in.

Q: Can we talk about record music executive, John Hammond, Sr., perhaps the A&R man of the century?

A: I visited him in the hospital, on his deathbed, years ago, and our final conversation was about Robert Johnson and Bob Dylan. Well, I think I ran into him in the early '60s. He knew my poetry quite well. But it was around the Rolling Thunder Review with Dylan that we got more intimate. I had already made one recording, William Blake's "Songs of Innocence and Experience," in 1969, with some very good musicians, including Julius Watkins on French horn, Don Cherry, and Elvin Jones. And also Herman Wright, a bassist that was suggested by Charles Mingus. Mingus encouraged me to do the Blake. So I had something to play. It had been put out by MGM Records, but disappeared out of circulation when Mike Curb bought MGM and denounced all the dope fiends who were on his roster and wanted to ban them, so then re-issued it with a beautiful cover, with a picture of Judge Julius Hoffman, on their archive series.

I was on the Rolling Thunder tour, doing a little singing, and I had a whole bunch of new material I had done with Dylan in 1971. In 1971 Dylan and I went into a studio and improvised. I had forty minutes of music with him. So I brought that to Hammond in 1975, after the tour. I had a bunch of new songs and he said, "Let's go in the studio and make an album." I had some musicians who had been with me since 1968 or 1969, since the Blake. David Mansfield from the Rolling Thunder tour, and a wonderful musician, Arthur Russell, who Philip Glass has just put out posthumously on Point Records. Arthur Russell lived in my apartment building, upstairs, and had accompanied me across country on tours, and managed The Kitchen in New York. We had a good little group of musicians. Dylan made a record in the Columbia Studios. It was the first time I didn't have to pay! Then, Columbia wouldn't put it out because of dirty words, they said in those days. The anti-smoking, "Don't Smoke" poem. So things were in a stasis, but I continued recording myself in 1981, did a whole series of recordings with David Amram. By this time I was working with Steven Taylor, now the lead guitarist of The Fugs.

So we got together at CBS Studios and did another forty minutes of music, and later, John Hammond put the two together. He had left Columbia and started his own label, John Hammond Records, to be distributed by Columbia. So he not only put out what he did with me, he put out a double album, and he got Robert Frank, who had done the [Rolling Stones'] "Exile on Main Street" album cover, who's an old friend, to make a composite for our cover, and there was a really good playlist inside, and the text was a good deduction. However, the record didn't sell. Before I had a chance to rescue the further 10,000 copies they [Columbia] had, they shredded them, so they were gone, and a rarity now. So what this four-CD box set is, is a summary of all the studio recordings I did, plus a lot of other stuff that was never done in a studio, but done in readings, plus another album with Blake, including Dylan on Blake, and a duet with Elvin Jones, including some work with Dylan out in Santa Monica in 1982 in his studio, the live Clash cut, and an excerpt from the opera I did with Philip Glass. So the range runs from *a cappella* up through folk, punk, dirty blues, classical, collaborations with Dylan, some rap, percussion, and vocal with Jones. David Amram was on it as well.

First of all, I grew up on all blues, Ma Rainey and Leadbelly. I listened to them live on radio station WNYC, back in the late '30s or early '40s. So I have a blues background. There's some sort of Hebrewic cantalation relation to the blues that I've always had. So the first thing on the collection is "When The Saints Go Marching In," that I made up *a cappella* when I was hitchhiking and recorded in Neal Cassady's house a year later. Then things like my mother taught me. "The Green Valentine Blues." Just coming from everyone who likes to sing in the shower. Then there was the poetry and music, King Pleasure, and the people who were putting together be-bop, syllable by syllable, like Lambert, Hendricks & Ross. I knew them in 1948. We used to smoke pot together in the '40s, when I knew Neal Cassady, around Columbia when I was living on 92nd Street.

Q: Hey, I met drummer Freddie Gruber last week. Buddy Rich's main man. He told me you tried to hit on him once.

A: [Laughs]. I had a crush on Freddie. I saw him recently. Around 1944, '45, Kerouac and I were listening to Symphony Sid, and I heard the whole repertoire of Thelonious Monk, "Round Midnight," "Orinthology" and all that. I actually saw Charlie Parker, weekend after weekend a few years later at The Open Door. And in the '60s, went night after night to The Five Spot to hear Thelonious Monk, and actually gave Thelonious Monk "Howl," and got his critique on it two weeks later when I saw him again. "What did you think of it?" He said, "Makes sense." In 1960 I delivered some psilocybin from Timothy Leary to both Thelonious Monk and Dizzy Gillespie. And Monk said later on, "Got anything stronger?" Later on, I spent an evening with him on what is now Charlie Parker Place, around 1960. Also in San Francisco, in the mid-'50s, there was a music and poetry scene. Mingus was involved with Kenneth Rexroth and Kenneth Patchen. And Fantasy Records documented some of that. The Cellar in San Francisco. By that time, I didn't know how to handle it, so I never did much of that myself, 'cause I was more funky, old fashioned blues. I couldn't cut the mustard with free jazz.

So then in the 1970s, I began turning on to Dylan. I knew him in the '60s. He taught me the three-chord blues pattern. So he was my instructor. I began singing in India, Mantra, and in the great '60s, I began transferring the sacred music idea to Blake, and began transferring that to folk music, and then got together with Dylan in the early '70s. Influences by Happy Traum and Rambling Jack Elliot, whom I've known since the '40s, and Derroll Adams. So finally, the amalgam got together, and it was very simple-minded blues. Also improvisation, which was important.

Q: What happens when the beat or the music collides with your words and voice?

A: Elvin has a very interesting attitude. He feels that he's not there to beat out the vocalist. He's there to put a floor under them. He's there to support and encourage, and give a place for the vocal to come in, not to compete with the vocal, but to provide a ground for it. He's very intelligent as a musician. We did it once together in 1969 on the "Blake" album; there was military type drum, and then this recent rap song. I've got some other stuff we haven't put out with Elvin. I've rarely found opposition to the music because the musicians were very sensitive, and built their music around the dynamics of my voice.

Q: You write something on a piece of paper. Other people, musicians, come invited to participate and collaborate. Does the original intention become a different trip once there is music and other elements involved?

A: Well, it widens it into a slightly different trip, but the words are pretty stable, and they mean what they mean, so there is no problem. The interesting thing is adjusting the rhythmic pattern and the intonation to the musician's idea of what is there. That's pretty good, because I'm good as an improviser, I can fit in, as you can hear on "Birdbrain." Where I can take a long line or a short line and fit it in sixteen bars without worrying about spaces and closed places.

Harry Smith, before he died, came out to Naropa, where he was the resident ethnomusicologist and philosopher. He won a Grammy in 1991, the year he died. Harry recorded me for Folkways. So for a blues pedigree, that's pretty good.

Q: I was talking to John Sinclair in New Orleans. He mentioned you read or performed at a rally for him with John Lennon in 1972, and played "September on Jessore Road" for John Lennon.

A: John Lennon suggested I do it like "Eleanor Rigby," with a string quartet. In 1982 I'm in Amsterdam with Steven Taylor at the One World Poetry Festival, and the organizer said, "Would you like to have a symphony orchestra or a string quartet?" so in two days, Steven Taylor wrote out all the parts for the Mondrian Orchestra, and we recorded it.

Q: What kind of impact did FM radio have on you as a writer and reader/performer?

A: By the time I got around to getting on the radio, it was actually an AM station in Chicago with Studs Terkel; I recorded the complete reading of "Howl" in Chicago, later used for the Fantasy record. It was broadcast censored. '59. KPFA in the Bay Area then started broadcasting my stuff in San Francisco, a Pacifica station. Fantasy put out "Howl" and that got around. Then, Jerry Wexler at Atlantic put out "Kaddish." It was radio broadcast from Brandeis University.

Q: Was there ever a conflict of written page origin then into audio land?

A: We wrote, and we were in the tradition of William Carlos Williams spoken vernacular, comprehensible common language that anyone could understand, coming from Whitman through William Carlos Williams through be-bop. We were built for it. I can talk. I'm an old ham.

Q: Does the vision change once it leaves the paper?

A: No. It doesn't make much difference. The method of my writing to begin with is that I'm not writing to write something; it's that I catch myself thinking; I suddenly notice something I have thought of when I wasn't thinking of writing, and then I write it down if it is vivid enough. And as far as the choice of what to write down or not, the slogan is vividness, is self selecting. So in a sense, the method is impervious to influence by the audience because I'm just thinking to myself in the bathtub.

So even if it's the most private, it's the most public, because as Kerouac said in "Pull My Daisy," "Everybody is interested in their secret scatological doodlings in their private notebooks." I mean, what do people really think about?

Q: As far as performance and poetry readings, when you read before a house, aren't you trying to keep the same original birthplace word vision and not really expand or bring in heavy theatrical elements?

A: I like to stick to something that is grounded in anything I could say to somebody, that they wouldn't notice I was really saying it as poetry. Intense fragments of spoken idiom, with all the different tones of the spoken idiom, which is more musical than most poetry. Most poetry by amateur poets is limited to a couple of tones, a couple of pitches, instead of an entire range, so that the poetry we do fits with the music because it has its pitch consciousness. The tone reading the vowels up and down.

Q: You document by date. Page and performance dates, calendar time and year attached to the writing. I produced a poetry CD a couple of years back with the poet Harry E. Northup. Harry is a date freak like yourself. In the studio, on tape, he would read a poem written in 1989, but we were recording it in 1992. And we've just done a new recording in 1995 but we still listed the poem birthdates in the liners, but not on the tape this time. I'm in conflict about this form of documentation. I'm still on the fence on this one.

A: Wouldn't it be interesting if you went to a concert by Dylan and he dated each piece . . .

Q: Explain the use of chronology in the '90s, reading original work written and created decades earlier?

A: My background was William Butler Yeats. Seeing the sequence of his development, maturation and growth over the years was really interesting as a novel. How he began as a vague, misty-eyed young 1890s devotee of Irish Mythology, and how he wound up, this tough old guy who put a skin on everything he said. So I like the idea of seeing the development of the mind, or of the voice, or of the thought, or of the poetic capacity, and I want to leave that trail behind for other poets so they could see where I was at one point, or where I was at another. My oration, my pronunciation or my singing, my vocalization differs, and it builds.

As I get older it gets more interesting with more and more tones, and more and more breath, and deeper and deeper voice and higher and higher voice. But still the original rhythms and the original ideas are from the original text, so you've still got a chronology going. So people could see the development of the mind. I'm not writing about the external world. I'm writing about what goes through my mind. So, at a certain period I'm interested in this kind of sex, another period, this kind of politics, another period, this kind of meditation, and I like people to be able to dig there's a development, and not a static process.

Q: Let's see . . . I saw you read in the late '60s, early '70s, maybe when I was in college in San Diego. San Diego State University. I do remember going with Leonard Cohen to see you read at The Troubadour in 1975. A year later or so, we all ended up singing on Leonard's "Death of a Ladies Man" album that Phil Spector produced; yourself, Dylan, Rodney Bingenheimer, Dan and David Kessel.

A: I like Phil. Get me a tape of that album. Dylan tried to get him (Phil) to work with me. At that session, Dylan said, "He's (Allen) got words! He's got words!"

Q: I really love Phil but haven't seen him in a while. I'm still amazed at your readings, not just the impact you have on the audience, but your paper trail, book catalogues, albums, vinyl, first edition printings, out of print classics people want signed. Old money. New money. No money. It's like "This Is Your Life" on parade.

A: Not quite. It's my mind on parade. That's what the mind is for, to show other people.

Q: It's obvious that people want to be writers again. I feel that.

A: They want to express themselves. Not just to be a writer to be a writer, but they want to be able to say what they really think.

Q: For years, and it's still evident today, there is still restriction on the radio airwaves, and a limited window when you can be heard. 6:00 P.M.

A: Most of the material on my four-CD box set might be banned from the air 8:00 A.M. to 6:00 P.M. I'd like for some FM station to play all four CDs one night, announced in advance so everybody could listen to it, and I think it would not only change heads, but expand people's emotional range. "All the time in eternity in the warm light of this poem's radio." That was 1953. So I was aware. I was laying out treasures in heaven, basically. I knew that after I was dead my stuff would slowly seep up, so I'm really glad I'm alive to put this (box set) recording together.

Q: Recently, you sold your vast archives to Stanford University for over $1 million. Seven-hundred fifty bookshelves, 14,000 titles. Like 300,000 items in a collection that covers your sixty-eight years. I know New York archivist Bill Morgan has spent fifteen years cataloging your possessions. The papers gave you props. They presented the acquisition as postwar American poetry and literature and American cultural history. Stanford's bid topped that of Columbia University, your alma mater. And I know the money will help you move from your Lower East Side pad to a loft where there is extra room for your stepmother. You have been in control of your own history and catalog destination.

A: I thought the whole '40s, '50s literary movement was historically really important, and was kind of a wall built against authoritarianism, that there would be a counter reaction and maybe a police state in America someday, building on the drug thing, and the suppression of literature. So I thought it would be best to build a complete archive of the whole transaction of the cultural change including all the printed stuff, tapes, newspaper articles, anything that had to do with cop-selling or cop-trading, or cop/mafia relationship, or CIA/mafia/cop relationship, or repression of literature or censorship, or foreign reactions to Beat Generation translations, interviews. So everything was put together as a cultural, historical resource.

It's all on computer now and retrievable. I had it up at Columbia all these years and it's been used for endless books. *Acid Dreams*, *The History of Marijuana*. Researchers for biographies on Burroughs, Kerouac.

Q: I know you don't have seller's remorse. You wanted it done this way. You orchestrated the collection and the housing, right?
A: Yes. I needed somebody to service it, take care of it.

Q: Why them?
A: They were the ones to pay me enough money to pay back the expenses I took over thirty years, which amounted to probably a good deal more than I ever made in one spot.

Andrew Loog Oldham:

Stoned (Out of His Mind)

I interviewed Andrew Loog Oldham for the first time in the autumn of 2000, right after his memoir, *Stoned,* was published in the U.K. by Secker & Warburg. People are still talking about this wonderful and insightful film/fashion/music print trek of Brit pop circa 1960–1964, of ALO, perhaps best known as the man who helped create the Rolling Stones as their manager and producer. *Stoned* will go a long way in further educating the music historians and pop culture documentarians on the impact this lad had on your record album collections.

In January 2001, St. Martin's Press in the U.S. published *Stoned.* Stephanie Zacharek, a staff writer for *Salon Arts & Entertainment* in January, 2001, reviewed *Stoned* as a "shiftily entertaining biography. You could argue that the Stones would have become what they did without Oldham. But you'd be wrong. *Stoned* is a book written by a guy who has never pretended to be anything but a raconteur and a bullshitter supreme, but even if it's not 100 percent true, it's still 100 percent believable. Part of what makes it so credible is Oldham's unerring belief in the fact that he himself is unequivocally interesting, and whether or not you've ever cared much about him (or have heard of him), by the sixth page he has you convinced you should."

May 2001 saw the publication of *Stoned* in U.K. paperback. In July 2002, it was issued in U.S. trade paperback. His latest work, 2*Stoned,* came out in hardcover in Fall, 2002.

With *Stoned,* the 1944-London-born Andrew Loog Oldham brings the reader into his world just before his act, the Rolling Stones, came to America. Andrew's abilities to detail an environment are smashing. He sets

Andrew Loog Oldham in his home library, Bogota, Colombia, 2001.
Photo by Alfonso Durier (©2001).

the scene, the tone and the moan for us to investigate a post-WWII era England and the many major players in the late 1950s and early 1960s rock world. As a woman I once dated said while applying her make-up one morning, "It's all in the foundation, dear."

Stoned might influence future authors to conduct even more foundation work and research in their craft. You know, really show the backdrop. No more of this "cut to the chase" stuff.

A cover blurb on the *Stoned* sleeve from ALO serves as a teaser: "People say I made the Stones. I didn't. They were there already. They only wanted exploiting. They were all bad boys when I found them. I just brought out the worst in them." If anything, *Stoned* really proves how ALO, the Rolling Stones, and a few hundred plugged-in kids and tastemakers in the U.K. really shook up the traditional record and music business and changed the world.

We all got a taste of ALO's literary endeavors many years ago when we scanned the liner notes of the Rolling Stones albums he produced and annotated. Those short paragraphs were often cryptic messages, mixed with current band profiles, that were describing the sounds you would hear on Decca or London label vinyl. He's shown tremendous growth as a writer with *Stoned*. Even the photos Loog has provided illustrate the fertile and exciting environment he chronicles.

A large portion of this interview, not counting the new segment on 2*Stoned* (ALO's second memoir covering the 1964–1967 era), which was conducted with Andrew in late summer 2002, appeared in *discoveries* magazine a couple of years ago. The music web site www.rocksbackpages.com also displayed a chunk of the text. I felt obligated, and it was very logical, to tack on some new questions and responses with ALO about 2*Stoned* for *This Is Rebel Music*. Phil Spector might publish the song, "He's a Rebel," but Andrew Loog Oldham has had for years a non-exclusive lease to utilize the living copyright the way he worked the music business and life around him in those "daze."

The first *discoveries* Q&A Loog cover story I conducted captured a guiding light record producer and literary talent, someone who influenced my own budding music journalism aspirations (along with copies of *Playboy, Sports Illustrated, KRLA Beat, KGFJ Soul, EYE, The Herald-Express/Examiner, Ebony, Surfer, Melody Maker, Hit Parader*, and *West*), from the seminal liner notes he wrote on those first batch of Rolling Stones albums in the mid-'60s.

ALO was a walking time bomb around and inside the Rolling Stones' circle. A fan with a plan becoming the band's manager and producer from 1964 to 1967. Andrew Loog Oldham served the vibe, pop music, and really housed rock-'n'-roll in body and soul. He was a potent member of the Rolling Stones team, for anyone interested in keeping statistics.

In 2002, Andrew Loog Oldham asked me to be one of the contributing voices for 2*Stoned* (now published by Random House in the U.K.). I was delighted and supplied him with a half-dozen pages describing *my* Los Angeles and Hollywood teenage neighborhoods, 1964–1967.

Back to the first book, *Stoned*. This is a new kind of pop/art/cinema/song/fashion expedition text-book that has longed to be written and published. Andrew, like so many times before, has done it first. As *MOJO* magazine offered in their book review, "A fantastic evocation of an oft-forgotten period in British history and a sizzling read for '60s spotters."

Andrew Loog Oldham might have left the audio and producing/

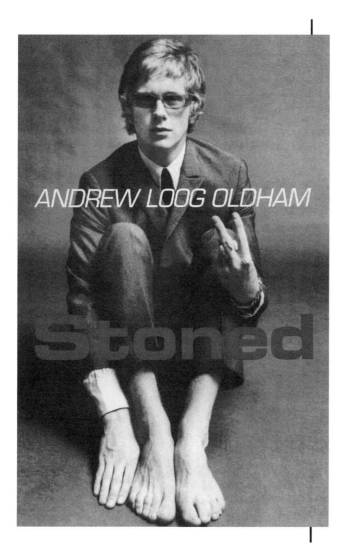

Cover of *Stoned*, courtesy of The Random House Group Limited. Photo by Crispian Woodgate from the Andrew Loog Oldham Collection (©1964/2000).

managing playing field of the Rolling Stones around 1967, but don't ever think he was out of the music game, even if he was almost out of the game of life.

The Andrew Loog Oldham Orchestra recorded four LPs: "16 Hip Hits," 1964 (which featured Mick Jagger, Kim Fowley, John Paul Jones, and Jimmy Page), released on Decca; "East Meets West," 1964 (a Tribute to the Beach Boys and the Four Seasons), released on Parrot; Lionel Bart's "Maggie May," an orchestral homage to the composer's stage show of the same name, released on Decca in 1964; and "The Rolling Stones Songbook," released on Decca and London in 1966, from which the track of ALO's arrangement, "The Last Time," was used by The Verve on 1997's "Bitter Sweet Symphony" (yes, the matter of the recording is still a U.K. High Court matter, the musical copyright having been settled in ABKCO's favor).

Other recordings that made a dent in the '60s include Marianne Faithfull (Decca) '64, Gene Pitney (Musicor) '64, The Poets (Decca and Immediate) '64–'66, Dick and Dee Dee (Liberty) '65, and Del Shannon (Liberty), recorded in 1967.

Oldham also gave the rock-'n'-roll world the trend-setting Immediate Records label in the 1965–1969 era, the first pop independent record label in the U.K. The mainstays of Immediate were the Small Faces, the Nice, Amen Corner, Fleetwood Mac, P. P. Arnold, Twice as Much, Duncan Browne, the Aranbee Pop Symphony Orchestra under the direction of Keith Richards, Eric Clapton-Jimmy Page-John Mayall-Jeff Beck and the British Blues Anthology, Humble Pie, and Chris Farlowe (1965–1970).

In the 1970s he produced albums on Donovan, Jimmy Cliff, Benny Mardones, Humble Pie, and the Werewolves. In the '80s he produced Bobby Womack's "Poet 2." In the mid-1980s Andrew was very involved in the presentation and remastering of the prestigious ABKCO boxed set collections, active studio involvement and preparation of many titles, including "The Rolling Stones Singles Collection/The London Years," "Marianne Faithfull," "Herman's Hermits," and seminal Sam Cooke packages. Mr. Oldham is one of the architects of the musical soundtrack of your life.

From 1989–1996, he's been behind the board with top-selling band, the Ratones Paranoicos, all gold and platinum LPs for the Sony Music label in Argentina. The group appeared with the Rolling Stones in 1994, and with Oasis in Latin America in January, 2001. In 1994, Andrew Loog Oldham charted in Argentina with a duet with Charly Garcia of "Sympathy for the Devil" on Sony Argentina. Charly has been the Elvis/Johnny Hallyday of Argentina for twenty-five years.

I met Andrew Loog Oldham in late 2000 at the Brian Wilson "Pet Sounds" concert at the Hollywood Bowl, sitting with Lou Adler in the box seats right in front of me.

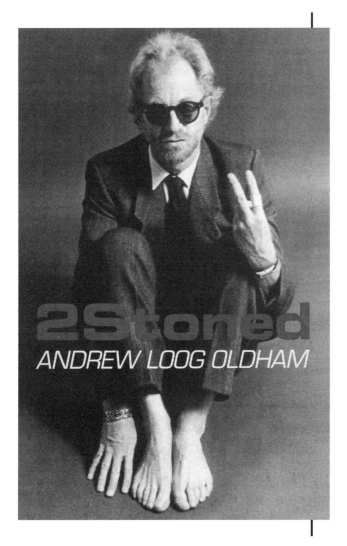

Cover of
2Stoned,
courtesy of
The Random
House Group
Limited.
Photo by
Alfonso Durier
(©1983).

Andrew and I later made arrangements to conduct an extensive question and answer session to discuss his terrific *Stoned*, and a follow up arrangement was made for a meeting and nosh when an advance copy of *2Stoned* was ready for publication.

Then a year later—Summer 2001, to be precise—I met up with him in a West Hollywood hotel, and later a dinner with him and his family at a Beverly Hills restaurant to examine the regional aspects in *2Stoned*. And I thought *I* was the Ambassador of L.A.—Andrew Loog Oldham has a free pass to Angels Flight anytime!

Andrew currently lives in Bogota, Colombia.

Q: Before you start talking about your book, *Stoned*, I know in the mid and late '80s you remastered for disc via ABKCO many seminal box sets and repackages on the Rolling Stones, Herman's Hermits, Marianne Faithfull, Phil Spector, the Animals, Cameo Parkway, and Sam Cooke. What were some of the many memories and feelings you had during some of the playbacks when you were assembling these sets?

A: The period was from 1984 through '87, and Cameo Parkway even earlier. The most interesting section of the Cameo Parkway assignment was having the opportunity to study the formative "grope and learn" years of Gamble and Huff out of writing and performing and into producing. Chubby Checker and Dee Dee Sharp were not that interesting, Patti LaBelle & the Bluebelles a ball. There were some great efforts and some panics on the Gamble and Huff front, such as some of the white-originated psychedelia Norman Whitfield engaged in successfully at Motown with the Temptations. I remember one effort by G and H in which it sounded as if they'd been so smoked out by the intro to the Lovin' Spoonful's "Summer in the City" that they'd just decided to use it *"en total."* I guess it would have sounded new on their side of the tracks anyway. There were some other gems including an LP Clint Eastwood had made whilst he was Rowdy Yates—Merv Griffin was another Cameo star.

None of the work I did on Cameo Parkway ever came out. I did the work with Phil Chapman, a great English engineer from the Olympic days. I hope it does, it's an incredible period of naff America.

With the Herman's Hermits remastering, I was able to work my respect for Mickie Most and affection for Peter Noone. These two guys had a great run together and nailed down that American affection for British song and vaudeville that survives from Bob Hope to Stanley Holloway to that Michael guy with a million electronically enhanced Irish tapdancers. Mickie Most was a great songsniffer, one of the best. "I'm into Something Good" and "There's a Kind of Hush" are great records.

Marianne Faithfull will understand that she was not such a pleasure. Drugs I was taking amplified some poor choices of key and material in her early work after "As Tears Go By" into a nightmare. I recall dying my hair orange and black from the shock. "As Tears Go By" and "Come and Stay with Me" held up. Our version of the Ronettes' "Is This What I Get for Loving You, Baby?" did not. It was all very stiff and "Ritalin." She had had the hits, but for what we were about to receive should not have included an album.

The Phil Spector experience was remarkably cold. I was only involved in sequencing and mastering a couple of the albums. There were no great surprises, just a helluva lot of musicians on each track.

There were some little secrets that are Phil's to speak of and not mine to tell. The records were great, are great and always will be great. I remain a greedy, optimistic fan of the man.

The Rolling Stones was an emotional experience that drove me to the edge of madness; the madness I tell of in the preface of *Stoned*.

I was at a very fragile and wired time. I did a great job, but finished the project more than a little fried. The actual listening of the Stones masters as produced by myself, Jimmy Miller, Glyn Johns, and the Dimmer Twins themselves was amazing. It was like being let back in time into the studio and hearing the canvases wet again before they dried, and that, given my condition at the time, was wearing and not possible to confront and handle.

To do the work, however, I just remembered what the vinyl sounded like and what it had been heard on and adapted it up to present-time; you also had to allow what people thought that the records had sounded like and remember that their experience was mainly compressed radio—so I let a little of that in.

I did the CDs in Hanover, Germany, with a great Dutch engineer who used to do concerts and had done the Stones in the early seventies. I finished the project with Tom Steele at Frankford Wayne in New York. Another great assist came from Big Dom at Bell Sound who had done all my original mastering and still had his notes and recall.

Q: You were in such a rare position of knowing many of the artists, producing the actual recordings on some of them. Did you go through a series of mixed emotions when doing these projects?

A: I try not to "miss" anything and stay in present time. My late Colombian friend and magician, Fernando Harker, once reminded me not to have tears for things that did not have tears for me. That data meant a lot to me and saved a lot of drama. I regard my job as very simple and very present time. I have to fill in a certain space in people's lives—in time and in actual musical space. Making the original recordings with a self-contained entity like the Stones, the job is just as simple until you get cocky, and that is to provide the space, environment, and people in which and with whom they can realize their potential and make universal noise. In the '80s when I remastered the ABKCO set for CD, I measured the space again. I studied on what equipment the music would be heard and filled up the space in the proportions the music demanded. It's quite simple.

It remains a privilege to be able to be engaged in what Graham Greene termed edutainment—it always was. Even when I was not at my best, I attempted to rise to the standard required, out of respect for the form, the song, the artist and the consumer. I am a consumer and I relish the pleasure of having my life changed by a word, sound, phrase, space or thought and idea . . . or a pair of shoes. Excuse me if I enthuse about the wonder, but, as you know, I only recently got the wonder back.

Even whilst I was selling the Stones, I could still have my life changed by John Lennon, Brian Wilson, or the Shangri-Las, and it was wonderful. Sound and vision remain the great communicators, and electricity the mother and pluralplication that allowed art to move off of the ceiling and into the home and the concert hall. The wheel helped too.

Q: You must have really enjoyed preparing the Sam Cooke packages.
A: Sam Cooke was the great experience of my remastering period. I'm one of the few lucky young white zits to have seen him on the Little Richard/Jet Harris tour promoted by Don Arden in England in 1962.

I'd always regarded Sam Cooke and Elvis Presley, and later Bob Dylan, as the real self-producing artists of the era. Sinatra and Bing Crosby had to be the guv'ners—Keith Richards and I got to watch Mr. Sinatra record, that was an education in form and producing thyself. It's an art that Julio Iglesias and Lionel Richie mastered in the '80s—to know thyself and how to dress yourself in sound, song, and polish every word so that it belongs. It places you above anything that can be deemed the A&R domain.

You have that uncanny period of time where you are at one with the audience.

You only have to listen to the Sam Cooke studio chatter and Sam's instructions to know this was the reality of Sam Cooke. He wore the band like a glove. He knew what fit his hand and his command of who he was spot on. Being able to work on remastering Sam Cooke was a joy—the "Live at the Copa" recording remains an uncanny experience. I spent a lot of time getting the knives and forks balanced in character. The original 3-track recordings were perfect—you just had to allow for the new medium of how and where the work would be listened to and on what. I did the work with Steve Rosenthal and Jody Klein at the old RCA studios on 6th Avenue in New York. There were still a lot of the old guys around, original engineers from the day, they were so graceful and wanting to be of help. Now, RCA Studio A was the same dimensions as the RCA Studio A in Hollywood; so the nature of my beast at the time being so, I invited some Colombian visionaries I knew at the time and we seanced and got in touch with Sam Cooke in RCA Hollywood in 1963 during a recording and got his approval as to what I was about on his behalf.

Q: Why did you write the book? What was the actual time period from start to end on *Stoned*? Did it take a few years to put this together?

A: It took twenty-one years to put it together, thirty to blow it apart, and another five to put it all back together again into *Stoned*.

Q: Did you always want to tell it in first person narrative? Were there a series of rough drafts? Please take me through the process and construction of *Stoned*.

A: A young man named Simon Dudfield entered my life in 1991 and wanted to write a book about my life. In 1996 I agreed to let him do it. When I read somebody else's—his—take on how I felt and what I did, I had to take the work over myself, and Simon graciously agreed and that's how the work was born. Simon went on to interview the "voices" that speak throughout the book; and Ron Ross, whom I'd met at the end of the '70s when he worked at RCA in New York on Bowie, Lou Reed, Iggy Pop, and then the Werewolves for me, became my Max Perkins and became my editor in the true Dede Allen sense of the word. I hope the book feels like a movie, successful time-transportation, because that's what it is for me.

Q: Did you keep a diary of life in the '60s? Did you keep a file or retain your own clippings?

A: No, I only kept a diary when I met my wife Esther—I'd finally met somebody who made every day count. I had kept a lot of press cuttings, ads and business mumbo-jumbo, but none of it really helped. What did the work was my mind—I knew exactly what had happened and, now that I had decided to survive, could tell it very well. I did spend a lot of time with the late Tony Secunda in the early '90s and with Dave Thompson in Seattle. I was taking an awful amount of drugs and wrote up the years that will form the second part of my triography, 2*Stoned*. Once I'd removed the drug editorial, psycho baggage and babble, perceived pain and ills done unto me and flattened out the data into actuality, it makes a valid part of 2*Stoned*.

Q: Did you always make it a conscious effort to write about a subject-specific period that ends in 1964, and plan another volume dealing with your life 1964–1967?

A: I always had three possible endings. The first was ". . . And then I met the Rolling Stones," the second was ". . . And then we went to America," and the third, ". . . And then we recorded "Satisfaction." The first might have been a bit cheeky and the third would have been kinda like the end of "Thelma and Louise." It worked out to be a version of the second as a natural piece of the working process; the words, like a basic track in the recording studio, just suggested, no, demanded, by their very being that this was the moment to fade.

The book is not about the Stones, it has five chapters on my early days with them. Those five deal with my meeting them in early 1963, to our first recorded and career efforts through the spring of 1964 when the Beatles have just conquered America and changed the rules of engagement. The Stones and I are nervous and just about to go on our mostly disastrous first American tour. You see, before the Beatles went to America, the best possibility that pop music offered was not having to get a regular job. You must remember that Ringo would have happily called it a hard day's night if he'd made enough money to open a ladies' hair salon and settle down with Maureen. Life was that simple until America entered the equation.

Q: *Stoned* is not a book about the Rolling Stones. Your writing obviously proves this.

A: If you want a *Rolling with the Stones,* stick with Tony Sanchez or Chet Flippo. They do that very well. I don't. This unfortunate mislead is almost a tired re-play of the first Rolling Stones LP when it got released in America. In England I had created some controversy for the group, got a lot of press and pre-orders by refusing to allow the album to be titled or even have the Stones name on it. It was no master stroke—doing it the normal way would have just felt so ordinary and that was not the way I wanted to introduce the Stones to the LP world.

The Decca arm in America, London Records, stuck the stupid title across the top, "England's Newest Hitmakers," and almost relegated us to the Freddie and the Dreamers trenches the same way that *Rolling with the Stones* is one, misleading, and two, sounds like some roadie, drug dealer, or war-zone journalist telling all. That was not my job description—I told the Stones who they were and they became it. And when they no longer needed telling I get to in *2Stoned.* If *Stoned* is *Little Women,* then *2Stoned* is *In Cold Blood.* It's almost bizarre how you can't run the past without a present day version of "then" rearing its head to test you. *Stoned* does tell you what we did and how things felt for the Stones and me in that first electrifying, exciting year, working and getting known in the U.K.

I've also told of the state of our nation and the time and conditions into which all of us rock-'n'-pop war-babies were born. Soho was the playground, London was where we made all the pieces fit, and I've tried to bring that feeling alive on the page—the growing pains of pop and vision. It cannot be that dissimilar to your first Manhattan

(l to r) Phil Spector, Gene Pitney, Brian Jones, Andrew Loog Oldham, Keith Richards, Charlie Watts, Bill Wyman, and Mick Jagger, circa 1964. From the Andrew Loog Oldham Collection, origin unknown.

stride, except it all happened in a time when long-distance telephone calls were something your elders made when somebody had either been born or, more often, had died.

It was an age of innocence that ended when America became a possibility. I've tried to write a book of British popular music and filmic influence as I, the Beatles, Who, Stones, et al., were born into it. How Vaudeville and World War II begot a middle class trad-jazz, which begot skiffle and imitative well-meaning pop, and eventually this little cluster of about 300 white kids with a passion for Rhythm & Blues. How before the Beatles there was a Jack Good, Eddie Cochran, Little Richard, Buddy Holly, Billy Fury, Marty Wilde and Cliff Richard & the Shadows that ran that first all-important mile. How much bigger than life, defining our behavior, up there on the screen were Elvis and Jimmy Dean.

I worked as a press agent for the Beatles, Chris Montez, Bob Dylan and the Little Richard/Sam Cooke/Jet Harris tour before I met the Stones. I worked for fashion designer Mary Quant in 1960 when fashion was the pop business—the only pop Britain had. It was a time when American Cinema gave us hope and attitude, and the pill gave us time and disposable income.

Q: One of the best things about *Stoned*, forget any mention of the Rolling Stones, is that the book reinforces the power American music and movies, foreign films, and U.S. independent cinema had on your life. I don't think there's a better book around that really explains how these components charged and changed lifestyles and subsequent rock-'n'-roll individuals' music and art results. I mean, Johnnie Ray and John Cassavetes blew your mind, as well as the big studio film musicals and "The Sweet Smell of Success."

A: The art of the American song fired our imagination and the French New Wave Cinema gave birth to the British working class theatre and cinema, and in my case, along with the immaculately vain Laurence Harvey and the inspirational "Expresso Bongo," Jean Claude Brialy in Chabrol's "Les Cousins" gave me attitude, cheek, a dress code and verve. There are many life-forming images I've brought to *Stoned*. Picasso checking his work out, smoking a spliff off the Croisette in Cannes, where I was working the pavements and the tourists. The Antibes Jazz Festival, where I got my first look at the results of smack as Ray Charles shivered in an overcoat in the warm Côte d'Azur sun. The joy of Les McCann, whom you know Harvey, whose elegant innovations glissed and glided across the Mediterranean blue like forever birds of rhythm and grace. I was a gofer there, fetchin' sandwiches for the likes of Mr. McCann. He called me Sea Breeze, 'cause I was gone and returned in a breeze. I remember the grace of McCann, not too many men look you in the eye when you are delivering a sandwich. This was my first summer of love.

Q: Did you have any false starts in the actual writing?

A: No, I had done my homework, studied the masters who would have cause and effect on my work and I was prepared.

Q: Like who?

A: The main masters were Graham Greene, Anthony Burgess, and as form, the *Edie* book by Jean Stein as edited by George Plimpton. The examples of the autobiographies of Terence Stamp and Dirk Bogarde as regards taste, truth, and decorum were of great assist as standards that are possible and what one should aim to maintain. Then there was the forever influence of cinema as rhythm to the word—a constant source of revival and idea. I was also assisted by reading all the *Paris Reviews*; by the time I started writing, I'd stopped reading finished works, for they would confuse and complicate what I was about. But I found the process of work as detailed in the *Paris Reviews*, with all the great writers, an incredible source of light, work-ethic, order and encouragement.

Andrew Loog Oldham

Q: I was very interested in your relationship with your mother. She made an impression in the book.

A: My mother gave my life form—something to work with and against.

Q: How did *Stoned* come together? Did you do a formal book proposal? Were you turned down all over town? I really like the music era you emerged from, especially the U.K. music/pop world just before The Beatles and Stones were released on disc. Did you find publishers and houses not understanding the pivotal and seminal U.K. pop/fashion/cultural landscape of the very early Sixties?

A: I produced *Stoned* the way I was fortunate enough to produce records—as a finished master. This is it—what you see is what you get—words, music, image intact. I was not interested in writing about just what I had done, I wanted to explain the life that made us do it—and gave us the space in which to breathe. The independent film mavericks that gave light to what I pursued in the record business. The examples as I perceived them of Bryna, Hecht-Hill-Lancaster, and the Woolf brothers. If anything from my world and the telling of it serves some young pup into tomorrow's version of what we did yesterday, then the tree was worth chopping. I can afford that position and enjoy it. I look forward to being a very young old fart with a doctorate.

Q: Perhaps I'm talking from a U.S. viewpoint, but there seems to be a tendency to hide and not acknowledge the British pop scene/music before the February 1964 Beatles U.S. visit. I mean, even music periodicals, and especially TV documentaries. MTV and especially VH1 in the U.S. seem to think the whole world began in 1975.

A: *Stoned* acknowledges and applauds the very essence of which you speak. I live in Colombia and I don't follow VH1. If I want to watch soap operas, I'll stick with Aaron Spelling. VH1 is a little too close to home to make healthy viewing for the likes of my mind. It has so many hours to fill, it more than over-dramatizes a very simple tale, that of popular music. I like the records but I can't handle that much time on "Cat Stevens: The Story." God bless those who can. He had some hits, some national anthems, took over the world, went mad, and found himself after nearly drowning in Malibu. A little too familiar to make comfortable viewing for me. I prefer "Law & Order."

I do agree with you about the time squeeze. My friend, the same I mentioned to you before, the late great Fernando Harker, was about five years younger than me and that's the five that made the difference. He would "bail" on asking me about the Beatles, Pink Floyd, acid, love, and peace and I would have to point out that love and peace came when fame didn't deliver, and that, on the way up, John Lennon was as ruthless as the likes of Fernando. John just carried a guitar instead of a gun.

It's the same with Marianne Faithfull if you are the left side of fifty. Her life gets concertina'd into heroin overdoses in a poor choice of location; an affinity for Mars bars and throw rugs as opposed to Sunday tea, and a dramatic relationship as cultural *au pair* to the young man Joan Rivers so aptly described as "child bearing lips." The fact is forgotten that Marianne had, between August of '64 and the summer of '65, four Top Ten hits in the U.K. and that is no Jonathan King, and certainly up there with the boys.

Q: Are there any other music books or biographies out that influenced or impacted *Stoned*?

A: I've covered that above. Oh, probably Nick Tosches' *Dino* as well. The wonderful image of how he'd given more than 100 percent of himself away at one point on the way up. Pete Hamill's *A Drinking Life*; *Strange Life of Ivan Osokin* by P. D. Ouspensky, Gabriel Garcia Marquez's *News of A Kidnapping*, all great powerful flat data, and Mario Puzo's *Godfather*—the most moral read this side of the bible. They all provided great images, but it's Graham Greene and Anthony Burgess that amazed me into wanting to make my words work.

Nothing to do with influence, merely plugging others if I may, I recently read Bernie Brillstein's memoir, hated it at first, found it utterly self-serving, all the Brad Grey afterthoughts. But I gave it a second chance by flicking through the index to find people I was interested in and found it an endearing tale of a man in love with the show and business in a very moving way that I related to and recommend.

I was also taken with *Dusty* (a book about singer Dusty Springfield)—a terrifying read about a great talent who abused herself, presumed an entitlement based on great pipes, never had a manager to slap her around, and went to America—Los Angeles of all places—and got lost. Tragically, and this was the painful part of the read, she never got a life or a career. To have grown up gay in the British fifties was a big deal and something "to get over and settle down." It's hard to recall but homosexuality was against the law. I was glad Penny Valentine informed us on the dust-jacket she lives in North London with her son. I live in Bogota with mine. Who knows? Maybe Brian Epstein is managing Dusty now. "C'mon, Dusty, St. Peter's got two tables, it's a full house, you look great!" "Oh, Brian, are you sure?" "Yes, now get on the fuckin' stage, girl, or I'm calling Peter Grant . . ."

Q: In the book, *Stoned*, you used a process where, in addition to your research and writing, you quoted other published works and integrated some pre-interviews with some contributors. Was this by design? Was it just the case, like with Marianne Faithfull, where she said it earlier in her own book, and how could you improve on it?

A: That was the case as regards Marianne. The Stones, as you are aware, would not speak about our time together and that remains the privilege of the act. Nik Cohn was a combination of his books and present-time interviews, as was Mary Quant. Vidal Sassoon I interviewed myself. The other voices, Pete Townshend, Chris Stamp, Lionel Bart, Tony Calder, Mickie Most, Peter Noone, Alan Freeman, all provided valuable memory about times and circumstances I was either too busy "doing" to recall and re-tell, or too stoned to recall that well, as in the case of my then girl friend, later first wife. I have a very healthy respect for my accomplishments; but it's healthy, so I would get bored with an "I did this, I said that," format. I thrive on and feed off the collaborative art. The other points of view were ammunition and tension, full of surprises, education and turns. Mickie Most's recall of how he felt walking through Soho with a recording contract in his pocket is just such a magical filmic moment. John Paul Jones' description of the rules of music and conduct in the Soho of '59 through '61 really breathes and takes the reader onto the streets of which he speaks. With Pete Townshend, John Paul Jones, Chris Stamp, and Philip Townsend, I spent a long time trying to capture my boyhood chum, Peter Meaden, who was such a big influence on us all. Peter managed the Who when they were known as the High Numbers. He was a kind of pill'd-up Johnny Boy in "Mean Streets"—a vision ahead of his time and mind.

Q: Do you write on a computer, type or by hand?

A: I type with Juan Finger. The computer allowed me to stay at home and reach out into and be in the world. I walk the dog at 5:30 A.M., I have some liver or steak for breakfast. I then sit down and write, having either something to write about or until I've found something that works. It really doesn't matter which, you have to do it every day. The joy of writing is a well-kept secret misrepresented by all the propaganda about writer's block and bleeding onto the page. It's a wonderful, heady experience, wherein a word can distort or define a truth, and with each word you have that choice to make. You can sit there all morning, writing thorough rubbish, looking for that word or phrase that puts you back into play. You can be done, and realize the placement of one word can change the truth. It's a wonderful occasion in which the word is king but you have to run an ethical empire.

    2*Stoned* is a tad tougher than *Stoned*—it's about blowing it as opposed to finding it— about America as a reality as opposed to a dream. But the process is still as magical as that first school job delivering morning newspapers on a bike. It's the same job. You work, you have a result and you deliver that result. You have to keep it simple and enjoy the game.

Q: Can you describe the editorial process? I imagine you had to cut some words. Did you do a longer book and then trim from that existing text?

A: I'd cut the tracks, done the vocal, done the overdubs. Now it was about the mixing—serving the voice and the song. We had to be able to eliminate the detail that may have passed muster at the dinner table but got in the way of the flow and rhythm of the book.

Q: How did you actually collaborate with some of the people in the book? Did you do some interviews? Use the phone a lot?

A: The phone bill could remove major debt from a third world nation. Tracking down some of the people, like Jet Harris, the bass player with Cliff Richard and the Shadows, was a pilgrimistic must—he'd been a hero to me and to the likes of John Paul Jones. Jet was the James Dean of British Pop. The chase and tracking down of people I had spent a lot of life-forming time with was a movie in and of itself. I provided Simon Dudfield with the background on my interactions with these people and how they'd affected my life and how I may have had cause on theirs. That was seventy percent of the voices. The remainder came from actual books, as in the case of Marianne and Mary Quant, although Mary was part voice, part book, and the remainder provided their own essays. John Paul Jones gave a fabulous backdrop into the London we discovered at fifteen years of age, and Pete Townshend just wanted a hotel room, a pot of tea and cucumber sandwiches, then played mum and gave his all. It was an engaging process. I couldn't wait to read the results. You have to remember that a lot of the voices had, like me, been so busy "doing," that we'd never had time nor reason to compare notes. The agenda was not me, it was the time. It's like a huge tracking shot through a coming of age.

Q: The book reinforces how vital fashion was to pop music. Elaborate on this. MTV has fashion specials and programming around clothes and style. The collision of fashion and music was really detailed in your travels and *Stoned*.

A: It was not a collision, it was a union. The British fashion business was the first pop business. Look at the photographic work of Terence Donovan and Bailey in 1960, 1961 in *Vogue,* and you'll see the first Beatles and Stones covers and the clues at all early video attempts. Vidal Sassoon exported his haircuts, Mary Quant exported the miniskirt,

David Bailey was already traveling the world for *Vogue.* At the same time, poor British pop music had its moments, grand magical moments like Jack Good's TV shows, "Oh Boy!" and "Boy Meets Girls," but the music we had was hardly exportable. All that ever got out and onto the Ed Sullivan TV show and the American airwaves were the one-offs and the freaks—Acker Bilk, Jackie Dennis, and Laurie London.

Q: I'd like to ask you to talk about survival. You were in a different state of mind before you undertook the journey and the obligations of writing this book. As you were writing *Stoned,* and in a new health environment, did events and people become bigger and more dramatic in context? Does memory return?

A: Memory never goes. It just gets adjusted by the drugs and alcohol; it gets given a point of view that is not reality—what actually went down. The electric shock treatment didn't help either. And that is all I had to remove. Therefore it did not get bigger and more dramatic in context, it just gets back to being flat data and being real. One U.K. reviewer confused that ability to de-dramatize with the lingering effects of coke. I think he may have been speaking from experience, but for me it's just not like that. In 1997 I rid my body of the remaining toxins that still lived in my body and affected my thoughts, actions, and ideas. That's when I could really tackle the book.

Q: Personally, I thought you would be a lot more bitter about some of the actions and scenes around your life covered in *Stoned.* Do you process the anger?

A: Not me, honey. Look at Richard Ashcroft. The poor lad experienced fame and being bitter in the very same beat. You made a record and millions of people listened and beat as one. It really does not get much better than that. When all is done and over about The Verve using my recording as the backing track for "Bitter Sweet Symphony" and passing it off as a sample, it remains one of those great pop moments that rise above the charts and into the time of our lives. I know how he made the record, and I'm the Tommy Dorsey Orchestra and he's a very young Blue Eyes . . .

As for advice, I'm only really qualified to talk about survival and the potential of the opposite for a drug addict and alcoholic. The rest is written in *Stoned* as experience. I would try to be an example by my acts, not give advice, save perhaps that the preface of *Stoned* might serve as a warning . . . And a great tracking shot *a la* "Goodfellas" into the Copa.

Whether you are a writer or a shoe repair artist, the meat and potatoes should be in the moment of work. The applause and recognition should be no more than the veggies or dessert. Any other split of percentages is dangerous. Or as Keith Richards once said in a beautiful display of self-protectory candor, "Art ? It's the diminutive of Arthur . . ."

Q: I've always felt some of your contributions to the Rolling Stones have been overlooked.

A: I can't go over all of that better than I have written it up in *Stoned*—so I'll leave it at that. Every dog has his moment. I'm a lucky dog enjoying another day. The bottom line is that the Rolling Stones and I know exactly what I did do, and what I did not, where I was great for them and where I was not. I hope that they read *Stoned* and enjoyed my take on our shared good lot . . . and if they didn't, they didn't. My universe on it is clear.

Q: I had a brief chat with you at the recent year 2000 Brian Wilson "Pet Sounds" concert at the Hollywood Bowl. Can you talk about Brian Wilson and your relationship with "Pet Sounds?"

A: Brian Wilson's "Pet Sounds" changed my life for the better, and traveling to the Hollywood Bowl was a privilege and a pilgrimage. For me it was like going to the Vatican and seeing the Pope. "Pet Sounds" changed the possibilities of pop music and the potential of what could be done in the long-play form.

On the personal side it spoke for me when I was too busy to have a personal life. The sound and music, the words of Tony Asher blended into the melodic slices of Wilson, spoke of the pain and coming of age in a way that allowed all young ambitious dudes to let him speak for us whilst we hid whatever and hung tough. It was my "Primal Scream." It certainly got Paul McCartney to work on another level.

The Hollywood Bowl "Pet Sounds" experience will fill my trunk for another thirty-four years. Thirty-four years before, Lou Adler arrived in London with an acetate of "Pet Sounds," he came to my house from London Airport, I sat in smoke with Paul McCartney and that first listen changed our lives. And thirty-four years later, Brian duplicates the record live and in perfection! Just wonderful.

Q: You have a wonderful anecdote about Lennon and McCartney running into you on the street and giving you and the Rolling Stones a song to record, "I Wanna Be Your Man." Can you talk a bit about your stint with the Beatles and their manager Brian Epstein? What did you learn from Epstein?

A: Yeah, I'm told Paul has revised bumping into me into bumping into Mick.

What did I learn from Brian? Oh, the danger of being in love with the act—a lesson I'm glad to say I didn't learn. That paisley scarves didn't suit me. That if you've been lucky enough to have had an education, use the accent—it works.

Brian was a lovely, passionate, but tortured man who probably should have died a few months earlier whilst he was still king and did not, propelled by self- and over-medication, perceive of himself as a rejected old queen supplanted by some tatty little guru who in any other decade could not have got a job as a head waiter.

Tough, yeah, but with love. The recent revisionist shit about "Our Brian," with his life and too many old queens' wishful thinking served up as British Christmas TV fodder, is vomit-laden and appalling. Does Paul McCartney really have to look so available and flirty and explain Brian's predilections whilst a nation burps up turkey? John Lennon had a much blunter take on it all.

Let us look at the bottom line: Brian was a passionate man who would not take a "no" on behalf of his lads, and that is how we got to hear the Beatles' music. End of story. The rest is all *schaudenfreuden*, anal-retentive scatology and self-serving revisionism. My book celebrates the few months I worked for the Beatles and applauds the Brian I experienced and worked for.

Q: I liked the part where you talk about your brief gig doing PR for Bob Dylan's debut BBC TV program. Can you expand on that show and the Dylan and Albert Grossman relationship? Were you a fan of Dylan even then? Did you like his later music?

A: Not really. I've always preferred the idea of Dylan and what he did for America and the world with word and imagery, as opposed to the actuality. I loved his late seventies on-stage Latin cowboy *shtick;* I loved "Oh, Mercy" and "Gotta Serve Somebody," but there were a lot of years in there where he seemed in need of a life. I loved him forever young once again in those January '98 shows with Van Morrison. But, like Bruce Willis, I like the idea rather than the detail. They are both American heroes and I respect their cause and effect on American and wannabee lives. They give hope and they explain in a few chosen words. That's not a bad gig to get paid for.

Q: Do you still talk to members of the Stones?

A: As regards the Stones *en total*, to quote Sir Cliff, "We Don't Talk Anymore . . ." But the other Mr. Richards and I continually wish each other well via third parties, and hug on the rare occasions we do meet. I embrace the very idea of him at least once a week.

Q: Did you feel the *Stoned* format gave you ample opportunity to chronicle and reflect on your initial period with the Rolling Stones? Does the print text mirror your early life with the group?

A: It was the perfect time and forum and I'm very proud of the total result, or I would not have had it published. I applaud the time, the opportunity, I applaud my England and I hope it shows. I had a dream a few years ago, prompted, as I recall, by that funny Keith Richards and Elton John spat about songs for dead blondes. In the dream I'm in some awful early-Jewish brocade-driven living room, probably Elton's, overlooking Regent's Park, and Sir Reg is whispering in my ear, "Andrew, you really should come home again . . ."

And I answer, "But I have, my dear, I have . . ."

Q: You've just put out 2*Stoned*. Do you think your oral history format makes it easier for us to glimpse the world(s) you've lived in? And does it make editing easier? Are you really sold more than ever on the oral history forum, of course with yourself being principal moderator and writer within the pages?

A: Yes, I'm sold on the oral history form . . . It has really worked for me with *Stoned* and 2*Stoned*. As you know, Harvey, I was influenced in this way to go by the 1981 book, *Edie*, by Jean Stein, edited by George Plimpton. I was first attracted to the cover and the accrediting of Plimpton in the same way that I was attracted to the Phil Spector 45 labels and the giving of credit to Larry Levine, Jack Nitzsche etc. Then I got taken with the style of the book and, when I started in on *Stoned*, I used *Edie* as my role model, figuring that the only difference was that I was alive whereas *Edie* was dead. What works for me is that I'm able to have all these other points of view and truths. The Robert Evans bio, *The Kid Stays in the Picture*, has a great first line in the preface, "There are three sides to every story: yours, mine, and the truth." It's the first line of Chapter 1 in *Stoned*. It's so true I decided to have these other truths; it makes my life more interesting and brings a greater range of textures and experiences to the books. It also allows me to catch up with other people's '60s.

What I mean is that we were all so busy "doing" in the '60s, we didn't have time to sit about. The experiences of Pete Townshend, Chris Stamp and, in 2*Stoned*, a lot of the same voices from *Stoned*, like Pete and Chris, plus those who come into this American volume, like Lou Adler, Al Kooper, Herb Alpert, Allen Klein, Toni Basil, Roger McGuinn, Nona Hendryx, Kim Fowley, and a lot of other players, including your goodself, give the reader a panorama and sweep I alone could not give—in that I was just about "me," and as much as I love me, I'd really get

Andrew Loog
Oldham at
home in Bogota,
Colombia, 2001.
Photo by
Alfonso Durier
(©2001).

bored with a process that only covered the "I did this, I thought that, I did great, I fucked up" scale . . . I mean, if there were only a couple of hundred people really involved in the '60s, I've got quite a few of them in 2*Stoned*.

The editing was a bitch, and on a few days I felt I had my own "Heaven's Gate" in my hands. You are right, you've read the rough cut. It's a big area of time and experience to edit down into one run, to get into one cohesive cut. 2*Stoned* basically covers where *Stoned* leaves off, from the spring of 1964, when the Beatles have just conquered America and the Stones and I are waiting, nervous and excited, in the wings, waiting for our turn, knowing full well we have not got the vinyl legs to cut it. The book covers from that time to us taking America, to America taking us and my leaving the Stones. In addition it has a device I used to keep my interest up, which I called "drug-cuts," as opposed to "jump-cuts,"

Stoned (Out of His Mind)

in which I cut into the future and write about the consequences I set up and lived through as a result of having "had it," in so many people's perception, by the age of 23, which was how old I was when I left the Stones. That was the bitch, editing that into a smooth one-thematic mix. I worked first on this with David Dalton, a great mate and a talented git. He was very good for the process in that he helped me fine-tune and hone many of the key "you-are-there" scenes, you know, recording moments, magical moments that run a thin line in audience participation or leaving them out in the lobby. David helped me add so much in making those pages work. He also had too much love and respect for what I'd been about. I ended up joining him for a while in that domain, and we ended up adding 150 pages instead of cutting it down.

I now needed a talented, warm, musical, filmic, cold-hearted butcher, as the book was taking on elements of *In Cold Blood,* as opposed to *Stoned* being more akin to *Little Women* . . . or just like the jump from "That'll Be The Day" to "Stardust." I found it via my mate and socio, Doc Cavalier, up in Connecticut. His artist, Christine Ohlman, great and immaculate singer, the Beehive. Well, we had all known each other since I lived in Connecticut in the early '70s when she was in the Scratch Band and I was scratching my runny nose. Anyway, we had in the past few years been circling the wagons on doing something to do with the word. She's a graduate of Boston University in writing and journalism, and we just decided to go for it, get the "Heaven's Gate" out and musical-flow the time and wordplay back in focus.

So it went in three increments: I put it together, Dalton and I re-filmed it, and Christine and I called the meeting to order. Just like *Stoned*, it was still like making and mixing a record, though this time it's less "I Fought the Law" and more "River Deep, Mountain High."

Q: I know you've met many fans of your work with the Rolling Stones, as well as professional musicians. I can imagine some of the comments you've received over the years about that band and the era, also including your vision at Immediate Records, the Small Faces on your label. What kind of things do they say? Do any of them comment on your liner notes? Do some patrons and hardcore record fans and recording artists like DJ Little Steven talk production and still marvel at the LPs' artwork?

A: Oh, lots of that, some wonderful exchanges. Little Steven was a recent treasure you set about . . . a *bona fide* piece of the American rock-'n'-roll aura, a worker and a survivalist. His ride is wonderful, his musical focus a treat, his "Sopranos" work a wonderful call and report on the behalf of whomever thought of him and gave him the gig, not unlike what would have happened if they'd cast Keith Richards in "Lock, Stock, and Two Smoking Barrels" instead of Sting . . . But then I guess Sting cast himself. We are not all Rolling Stones; Little Steven is a worthy pebble. I'm glad the tide preserves him.

Q: We now live partially in a reissue/re-release/repackage society in terms of box sets. Do "best-of" packages make you consider or reconsider any of the achievements? Specifically, in writing *Stoned*, or really *2Stoned*, the 1964–1967 era, do you play the records in terms of research even? Do you look at film clips, even for research? What are your research methods? Probably just in your head, right?

A: Writing the books and playing music is not on. It would be like recording the Stones and having the radio on in the control room. I even had to stop reading. Yes, by the time I get to the studio, or to the page, it's all in my head, aided by the trunks of hand-writings I'd kept, that once they'd been drug-dusted and cleared of aberration and inaccurate perceptions, were fit for the page.

Q: As manager-producer, you did help inject an outlaw element into bands' endeavors. Probably media ploys, but you did sense and add to the group, in areas of image and some of the recordings, a "rebel" posture. Hard to believe, and maybe you can discuss this a bit, but the Rolling Stones not taking a courtesy bow at a London Palladium TV show was considered rebellious.

A: That's in *2Stoned*, it's best left there, as it is. Writing *2Stoned* and finishing it has made it hard to answer that kind of leading question. Before I did the book I thought I knew all the layers—I was wrong. Suffice to say there is somewhat of a case to be made of "I Was, They Became, I Got Lost." Kinda Buddy Holly, "Fool's Paradise."

Q: Did British actors like Dirk Bogarde and Laurence Harvey, and perhaps artist Francis Bacon, inform your own sensibilities to work in the outsider forum? There's a lovely section on Laurence Harvey in *2Stoned*. I know films did have an impact on your psyche and how you perceived America when you and the Stones came to America. It seemed, from clothes to actions, you and the band, attitude and product, absorbed America. They were active musicians, you were more oriented towards cinema.

A: They were not mavericks and outsiders. They all wove their magic and talent within the system. Francis Bacon was another story, an avalanche of man and art whom I was lucky enough to meet because he lived next door to songwriter Lionel Bart, a great old mate who wrote all the early Cliff Richard and Tommy Steele hits before moving on to "Oliver!" The

Stones and I adored America from our different perches that tweeted pretty well for that while . . . Kinda like Willie Dixon meets the Ronettes.

Q: Keith Richards, Marianne Faithfull, Jack Nitzsche, and Jack's stint arranging for Phil Spector, are presented in *This Is Rebel Music*, in addition to Berry Gordy, Jr., and Chrissie Hynde of the Pretenders. The above-mentioned are included in *Stoned* and especially woven into *2Stoned*. They have appearances in *Stoned* and are larger factors in *2Stoned*. Do you feel any different about them after writing these books?

A: Naturally I'm more interested in talking to you about Berry Gordy and Chrissie Hynde, both of whom I've only met once but have enjoyed enormously. They both sit on that fence of artists with that required self-entrepreneurial streak that separates the wheat from the sheep. Mr. Gordy when he was telling Paramount what to do on behalf of "Lady Sings The Blues"—Miss Hynde I met this past January at a Landmine concert in London. I must happily admit I was quite the tongue-tied fan which was a great pleasure and a nice emotion to experience again.

As for Keith, Marianne, and Phil, in *2Stoned* I've defined them as to the part they have played in my life, and now we'll see what part I remain in theirs. Jack Nitzsche, having dropped his body, is a different story, and I've tried to define his really important contribution to that first golden run I had with the Stones, in which, in the kudos division Jack has often been left out in lieu of Brian Jones.

Q: I'm glad *2Stoned* gives a display of how vital and important Jack Nitzsche was in the studio with you and the Rolling Stones. In my book, Jack addresses the "Performance" film and his soundtrack album. Was the car in "Performance" your vehicle?

A: I didn't see "Performance" till the late '70s. Didn't like it then, don't like it now. It's an ode to being unable to produce. The car, the Rolls Royce Phantom V, was identical to mine in the same way that James Fox was playing me. I deal with all that in *2Stoned*, and the inability of pop stars to retain their rhythm and charisma in the celluloid world, that's kind of akin to Kevin Bacon singing.

Q: I had a chat with composer-arranger and songwriter Van Dyke Parks last week at a party in a restaurant in Beverly Glen. He went out of his way to explain to me how essential and important it is for writers, historians and authors these days to do something about the rampant revisionist history he sees, especially in pop and rock music documentation. He told me I was one of the last of a dying breed. This stemmed from a letter he wrote to the *L.A. Times* recently, pointing at their pop music critic, who made some errors in a story, going on to the *L.A. Times* about "God [*sic*] is in the details." I tend to agree with him. I know you've been slighted in this area and know you don't lose sleep over it but . . .

A: "There are no victims, only volunteers." Don't know where he got it from, but I thank "Doc" Cavalier for bringing that staple diet into my life, plus so many other things. I don't know about Van Dyke Parks, I know even less about Randy Newman. Let's get real about this: Writing two books allows me to clean my house and present that world to the world in a way I hope will be evolvingly useful to the present and the future. I'm a reference point of a great, perhaps important time for a lot of folks, and I've managed to survive it and to get referenced in my own words.

Q: Producer Phil Spector informed your rock music tastes and influenced your music business flair. You detail it a little in *Stoned*, and he is mentioned briefly in *2Stoned*. To this day you still communicate with him a little. What impressed you the most about him and his productions? Some of the images and scenes in both your books are as explosive as some of Phil's recording statements.

A: I love Phil Spector. As you know, Phil wrote me a very gracious communication when my mother passed earlier this year. I treasure that reach. I don't just communicate with him a little, I communicate with him in the higher tone sense daily. How can you not with a man who wrote, produced, and redefined the music industry in as many ways as the Beatles did? He influenced me in a way Keith Richards described as embarrassing, but when you come out of the other side of it all, there's nothing embarrassing about it, or Phil's influence on me. He inspired me to produce and the work still stands today; he inspired me to work the way the Stones inspired a whole world to play. Between 1957 and 1966 with his own national anthems, and then again when he provided the environment that assisted John Lennon and George Harrison in getting their finest work done, Phil Spector provided a major soundtrack to our lives. In so many thrilling, productive ways, life has just begun. I look forward to joining him on the other side of 60 and continuing to rejoice in our good lot—we were all a bunch of maverick whores who survived the big clap. That's part of the wonder of it all!

Steven Van Zandt:

Little Steven Doing Big Things on the Radio

Most rock-'n'-roll addicts and music fans know Little Steven (Steven Van Zandt) as the longtime guitarist with Bruce Springsteen's E Street Band, and cable television viewers from his role as Silvio Dante, the manager of the strip club Bada Bing, on the ground-breaking series, "The Sopranos." Some might remember his pioneering efforts in putting together the "Sun City" Artists United Against Apartheid project.

Over the last twenty years he's released five solo albums, often under-scored by topics of sex, politics, and religion: "Men Without Women," "Voice of America," "Freedom—No Compromise," "Revolution," and "Born Again Savage."

In April, 2002, Steven emerged once again on the radio dial, hosting "Little Steven's Underground Garage," a weekly two-hour rock-'n'-roll blow-out heard all across the U.S. on over 115 radio stations and counting. His program spreads the garage rock gospel, in addition to tracking classic album selections and roots music from the Who, the Kinks, the Beatles, the Dave Clark Five, and the Rolling Stones.

"What is garage rock?" many of you might ask. "I can tell you what it's not," Steven informed *Entertainment Weekly*. "It's not synthesizers. It's not drum loops. It's not keyboards in general, unless it's a Vox Continental or Farfisa organ. It's guitars, bass, drums, harmonica, and maracas. It's real people playing real music. It's primitive."

Steven Van Zandt was born November 22, 1950, in Watertown, Massachusetts. He became a teenager the day John F. Kennedy was assas-sinated in Dallas, Texas. He grew up in Middletown, New Jersey, and was

Photo by Ronnie Farley, courtesy of Renegade Nation.

in a garage rock band, Source, when he first met Bruce Springsteen from nearby Freehold, New Jersey. Van Zandt now resides in New York City.

I first met Steven Van Zandt in 1975, when he played Hollywood's Roxy Theater as a member of Bruce Springsteen's E Street Band. Actually, I had heard about him around 1973, when Steve Van Zandt was playing briefly with local keyboardist Joel Warren in Dion DiMucci's backing group in Las Vegas. Van Zandt has known Bruce since he was sixteen years old and Van Zandt put him up at his pad when Bruce's parents moved to California.

Initially, we did a small chat for *Melody Maker* at the time, took a dip in the pool at the Sunset Marquis Hotel, and later (Miami) Steve and Bruce went along with me to Gold Star Studios to attend a Phil Spector recording session with Dion.

We all had a blast, and during their next L.A. visit, E Street Band drummer Max Weinberg called me and asked if he could meet legendary session "Wrecking Crew" drummer, Hal Blaine, whom I knew from playing percussion on a handful of Spector's 1975–1979 productions. Hal was very gracious and invited us up for lunch at his Hollywood Hills home. Max made arrangements to interview Hal, and he's one of the voices in Weinberg's wonderful book on drummers, *The Big Beat*.

I later went on a couple of Springsteen tours for *Melody Maker*. Van Zandt was working with and producing Southside Johnny and the Asbury Jukes, an endearing bar band outfit around the same time, and thanked me on their second album sleeve. I went to Asbury Park to interview both Van Zandt and Southside Johnny in the late '70s for *Melody Maker*.

Steven Van Zandt has become an acclaimed record producer for artists such as Springsteen, Darlene Love, Lone Justice, Gary "U.S." Bonds, Michael Monroe, Lords of the New Church, and the Arc Angels, while also writing songs for Love, Jimmy Cliff, Southside Johnny, and Brian Setzer. He left the E Street Band in 1982 and spent the '80s immersed in international politics, returning to the band for the 1999–2000 world tour.

Van Zandt's most impressive undertaking was his leading role to further human rights spearheading the hugely successful anti-apartheid "Sun City" project, and establishing the Solidarity Foundation in 1985 to support the sovereignty of indigenous peoples. Along the way he has been honored twice by the United Nations for his human rights achievements, and received the International Documentary Association Award for his film, "The Making of Sun City."

In 2001 Steven contributed "Affection" to the second "Sopranos" soundtrack collection, "Peppers & Eggs," performed with his '90s garage band, the Lost Boys, and he wrote the foreword to Richard Neer's book, *FM: The Rise and Fall of Rock Radio*.

A couple of years ago Steve joined forces with music promoter Jon Weiss of "Cavestomp!" They produced and presented a series of live garage rock concerts in New York, downtown at the Village Underground music venue. Seventeen sold-out shows followed, showcasing fifty new bands along with such well known and legendary pop and rock figures as Barry & the Remains, the Troggs, the Pretty Things, and Dave Davies of the Kinks.

I'm delighted by the success of his weekly radio show. New ears are discovering "Little Steven's Underground Garage" and DJ Steven Van Zandt's extensive knowledge and passion on the re-emerging genre and guitar-driven sound and pound.

I hadn't talked to Steven in over a decade. In early 2002 Steven phoned, he must have heard me playing the Impressions from 3,000 miles away, and asked for some help in locating producers Andrew Loog Oldham and Shel Talmy for his radio program. He often spotlights their seminal records in his shift.

It was pretty easy to accommodate him and a pleasure to help. I share an office with one of Talmy's engineers, and I'm one of the oral histories, along with Herb Alpert and Lou Adler, in Andrew's 2Stoned book. I arranged for Little Steven to meet ALO in New York, and Steven later did a phone conference with Shel in L.A. In August, 2002, Little Steven hosted a tribute segment on his show to arranger-producer, Jack Nitzsche, and utilized some of my previously published Nitzsche interviews and research in the touching audio salute. I'm thanked each week on his radio show.

For this book, I wanted to formally interview Steven about "Little Steven's Underground Garage," his life as a DJ, reflections on the Sun City group effort, politics, observations on 9/11, and his gig on "The Sopranos."

We talked for a couple of hours in July, 2002. In August I went to see him play with Bruce Springsteen & the E Street Band, when they stopped in Inglewood for a concert at The Forum. Little Steven, always very cordial, invited me to his meet-and-greet gathering at the venue before the concert, and following their terrific gig, I attended his post-show reception at a Mastro's Steak House in Beverly Hills.

Steven Van Zandt has a spiritual and physical bond with music and is concerned about its destination. Rock-'n'-roll is in good hands with him.

Q: On the TV broadcast telethon, "America: A Tribute to Heroes," a benefit for the 9/11 victims, with Bruce Springsteen and the E Street Band, you started the show off performing "My City of Ruins." Tell me about the experience of being involved with the event and your immediate feelings about the tragedy.

A: The mechanics of how that telethon came together, I really don't know about. For myself, the day this thing happened, the shock sort of wore off, and you stopped waiting for the next explosion. I watched the second one happen—I saw the first plane in the building on television, and I figured that the pilot had had a heart attack in some Cessna, and hit the building. What else can you think, right? Then I saw the second one hit, and I realized, "This ain't no coincidence, that's for sure." And then it was like, "Okay . . . we're in a war now . . . a war has begun." Anyhow, ten to twelve hours later, I was on the phone to everybody, tryin' to figure out what to do, and how do we deal with this. Your first thought is some kinda concert . . . but it just didn't feel right to me, and nobody I spoke to, we didn't quite know what to do. There's a certain celebratory aspect to a concert that just wouldn't be appropriate, obviously, for something like that, so "What the hell do we do?"

So we waited a few days, and somebody came up with this thing that turned out to be really, really well done, and managed to get the right mood, that would work as a catharsis and at the same time, be able to perform, but it really wasn't a celebration. It was a very, very difficult thing to pull off, actually. I thought it was very, very well done and all of the artists just picked the right songs, and they had the candles there . . . it was just a very, very difficult thing to pull off.

Q: Did you get the feeling, individually and collectively, that there was a sense of helping heal the city?

A: Yeah, yeah, because that's what we do, that's the job description with a performing artist; you have to be that thing that helps to heal in times of suffering. Sometimes it's there to celebrate . . . but you are sort of the "voice of the community," or the sounding board or whatever. In a funny way, I think that rock-'n'-roll became the church of the community. I know it has been for me . . .

Q: So when you left the soundstage and had some interaction with the other artists, was there a sense of healing? I mean, for somebody like you, who's been thematically occupied with "America" and studying America and international relations, did you look at America differently that night, after the show?

A: Well, for me, it wasn't quite as big of a shock as for most people. I've seen this sort of thing comin'. I mean, most of what I talked about and criticized was United States foreign policy since World War II, and I firmly believe that part of that led to this—although, of course, there's never any excuse for this kind of psychotic terrorism. But these things do not exist in a vacuum, they don't just sort of come from anywhere. There is a reason for this kind of thing, as sick as it might be, or

Little Steven with Bruce Springsteen and the E Street Band preforming at Madison Square Garden, New York, on Monday night, August 12, 2002. Photo by Rahav Segev/Photopass.com (©2002).

distorted or whatever. I've been trying to deal with most of those things since the 1980s, and all through my solo albums, and figure that stuff out. I mean, I knew there were problems that were gonna come, and actually, if you looked at what Bin Laden had been doing the last ten years, this guy was not the least bit secret about what was going on.

I mean, the Palestinian situation should have been dealt with thirty years ago, okay? Certainly twenty-five years ago, and certainly twenty years ago, and certainly fifteen years ago. It's the same fucking headlines for thirty years! It needs to be dealt with. When are we gonna come to a conclusion?

Q: In a nutshell, just tell me about the making of "Sun City" the record, the germ and the genesis of it. Your participation and coordination of that effort and how that all came together.

A: The reasons I got into politics, very briefly, were these: I had had rock-'n'-roll tunnel-vision all my life, and didn't know about anything other than rock-'n'-roll, didn't pay attention in school, the whole bit. Suddenly three things happened all at once. We went to Europe in 1980, became successful for the first time, and had our first hit. [During] that trip, the tunnel-vision I'd had all my life began to fade away, and I started to wonder what was goin' on in the world. The impact of bringing your personal rock-'n'-roll to Europe and to foreign countries had a profound effect on me—the thought that you could communicate directly with people of other countries, without using our government—without using any government—was amazing to me. It never occurred to me that rock-'n'-roll could do that. To hear them singing all the words to the songs, in every country where they barely spoke English, was quite profound when it first happened.

So that's happening, my tunnel-vision is fading, and a kid in Germany asked me why I put missiles in his country. I said, "I'm a guitar player, and I didn't put no missiles in your fuckin' country—what are you talkin' about?!" It stayed with me, and I thought about it, and I realized for the first time in my life—very late in life—that I am a citizen of America, the United States of America, and in fact, if we are a democracy, I *am* putting missiles in his country, ya know? And that made me wonder about what else we were doing, and what else I was doing. So I started studying foreign policy since World War II, and was very shocked to discover what was going on. I was brought up to believe that we were supporters of democracy all over the world . . .

Q: Could some of that influence have been—with the blinders on—coming from growing up in a Barry Goldwater Republican family?

A: Well, no, it really didn't. I think it had the opposite effect on me, actually. The effect of my father being a Goldwater Republican, and me being the only freak within thirty miles! I mean, we defined the generation gap. But the interesting effect of all of that, once we reconciled and all of that much later, was my sense of patriotism came from him, although his generation may have been of a more "blind acceptance" form of patriotism . . .

It just took a different form. For the '40s or '50s generation who had that "blind patriotism" to the country, it ended up being an informed patriotism, which involved questioning the government, criticizing the government, and not making (them) any less patriotic for doing so . . .

So I become obsessed with politics. I decide to learn that we are not the forerunners of democracy—to the contrary, we have been fighting against democracy for fifty years.

Q: Treatment of Indians, broken treaties, genocide . . .?
A: Yeah, forget it.

Q: Did it harm your rock-'n'-roll chops, say, instead of hearing a classic rock song or buying an R&B song, studying about Wounded Knee or Leonard Peltier?
A: No, because my music formation had happened. That was done. There was not a whole lot that informed me since 1970. So by the end of the '60s, I'd had enough (musical) input . . .

I discovered Noam Chomsky. All of a sudden it's like, "Wow, I have to do something about this, no matter how small or insignificant, I have to say something and write about it." So I began, and I outlined five different themes for five different records that were all inter-connected, and I began to write the political music. In the middle of this I put out my first record and my second record, and in between them, one of the issues—I had made up a list of all the issues (of) United States tax dollars, and we were on the wrong side of virtually every war. It was amazing, just an amazing discovery.

One of the things we were on the wrong side of was South Africa. I had actually gotten to the South African issue by studying American Indians, and realizing what the South Africans had done was to copy what we had done with the American Indians, for their black people. Our "reservation" system became their "homeland" system . . .

But anyway, I couldn't find out anything about South Africa. There was virtually nothing written about South Africa. So I had to go. I went down in '84, just as Soweto was occupied by the troops. I went back about four to five months later, which was really a surprise to all those people, because nobody ever went down there—and nobody had ever gone down there twice. Anyway, through various sneaking around, I found out what I needed to find out down there. It was a shock to see slavery. My generation, growing up, you'd only see slavery in movies . . .

Q: I myself heard about this stuff through rock-'n'-roll—I remember Dusty Springfield getting into government hassles in South Africa when she toured, and promoters asking her to play to mixed segregated cinema music venues. She declined, and they tossed her out of the country. And I think with the Byrds there were also some concerns about playing South Africa around 1968.

A: Yeah, and Ringo (Starr) told me that they (the Beatles) turned it down. I went down there, I saw it, and I realized that this is something that must be dealt with, and of course, our government was on the wrong side, and so instead of it being a song on my third album, "Freedom—No Compromise," I pulled it off the album and decided to have a few other artists on it. I was gonna have four or five artists at first on it, all representing different genres, and it grew to fifty artists and the whole thing. The strategy was quite simple, really, because you're looking at this terrible situation and wondering, "What can I do? Here I am, a guitar player . . ." This was a real "organizing" song, a real "union" song, one of those "war" songs. It was time to point the finger, name names and say, "Here we go . . ." I ended up using most of the reference lyrics, which I would normally change to something a little more vague.

Q: Not since the Bangladesh album and concert had I been hit by such an informed, group thing . . .

A: Well, it was directly related to George Harrison, of course. We managed to publicize this thing in a way that really got through. At that point, I knew revolutionary strategy from the battlefield to the television set, and this is what I tried to explain in South Africa and Nicaragua and everywhere I went. They sort of tolerated me, and "if he's that passionate about it, let him go . . ."

We just started getting calls from the whole world. They asked me to raise money when Mandela came over—which I never, ever wanted to engage in—but they were desperate—so Bobby De Niro, Spike Lee, Eddie Murphy and I raised half a million dollars for Nelson Mandela, and then, forget it. So now you're not only successful politically, but you can raise money too. Forget it, OK? You become one of the most popular guys on the planet! (laughter) So I was like, "Wait, wait a minute . . ." I learned what I needed to learn, and I now know how the world works. I learned a whole lot about myself, and now I can go back and make a living.

We were and are spiritually bankrupt, and in a state of confusion ever since the '60s opened up our eyes, and we never recovered as a culture. We've never found that *zeitgeist* or that paradigm or the next thing where people can relax and say, "O.K. . . . I know who I am, I know who our country is. We know who we are collectively." That's never happened. We started getting bounced around when politics started to really become show business, until the media became so powerful.

Once the news departments started getting put into the profit center, the moment they said, "We shouldn't lose money on the news department," that happened one day, and I remember when that happened, in our lifetime. Up until then, they were concerned with objective gathering of the news, as best as they could—not that they did that great of a job back then, either—but they were trying. Yes, they lost money, but this was for "the benefit of the community," ya know? But that went out the fucking window. We've been bounced around and manipulated here and there, so it's keeping us confused as well as . . .

But just to finish off the South African thing, obviously it always had to do with the economic boycott. So the strategy was, How do we make this economic boycott take hold, and bring this government down, when you're a guitar player? Okay? And the answer was, we would focus on the cultural boycott, and we'd use this Sun City Resort as a symbol of that, and then that takes hold, and eventually we will get to the economic side of the thing, and that's what counts . . .

The children of Senators and Congressmen started going to their parents, "what's this South Africa thing?" because we had so thoroughly gotten through the media, sideways, by the way, because no radio station would play it. Too black for white radio, too white for black radio. I had a very fateful meeting with MTV at the time and got them to support it and BET supported it, and that's how people heard the song. So, eventually it got to Congress and we overrode (Ronald) Reagan's veto for the first time in history and that was the end. Once the boycott took hold it was literally dominoes, and down came the government. It was one of those rare moments where you figure out a strategy and pull it off. Politically it was the ultimate sort of clean victory that you never ever see.

Q: And it was music-birthed.
A: Yes, that's right. Again, it was the same thing that hit me, like on that stage in Germany or Sweden. The power to communicate that we have. Music is not just some sort of distraction or background music, or purely for entertainment.

Q: I also know you've cited the work George Harrison did around the Concert for Bangladesh as an influence in your marriage of music and politics.

A: No question about it. No question about it. That was the first time where we connected those things together, man. Social concern and rock-'n'-roll were two different things, man. And that was big, and it stayed with me. That permanently affected me, and then when I had a chance to do it, I did it.

Q: Your solo albums always tend to be sort of thematic, almost conceptual in design. Why?

A: I decided early on. And I don't know why this is, there's not many of them, I decided I liked concept albums more than I liked the other kind. I don't even know why. There's not that many concept albums if you think about it. The Who's "Tommy" being the most successful and the most literal and the most coherent. I like something about having something bigger to say than just a collection of songs. From the moment I began my solo career, I decided that's what I was gonna do. And every record is specifically a concept record, not only within itself, but within the five themes.

Q: You have a song, "Affection," recorded with your current garage rock band, the Lost Boys, on the second volume of the "Sopranos" sound-track collection. And like most everything in your life, your current acting role in that television show came out of the rock-'n'-roll arena. A TV writer/director saw you induct the Rascals into the Rock and Roll Hall of Fame on a VH1 TV broadcast and wanted you to be in his new program, "The Sopranos."

A: It's one of those ridiculous cliché Hollywood stories you would not believe.

Q: But you had history with the group, and their drummer Dino Danelli was in your own band in the early 1980s.

A: Yeah. Right. This one is a moment where you start to believe in destiny. The Rock and Roll Hall of Fame didn't want to let the Rascals in. A friend of mine, Frank Barcelona is on the Board, and I told him, "If you come back from one more Board meeting and tell me the Rascals are not in the fuckin' Rock and Roll Hall of Fame, I want you to organize one of those special meetings and I want to come in and plead their case. I want to hear someone tell me why they shouldn't be in the Rock and Roll Hall of Fame. They are one of the best bands ever, and I may be the only ass-hole who has ever seen 'em play live." They were just fabulous.

We got them in. Frank then says, "You gotta induct them." I said,

"Frank, that's an insult to the band. Go out and get a fuckin' celebrity." I had a very casual relationship with the Hall of Fame people. Three months later they came back to me. I thought, "No one must give a shit about this band, obviously, and I don't know how many people must have turned it down [to induct them]. OK, I'll do it." It was the first time the Hall of Fame ceremonies were televised. It was always a private ceremony. I had the Rascals clothes made. The knickers that they wore. Blousy shirts they wore and a coat around it. Dropped the coat during my speech. The kicker is, David Chase, creator of "The Sopranos," is clicking around with his remote and just before I went on they showed on TV a video montage of the Rascals. He catches the montage. He happens to be a Rascals fan. Here's the Rascals on TV. That's weird . . . Unusual. He stops clicking around. It's a movie, man. I started to understand destiny. I come on and do my five minute comedy bit. He says to his people, "Find him. Get him on my new show." Now, they can't find me. I don't have any show business connections, right?

Q: Maybe they could have tried to reach your actor brother Billy in the Screen Actors' Guild directory.

A: [Laughs] Good one . . . They find me through the corporate papers of my Solidarity Foundation. Connect all the dots. A new TV show. "Send a script." It came and it was really good. The writing impressed me. I had some reluctance, because I didn't want to take a role away from an actor, and Chase said he'd create another role for me. And I've never acted and had no interest in acting. All I heard all my life is, "ninety-nine percent of SAG is outta work." Chase said, "Don't worry about it. I'm going to write a part just for you that doesn't exist in the script." The people I work with are really special. At our first meeting all we talked about was music. You can see that his vision for "The Sopranos" continues right into the music as well. And the soundtrack for the show has all sorts of music, from (Bob) Dylan to Johnny Thunders to Them. Being in "The Sopranos" is like being in a band, it's exactly the same dynamic. Everyone gets along. It becomes a family atmosphere you want to work in.

Q: With the success of your "Little Steven's Underground Garage" weekly syndicated radio program, now reaching over 115 stations across the United States, a two hour parade of classic pop, new tunes, wicked soul, rock, and overlooked music gems from the '60s, I also remember some sound checks on tours when you, Bruce, and the E Street Band would play some riffs from '60s U.S. rock acts, and British bands like Manfred Mann—"Pretty Flamingo," later including them in your show along with the Bobby Fuller Four's "I Fought the Law." Now, after the music shows you helped produce in the New York music venue, "Cavestomp!", things evolved and you now host the radio program, "Little Steven's Underground Garage."

[Mary Huhn in *The New York Post* reviewed the program and said, "It's a show that's hard not to respond to . . . Even stuff not familiar grabs you right away."

Kurt Loder on MTV News.com offered, "Can this be legal? Now you can get to know Steve Van Zandt as the coolest DJ in the country, a proud throwback to the late-night hipster jocks of long-gone 1960s and '70s FM radio."

Van Zandt also told Loder, "I love radio. But I just can't listen to it today. And I think there are all these kids out there now who don't know what rock-'n'-roll radio can be."]

A: A few years earlier, Richard Neer, a legendary DJ, came to me and said, "WNEW-FM is in trouble, would you talk to the general manager about being the program director?" I had a meeting. A moment that made me think. I have an affection for radio that I grew up on and can't begin to repay. AM radio, which everyone tends to put down, let me tell you, that was a ball. I was interested, I came up with a format, and garage rock was a part of it. Three or four categories. I had 1,500 songs or so, here's the idea, and eventually, the GM said, "We can go with this, but the DJs— we can't give them any freedom." And I said, "I can't take the gig without that. I want these DJs to feel they are communicating their personalities to the audience. That's what I grew up with and that's what I miss." It didn't happen and they became "All Talk."

A few years later, a friend of mine, Mark Greenberg, who introduced me to my wife twenty-five years ago at the Bottom Line club when we played there, and who was in a band in the '60s, told me there was interest again in his band in the "Nuggets" box set. John Weiss had started "Cavestomp!", a live music series re-uniting legendary '60s groups, and these new garage style bands that had started happening again. Other labels had been doing this sort of thing as well, and garage became institutionalized in my mind.

Q: A market existed, and new young bands emerging as well.
A: And all very connected. I thought, "This is fuckin' fabulous and wonderful." I got back interested in music for the first time in years. So John and I became partners in 2001. To do it right, we figured it out that we would lose $10,000 a show. A friend of mine was booking the Village Underground. My goal in life is to break even. I went to get some sponsorship.

I gotta tell you it was the easiest sell you can imagine. Unilever, Sundazed Records, Pepsi, sponsors all of which gave more than they could possibly make back by playing to these numbers of people. They were all interested in any kind of re-birth of rock-'n'-roll and that was the bottom line. Philosophically, they wanted to support this thing, ya know. Which was fascinating to me and I realized for once in my life I may have good timing [Laughs].

What I didn't know was, how many groups are there out there? We did twelve different headliners and it was a complete success. But more importantly, we put four new bands with every headliner. So, it was like fifty new bands. This stuff is so under the radar.

I'm not kidding you, man. The gigs were the most fun I'd had in twenty or thirty years. They were phenomenal. I spent a good deal of time e-mailing back and forth with Jim Lowe of the Electric Prunes, trying to get them to re-form. It was all personal. We got them to re-form. Phenomenal. We almost got the Sonics. We got them in a room rehearsing for the future. We got the Creation from England to come over and the Pretty Things. And half the audience was under 25. OK. And so all of a sudden I'm realizing this thing is real, and I'm gonna dedicate whatever I can and use whatever celebrity capital I temporarily have to make this move forward.

Q: You have made an impact in the music retail world.

A: The Whiz Records chain of forty stores now has a garage rock retail bin. They're one of our main sponsors, a local Tri-State Northeast regional record chain. As part of the deal, we went to them (and said), "Support us downtown at the Village Underground and put in a garage rock section and I will stock it. Sundazed, Norton, Bomp got in there for the first time. I stock like twenty records in forty stores and I'm looking for a national retailer.

Q: You were really impacted by the original sound and production of garage rock and the '60s AM radio dial, and the producers from that era like Shadow Morton, Shel Talmy and Andrew Loog Oldham. And your radio show also acknowledges them as well as other producers behind those records. I like it when a DJ gives a producer a taste once in a while over the airwaves.

A: Let me tell you something. The best Small Faces stuff was on Andrew's Immediate Records label, and he is very much not only part of garage, he's the father of garage. The Rolling Stones are the archetype, no matter what anybody says, they are the archetype garage band and he was very much instrumental in what they did, how they came across and what they sounded like and all of that.

And Shel Talmy's productions with the Who and the Kinks I play as well. I play all sorts of things: the Yardbirds, 13th Floor Elevators, the Monkees, the Standells, the Ramones, the Greenhornes, the Datsuns, Fonda, things from Rhino Records' "Nuggets" box, like Kim Fowley's "The Trip" and the Electric Prunes' "I Had Too Much to Dream (Last Night)." The Pretty Things . . .

Q: The Hard Rock Café, Pepsi/AMP (an energy drink manufactured by Pepsi), and Unilever (who have hundreds of divisions—your show is sponsored by Dove soap) are involved in bringing your radio program to a national listening audience. I think you're managing to demonstrate some creative partnerships where money helps finance the product. And you mentioned at one time to me you've found some people who are very passionate about rock-'n'-roll and specifically what you are doing.

A: And the fact that sponsors are supporting the radio show means there's a potential for mass appeal. It's not just me. For the first time in my life I see the purpose of sponsorship. Corporate support. Up till now, all I've seen is corporations supporting bands that don't need the fuckin' money, OK? The most successful. The big ones. I've never seen the corporations do what they should be doing, which is supporting the little guy, the underdog. The people who actually need the fuckin' money.

I've read the criticism on the internet about corporate sponsorship. "These corporations are involved . . ." If it wasn't for them, there's no show, OK? The infrastructure for rock-'n'-roll doesn't exist. It's gone. If you want to live in the past, or in fantasyland, go ahead. I have to live in the real world. And I've found sponsors who have a passion for music and rock-'n'-roll, which is interesting. The people who are running these corporations are the rock-'n'-roll freaks that we grew up with! The guy from Unilever wants me to play more Music Machine. That's what's so cool here. And all of a sudden there is a real purpose. They have a real purpose.

The sponsors said, "We dig what you're into here. We want to be involved." So we're trying to bring back rock-'n'-roll as everybody knows it. I went to the Hard Rock Café people. They had faith in me and the radio show, and hopefully there will be some local bands playing inside the Hard Rock Café.

Q: How has your playlist developed? Soul, girl groups, rare records, current crop sounds, original English invasion tunes, and Beatles and Stones hardly played on the FM dial.

A: I spent six months on it, and what worked together. I had a concept in my head and I wanted to really make sure that I hit the ground running 'cause I knew I wasn't gonna get a second chance. It had to be a combination of things I loved or I wasn't going to be able to sell this thing. It had to be something that really worked together. What happened next I was gonna play by ear. I knew I wanted it to be about the music, and not about me. OK? And I knew I was going to have to do it in a way that wasn't an academic atmosphere. It had to be fun. Blocks of tunes, and combine the different eras in the same set. And this is what is most important. The greatest thing that has happened to me is people coming up to me and e-mailing, "I'm not sure if that was an old song or a new song." I'm trying to show the connection between things and how they are connected and how they all strengthen each other and how there is a tradition that these new bands are continuing in. Let's support them and maybe we can actually resurrect an art form.

Q: And your shift puts some attention to all the band members on the records tracked. You mention the band members, the producer, the engineer, that never usually get mentioned. But in a lot of cases, they are people I know, or friends of friends and you treat it that way. Like a family gathering. But you consciously steer the show away from your life and interactions exclusively. You pretty much keep yourself out of the mix as the focal point. You are hosting the show.

A: Yes. The real point I hope is not that this is something I'm being nostalgic about, but something that was very cool then and is very cool now. You're gonna get something out of this now, just as I get something out of it now. I don't hear a song and think, "Where was I when I first heard this?"

Q: Initially, it was hard to get this format thing going. College radio and specialty shows on radio have tracked some garage sounds over the decades.

A: DJ Bill Kelly on WFMU has been an inspiration. He plays the more obscure stuff. At first, (producer) Dan Neer and I met with his syndicator, and I start to get a picture of what I'm up against here. And boy, is it scary. These guys who are in the business are saying, "You'll be lucky to get ten stations. It's going to be very difficult, nobody wants any syndication anymore."

Conglomerates own a lot of radio stations. Not only have they taken over horizontally, I find out they have taken over vertically. In other words, I find out Clear Channel now owns 1,200 stations, which is beyond belief, but they are creating their own content for syndication. So these PDs and GMs are afraid to take my show 'cause they might get their ass kicked from upstairs. This is what I'm walkin' into, right. So I decide every syndicator, and they're all nice guys, they really are, but they're telling me how they're gonna fail. And I'm like, "You know what? If we're gonna fail, I can do that. I don't need you to fail, OK?"

A depressing start . . . I said to Dan, "Let me ease your mind. We ain't taking no for an answer. This show is getting on the radio. I'm going to do everything I can do." So we started to attack this thing. We did a demo and people would look at the list of songs and freak out. "Don't look at the list, listen to the show." And what happened is guys started to listen to it and there is something going on with this music that they don't have. Eventually we started to win them over. Guys started to listen to our one-hour demo, whether they knew the songs, or knew the groups, there is something going on with this music that they don't have, that's not going on right now on the radio.

We started with twenty stations and nine weeks later we're at forty-four, ya know. Now it's over 115. I haven't heard a negative word from anybody. Amazing. I got everyone, including every station, to commit to a year. And I said I wanted to cut the commercials in half. Sixteen to eighteen minutes of commercials each hour is too much. I don't care what's going on in the corporate world, I guarantee you that even with half the amount of commercials, you'll be able to make the same or more amount of money, because I got a lot of people out there right now, ya know. I'm someone people are gonna respond to right now. That's what happened, man. We cut it down to eight minutes. They take half the time, I take half the time, and it really does help the flow of the show. I put five song sets into each show, man. I do play vinyl when I have to, two or three times on every show. I meet with the station people and we have a ball.

I'm getting 25,000 hits on the web site. As serious as I can be, and you know how serious that is, this is primarily about fun and about life, motivation, and inspiration. It's fun. I think everyone is responding that way.

Q: There's something about the radio and experiencing the audio world.

A: The medium itself I think is the last truly magical medium that can't be messed with. Movies are a magical medium, but we now have shows that explain to you why it's not magic. Every other show detailing special effects done, over-exposing actors, so you don't get the movie-going experience.

It's everything and everybody, that's what is remarkable. I don't mean to be blasphemous, but I look at rock-'n'-roll as a religion. For me it is that kind of thing. People become part of this religion regardless of their age, a certain common ground with this type or that, I can't explain, but I know it exists. It doesn't exist with other types of music, but it's sort of essential. Through this rock-'n'-roll thing that I either accidentally or through life experience have stumbled into here, this combination of things I'm playing just seems to have some common ground with people that cannot be explained. From fifteen to fifty-five, they react to it exactly the same way. This is cool.

Q: Is being a professional musician, a working musician for decades, a benefit in the radio world? Does it help?

A: I'm not sure if being a musician helps, but being a street survivor certainly does help. And keep in mind, we were street survivors before we were in the music business. We had to learn how to survive without the business for seven years, ten years, OK? The business was a pain in the ass, to be frank. I took a huge pay cut when I left the Asbury Jukes and joined Bruce Springsteen and the E Street Band. I never made that much money again for five years, because I was playing in Asbury Park for three nights a week, OK?

There's an accessibility now, as time goes on, it becomes really clear. What's really amazing to me is how my own perception has on one level stayed exactly the same, and on the other I'm starting to see how the Beatles become more of a garage band every year and at the time, they were very sophisticated. Now, you listen back, what a cool garage band this was. You hear the mistakes. And you hear guys playing. And regardless of everything, Ringo is playing those fuckin' drums.

What has happened is I'm playing some brand new songs, some garage songs I want to repeat. Two hours ain't enough for this shit, man. The rest of the country, the whole classic rock thing is playing 300 records and I got about 800. They are playing 300 records a day twenty-four hours, and I'm playing 800 two hours a week. Give me my own station!

Jim Keltner:

Remembering George Harrison

I talked to drummer Jim Keltner the week his good friend George Harrison died. We were scheduled to have dinner at his Los Angeles area home, and to discuss the impending 2002/2003 re-release of the "Concert for Bangladesh" album set that Harrison was working on at the time of his unfortunate passing. Keltner and Ringo Starr were the drummers for the historic charity event in 1971. Capitol Records had contacted me earlier in the year about doing some consultancy on the then-projected album reissue.

This chat and research discussion was originally planned for a *Rolling Stone* news story that the New York bureau had asked me to coordinate, about the late 2002 release of the live recording. At the time of this writing, the "Concert for Bangladesh" project is in a holding pattern as George's wife Olivia sorts out his recording legacy and select products that will eventually be made available in 2002 and 2003.

Jim Keltner, a veteran drummer and percussionist, had done hundreds and hundreds of studio dates over the decades.

His name can be found on recording session logs and recordings by Albert Stinson, Gabor Szabo, Cal Tjader, Don Randi, Gary Lewis & the Playboys, B.B. King, Johnny Rivers, Freddie King, Phil Spector, John Lennon, Yoko Ono, Jesse Ed Davis, Albert Collins, Bob Dylan, Joe Cocker, Dave Mason, Leon Russell, Neil Young, Harry Nilsson, Buddy Guy, Jerry Lee Lewis, Roy Orbison, Pops Staples, Steely Dan, Bobby Womack, Elvis Costello, Tom Petty, George Harrison, Brian Wilson, Mick Jagger, Bill Wyman, Charlie Watts, and the Rolling Stones, among others.

Alla Rakha with Jim Keltner at Madison Square Garden, New York, during the Ravi Shankar–George Harrison tour, 1974. Photo courtesy of Jim Keltner.

He's toured with Mad Dogs & Englishmen, Dylan, and Crosby, Stills, Nash & Young.

I've worked with and produced Jim Lee Keltner on recording sessions and known him for over thirty years.

When I briefly went to Los Angeles City College, he turned me on to the Barbecue Beef Tostada at Lucy's El Adobe Café on Melrose Ave. More recently, Keltner introduced me to green tea and antioxidants.

Jim Keltner is one of my favorite drummers and favorite people on the planet.

Jim and his wife Cynthia were extremely close to George Harrison, and in this painful time of grieving and reflection, it's to Jim's credit and our special friendship that he really extended himself to me as we jointly examined his life and working relationship with George Harrison in conversation.

Q: How did you first meet George Harrison?

A: It was in London, early 1971, at a Leon Russell session at Island Studios. George and Phil Spector and Klaus Voorman were all there playing acoustic guitars together.

Q: I knew George Harrison totally dug Delaney & Bonnie's first album, and he wanted them for Apple Records.

A: That's right.

Q: I've even seen some acetates or Apple label copies of Delaney & Bonnie for the UK market. But you also told me John Lennon was into that record.

A: Yes. I believe George turned John on to the record. George was also a huge fan of Ry Cooder. And that was a thing we had in common. He loved Ry and Bob Dylan. He was a great champion for all of us. After the earthquake in February of 1971 in Los Angeles, I told my wife, "Get the kids together and get on over here." We were there at a flat in Chelsea for a couple of months. During that time, George introduced me to Ringo and I played maracas on the single he produced for Ringo at Trident Studio, "It Don't Come Easy."

Q: I remember you telling me at a Spector session at Gold Star, when we were on the Ramones' album, that George and John were tight with Phil.

A: George and John both loved Phil. They loved his previous work. And they wanted a little piece of that. They wanted to see what it would be like working with him. George was really on top of it during that time. He was very clean and doing the worry beads and all that. He was probably at his physical best at that time. He was always talking music. I learned a lot from George about the American rock scene. He introduced me to my own scene. That happened because I wasn't familiar with it. I wasn't into rock-'n'-roll. I came out of jazz in the '60s. George was a very important teacher to me at that time.

Q: Run down recording the "Bangla Desh" song to me.

A: George called and said, "Let's do a single." So we went into Wally Heider's Studio 4 on Cahuenga (in Hollywood) and did "Bangla Desh" with George and Phil. Leon played and I think he helped arrange the song. The birth of the concert sort of started with this single. I loved the song. Then later we did two shows at Madison Square Garden in New York.

Q: One thing. I know we all used to sit around and listen to Ravi Shankar in the '60s. He was on the World Pacific label, same place as Lord Buckley. And I would imagine George brought you around again to Ravi in 1971, and actually introduced you to him. You also ended up touring with George and Ravi in 1974.

A: That was another thing that George brought to my life. Meeting Ravi Shankar and the great Alla Rakha and being able to hang out with them on the plane and at the gigs.

Q: I know "All Things Must Pass" blew your mind.

A: Enormously. Jimmy Gordon and Ringo played great on the record. For "Bangladesh" there was only one rehearsal. The rehearsal was in a basement of a hotel, or near the hotel. George was beside himself trying to put together a set list and trying to find out if Eric (Clapton) was going to be able to make it, whether Bob (Dylan) was gonna make it. Plus, George was nervous because he hadn't played live for a long time. He did a fantastic job. It was a benefit for a good cause and the first time I ever played Madison Square Garden.

Q: Was it pre-determined at "Bangladesh," and later evidenced on the album set, that you were to double-drum with Ringo?

A: Well, I think Ringo was asked by George, and Ringo said, "Yes, but only if Keltner will do it with me." Because Ringo was a little unsure about playing live with a big band. He hadn't played live in a while, either. So, when they asked me, I said, "Of course, but I want to stay out of his way." I didn't want to destroy anything of that great feel or his sound. When we actually sat down to play, I asked them to set me up in such a way that I could see his hi-hat hand. And after we played together at the sound check, I had to decide on a few things. And one of the first decisions I made was to not play the hi-hat much. So I played the hi-hat like I had seen Levon (Helm) of The Band do, which was to pull the hand off the hi-hat for the two and four, so that it didn't come down with the backbeat at the same time. And that helped me stay out of Ringo's way. But years later the cameraman told me, "You really caused me some problems when I was editing that film, because your hand coming up like that, I could never tell whether I was on the cut."

Q: How was George at "Bangladesh" as a bandleader? Talk about multitasking!

A: [Laughs] He was absolutely focused and fantastic as a leader. Of course he had Leon in the band. And Leon helped with the arranging and all.

Q: As you did a rehearsal and sound check for "Bangladesh," did the music and songs picked out and later performed sort of become larger in scope?

A: I remember that everything seemed to be fine at the sound check and that I didn't have too many concerns. When we started playing with the audience in the room it really did come alive.

George seemed very powerful that night. When you look at the picture of him then, he was really thin, ya know. But he was very powerful, and the songs, "My Sweet Lord," "Awaiting on You All," "Beware of Darkness," "While My Guitar Gently Weeps," "Wah-Wah," "Bangla Desh." Some great stuff. And very appropriate for the suffering going on over there. And don't forget Billy Preston with "That's the Way God Planned It." I loved being a part of that with George.

Q: I know you had to have seen every minute of Ravi Shankar's set.

A: Oh yeah! I was right in the back watching the whole thing and being amazed at just how powerful it was. I had been listening to Ravi and Alla Rakha for years and here I was seeing them up so close I could reach out and touch them. Alla Rakha and Ravi Shankar were telepathic. They played together for so many years it was awesome to watch it. Ravi was at his peak in terms of technical proficiency. Alla Rakha was as well. It was dazzling. It is something that will always be with me. They did a longer set than what was actually recorded. Between shows the hotel had an incredible hospitality room set up with incredible Indian food.

Over the decades I got to see George and Ravi a lot together. It was a father and son relationship in a way. He brought Ravi to the rest of the world in a very big way. One of my favorite things was being with George in the audience watching Ravi play. The last time was a few years ago in London. Sitting there next to George watching Anoushka (Shankar) play first, and dazzling everyone with her tremendous technique, and all these flashy things, and thrilling the audience. And then the old master, her father, makes everybody just sigh with a few well chosen notes. It was a perfect picture of exactly what you need to learn about in life. About youth, age, and wisdom, technique, soul, and all that. And George was at the wheel taking us there.

Q: Just about thirty years after the Concert for Bangladesh, you backed up Neil Young when he did "Imagine" at the TV telethon that benefited September 11th victims, beamed from the corner of Beverly and Fairfax at CBS Television Center in L.A. You've done many other large-scale concerts and special events helping others. But did you see any relationship between "Bangladesh" and the TV telethon for the NYC victims?

A: There's a thread obviously, and it's that show business goes out the window. There was no air of show biz. George always kind of brought that feeling wherever he was anyway. I've been telling people recently that I really took George for granted, because he was just Georgie, my friend,

Bob Dylan and George Harrison at the Concert for Bangladesh, Madison Square Garden, New York, August, 1971. Photo by Henry Diltz.

ya know. My beautiful, wonderful brother. And I read these things about him being kind of anti-celebrity and all that. I guess he had enough of that with the Beatles, ya know, so that the Bangladesh event seems like a warm and wonderful cause that everyone turned out for and no one was making any money.

Bob (Dylan) walked right by me on his way to the stage. I had already recorded with him a couple of months earlier so I sort of knew him. He walks out there on the stage with that little jean jacket on and puts the harp up to his mouth and starts singing and playing and chills ran up and down my arms. His voice and the command. It was awesome. And Leon decides to go up with his bass for "Just Like a Woman" and play with him. It was a tremendous moment. It was real dark on stage with a little light for them. Dylan was incredible.

Q: I wonder if George made sure John Lennon saw the Bangladesh movie of the event. I know you were recording with John at that time.

A: Yes he did, and one night at Record Plant somebody asked John, did he see the film. John said he went to the premiere and when he saw my face on the screen for the first time he stood up and yelled, "Hey—that's me drummer!" I fell on the floor.

Q: But in a sense you followed George and the evolution of "Bangladesh" as he and Phil were mixing the package at A&M studios. You were on the lot a lot then. Everyone always made fun of me since I was too young to drink at the time, but I could be trusted carrying the cans of master tapes from the shows. Later you were one of the artists on George's Dark Horse label.

A: That's right. And an interesting little aside. We were sitting in the kitchen at Friar Park (in Henley) one evening and he asked me, "What does Dark Horse mean to you?" He wanted to make sure he had it right. We talked about it a little bit and then he showed me some drawings he had of the logo. The Dark Horse with seven heads. Later on he signed the band I was with to his label.

Q: You also did a lot of recording with George over the years. Like the Traveling Wilburys. The recordings and the video. You got called to do the sessions and then the record blew up beyond expectations.

A: How could you go wrong with Roy Orbison, Bob Dylan, Tom Petty, Jeff Lynne and George Harrison in the same band? Watching them write and come up with songs around a table at Dave Stewart's home studio was fantastic, and something I'll never forget. The way they would pass the ideas around the table. It was really hilarious.

Q: You played on Harrison's "Cloud Nine" album. And his last real hit single, "Got My Mind Set on You." Isn't that a cover of a James Ray record? He did, "If You Gotta Make a Fool of Somebody." Maybe a B side of it. You physically played a drum machine on that track, right?

A: "Got My Mind Set on You" happened sitting around the studio one night. Jeff Lynne, George, and I were talking about drum machines, and George and Jeff were saying they didn't like drum machines because they couldn't swing like a real drummer. I just happened to have my SP-1200 sampler there, making samples and stuff for my own project later. But I told them, "I can make it swing." So I started this beat, and it was Gary Wright in the back of the room who said, "That sounds like, 'Got My Mind Set on You,'" and started playing the riff. He knew the James Ray song, and it went on from there. Everyone grabbed on to it. George actually started singing the lyric as much as he remembered, so I laid down the drum track in real time with my fingers on the pads. When I left they worked on it and next time I heard it was on the radio. The only song I didn't play on (on "Cloud Nine") was "When We Was Fab." Ringo was on that. And he played beautifully as usual.

Q: You and your wife Cynthia were close to George and his wife Olivia.

A: Well, Cynthia and I met George when he was with Patti Boyd. It was in 1971. Patti was a truly wonderful lady. So when they broke up I felt bad for George, because I thought, "Man, where do you go from there? How are you ever gonna come close to that again?" And then he met Olivia in 1974, and you could tell right away this was going to be it. They had such a great chemistry. At first I thought she was this beautiful Indian woman but then I found out she was a Mexican girl. And I'm half Mexican, so that endeared her to us even more. She was just exactly what George needed in his life. Her sister Linda was working for the label so we all spent a lot of time together.

Q: Linda, Olivia, and Cynthia are soulful L.A. girls. I know Cynthia, like Olivia, gave her man a lot of space to be creative and do his music.

A: Well, I believe that Cynthia and Olivia probably deserve a Purple Heart or some kind of badge of courage, or maybe a rock-'n'-roll Medal of Honor for getting through the seventies. And in Cynthia's case, the '60s and the '70s . With their families intact and still as beautiful now as they were then. Olivia had a solid upbringing as a California girl, so she brought a lot of that to George's life. And they both did a fantastic job bringing up Dhani.

Q: The thing about George not being on the physical planet. It was only a couple of years ago when we were at your home, listening to tapes, and I earlier had been at Ravi Shankar's house for an interview, and George supplied me with some quotes for that story. And he made us laugh. He said, "Well, at least at the Keltners' pad you don't have to take your shoes off." And I remember another time he brought you something that is still displayed in your living room. A piece of his studio board. Right?

A: Right. A piece of his recording console. He had such a generous heart. He loved to gift people with nice and unique things. He had his old board disassembled and instead of selling the parts, or throwing them away, he had them encased in a nice clear Plexiglas case. And he gave each of his friends who ever recorded in his studio one of them. And they were all numbered.

Q: Can we discuss his guitar playing?

A: Well, literally, every guitar player I've ever played with pays homage to George because they know what it's like to be the guy coming up with the parts. The second most important voice in the song, aside from the singer's voice, is the lead guitar, the way he frames the voice and how he plays the melody within the melody. The way he handles all those chores. That's a special gift when you're able to do that. George was probably one of the greatest that ever did that. Scotty Moore and Carl Perkins were his heroes. George was not what you'd call an improviser. He was a songwriter type of guitar player. He saw the guitar part as a piece constructed in his head and he would construct it as he went along and come up with these brilliant parts that will live forever. I mean, any Beatles record you pick up you'll see that. And, of course, any of his solo stuff as well.

Q: His sense of humor. You had some rave-ups with him over the decades.

A: Did I ever tell you the story about him pushing my Corvette?

Q: No. Tell me.

A: I was driving him home from a session at A&M one morning, back to his rented house in Holmby Hills, the old Burt Reynolds place. We ran out of gas on Sunset Boulevard right before his street. I pulled over to the curb and started to apologize to George. And he said, "Let's push it." So I got out and was guiding the steering wheel, and he went round to the back. So he's huffing and puffing, pushing this Daytona blue Corvette from behind. And the Starline tour bus drives by at that exact moment looking for celebrity houses and stuff and I yell to the bus as it drives by slowly, "Hey, there's one back there!" And I pointed to George. He looked up and waved. I always imagined somebody on the bus

George Harrison.
Photo by
Robert Matheu.

saying, "Hey, that was George Harrison pushing that car back there." And everybody going, "Yeah, sure."

Q: What are you going to miss most about George Harrison?

A: Oh man, I can't even be thinking like that right now. It's really difficult to imagine not seeing him bounding up the steps saying, "Hi Jim and Cyn." I loved his speaking voice as much as his singing. That great soft refined Liverpool accent. I think we're gonna miss that a lot. I can't stand the thought of never hearing him talk to me again.

Jack Nitzsche:

"Needles and Pins"

I last formally interviewed composer-arranger and multi-instrumentalist Jack Nitzsche in 1998 at his home in Beachwood Canyon. He died of cardiac arrest on August 25, 2000, at Queen of Angels Hospital in Los Angeles, the same location where I was born and where his son, Jack Nitzsche Jr., was also born.

Nitzsche was buried at Hollywood Forever, down the street from the now demolished Gold Star studios on Santa Monica Blvd. Neil Young provided dozens of red roses for the occasion. Conducting the service was Jimmy Bond, a jazz bassist who played with Lou Rawls and recorded with Phil Spector.

Spector gave the closing eulogy, and quoted from his composition, "To Know Him Is to Love Him." Jack Nitzsche Jr. spoke last.

Paying respects were Gracia Nitzsche, Don Randi, H.B. Barnum, Christy Bono, Jackie DeShannon, Nancy Sinatra, Carol Kaye, Earl Palmer, Lux Interior and Ivy from the Cramps, Pablo Ferro, Jon Hassell, Denny Bruce, Barry Goldberg, Gerry Goffin, John Byrum, Ron Nagle, Scott Mathews, Dan Bourgoise, Jewel Akens, photographers Julian Wasser and Robert Leslie Dean, actors Sean Penn and Don Calfa.

Bernard Alfred "Jack" Nitzsche was born April 22, 1937, in Chicago, Illinois, and lived outside Newaygo, Michigan. Around 1956 he moved to L.A. Over the past forty years, since he arrived in Los Angeles from Michigan after seeing an ad in *Downbeat* magazine for the L.A.-based Westlake School of Music, Jack Nitzsche has left an indelible mark on the music industry as an arranger, producer, and composer. You've heard his sound imprint. In the 1960s, he collaborated with Phil Spector on many

Jack Nitzsche during the recording of the Rolling Stones' "Aftermath" album, RCA Studios, Hollywood, California, December 1965. Photo by Gered Mankowitz.

records for the Ronettes, the Righteous Brothers, and Ike & Tina Turner. Jack had one of the first hit singles for Reprise Records with the instrumental, "The Lonely Surfer." He played piano behind Elvis Presley in the movie, "Girls! Girls! Girls!"

Jack Nitzsche arranged and/or produced records with Doris Day, Bobby Darin, Bob Lind, Tim Buckley, Marianne Faithfull, the Byrds, Petula Clark, Randy Newman, Thurston Harris, the Mighty Hannibal, Miles Davis, Soupy Sales, Roosevelt Grier, Judy Henske, the Everly Brothers, Duane Eddy, Harpers Bizarre, Gene McDaniels, Chet Baker, Mac Davis, Buffy Sainte-Marie, Tom Petty, Ringo Starr, the Lovin' Spoonful, Dorsey Burnette, Paul Anka, Bobby Vee, Leon Russell, Zal Yanovsky, Bobby Day, Gloria Jones, the Robins, Kathy Young, Timi Yuro, Chris Montez, Slam Stewart, P. J. Proby, Preston Epps, the Modern Folk Quartet, the Walker Brothers, Merry Clayton, Fred Neil, Art Pepper, Dr. John, Tammy Wynette, Toni Basil, the Monkees, Barbra Streisand, Leo Kottke, Chris Darrow, Jackie DeShannon, Ricky Nelson, Sonny & Cher, Michelle Phillips, the Tubes, the Neville Brothers, and Graham Parker.

It was also Nitzsche, along with Brian Jones, then of the Rolling Stones, and record producer Kim Fowley, who was instrumental in convincing Reprise Records' Mo Ostin to sign Jimi Hendrix to an American record deal.

The influential and historic music and recording personality became friends with the Rolling Stones on their first American tour in 1964, and subsequently worked on and contributed to nine of their albums. In 1970, Nitzsche created the ground-breaking score for the film "Performance," starring Mick Jagger.

Nitzsche brought Neil Young to the Reprise Records label. Earlier he'd worked on Young's cinematic "Expecting to Fly" composition during Young's Buffalo Springfield days. Nitzsche's producing, arranging and keyboard instrumental contributions on Young's debut solo LP had a major impact on that album recording. His string orchestrations and mathematical approach on Young's emotional folk tunes broke new sonic territory in the singer-songwriter form. Later, Nitzsche helped arrange some tracks on Young's "Harvest" album.

Jack Nitzsche continued producing albums with various artists well into the late '70s and early '80s, including collaborations with Willy DeVille and Graham Parker. Ben Edmonds, years ago at Capitol Records, when he was in the A&R Department, had helped arrange a "production deal" for Jack to work with new artists like DeVille.

Over the last twenty-five years, you have heard Jack Nitzsche's music more than you know. His extensive soundtrack work is as impressive as his career in rock music. His scores and compositional endeavors as producer-arranger include the feature films "Cannery Row," "Candy,"

"Jive," "Greaser's Palace," "When You Comin' Back Red Ryder," "Heroes," "Cutter's Way," "Stand by Me," "Breathless," "Without a Trace," "Mermaids," "The Crossing Guard," "The Indian Runner," "The Hot Spot," which earned a Grammy Award Nomination for Best Traditional Blues Recording, "Starman," that garnered a Golden Globe Nomination for Best Score, and "One Flew Over The Cuckoo's Nest," which received an Academy Award Nomination for Best Score. Nitzsche co-wrote "Up Where We Belong" for the movie, "An Officer and a Gentleman," which won both the Golden Globe and the Academy Award. Other films on his resumé include "Cruisin'," "The Exorcist," and the terrific atmosphere and tunes to "Blue Collar," where you get tracks from both Captain Beefheart and Howlin' Wolf. One of Nitzsche's own favorite created musical scores was to the film, "Revenge," which Tony Scott directed.

When I last interviewed Jack in 1998, he was working with rock singer-songwriter Charlie "C. C." Adcock, between his film and music schedule, and he still kept in touch with Willy DeVille.

You can hear on your radio the classic songs that he wrote, arranged, or produced: Bob Lind's "Elusive Butterfly," check out the strings, and "Needles and Pins," co-written with Sonny Bono, sung by Jackie DeShannon, covered by the Searchers and the Ramones. He also arranged "When You Walk in the Room" for DeShannon, and he was in the studio and arranging the music for Ike & Tina Turner's "River Deep, Mountain High," "Just Once in My Life," by the Righteous Brothers, and plenty of other Phil Spector productions, from "Be My Baby," sung by the Ronettes, to the Crystals' "He's a Rebel" and "Then He Kissed Me."

Nitzsche later wrote the choral arrangement for the Rolling Stones' "You Can't Always Get What You Want," from the "Let it Bleed" album that contained "Gimme Shelter." Nitzsche earlier had been a major contributor to both the "Aftermath" and "Between the Buttons" album recordings, also tracked in Hollywood at RCA studios. In the Stones' recorded catalog, Nitzsche's keyboard and percussion session work can be found on such gems as "Play with Fire," "Yesterday's Papers," and "Sister Morphine" on the "Sticky Fingers" album. He also played tambourine and piano on "Satisfaction."

Nitzsche was responsible for booking the Rolling Stones for the "T.A.M.I. Show" concert, filmed at the Santa Monica Civic Auditorium. Nitzsche also put the band together for the "T.A.M.I. Show." Check out their playing behind Chuck Berry during his set. The dude delivered a live action wall of sound that also backed the Supremes and Marvin Gaye for this amazing rock-'n'-roll event. Later, in 1965, Nitzsche took drummer Charlie Watts to a Phil Spector session at the famed Gold Star studios in

Hollywood. And in the early '70s in the U.K., Watts attended a recording session where Nitzsche conducted the London Symphony Orchestra for his own solo album.

His primary concern in the last thirty years of his life had been movie music. He hated what the music and record business had become, and he coveted his outsider artist-composer status, not dependent on record companies and corporations making creative decisions about his career. By 1970, Nitzsche had joined Spector in his growing disillusionment with the pop music grind. In 1974 he told *Crawdaddy!* magazine, "I'll work in a gas station before I go their route."

I first met Nitzsche as a teenager in the late '60s in connection with a Buffalo Springfield concert, and for decades went to recording sessions he produced or arranged around Hollywood.

During the '90s, we'd had some wonderful meals and conversations, and he'd been one of the few artists and people that had always encouraged my literary recording and producing collaborations. Imagine a world where he ran all the A&R departments . . .

In 1998, I rang Jack Nitzsche up at his Beachwood Canyon home. "Let's have a chat," I suggested. "Come by tomorrow," he answered. I think I secured our final interview when I reminded him I'm a Pisces. "Both my ex-wives and my son are Pisces," he smiled. Nitzsche was a Taurus, on the cusp of Aries.

Steering through SoCal, *en route* to Nitzsche's home, I played a cassette of Nitzsche-arranged-and-produced vocal and instrumental songs from various artists of the late '50s and early '60s, including Jack's legendary solo tune, "The Lonely Surfer," which appeared in the '90s Rhino Records surf music box set, "Cowabunga!" The tape made a lot of sense, blaring from my car speakers as I cruised past Gower and Franklin.

The last time I saw Jack, in 1998, he wasn't wearing his ever-present horn-rimmed glasses when he answered the door to his Beachwood Canyon home. That was new. Phil Spector gave Nitzsche the nickname "Specs" because of his glasses—which he never liked. The rest of him, though, exuded the same upscale-beatnik look as ever. He was decked out in black leather pants, Spanish boots, and a white oxford shirt with a puffy collar. His hair was long and straight and black. All of this, despite the looming of his sixty-first birthday at the end of that month.

Nitzsche's house looked like a residence inhabited by a beatnik movie music composer and record producer. Lots of CD and record racks, equipment, and a beautiful black grand piano in the living room. Scorebooks were spread out like a sushi dinner. Directly across from his Oscar hung the Gold Album for his work on "Phil Spector: Back to Mono (1958–1969)," for sales that exceeded 500,000 copies.

Doctor John, Tom Waits, Mortal Coil, Al Green, the Temptations, and Decca Country Classics were among the first batch of CDs to catch my attention. His bookshelves were lined with titles like *Marlon Brando, Women of the Beat Generation*, and a recent Dean Koontz title. "Braveheart" and "L.A. Confidential" were the two videos next to his VCR. A couple of paintings of Elvis Presley adorned the wall in the living room. A copy of Christopher Sanford's biography of Mick Jagger, *Primitive Cool*, sat on a table. On the floor next to a pile of 45s lay an illustrated drawing book of music personalities with Keith Richards on the cover, right next to the latest David Halberstam. Rock and read.

Jack Nitzsche's sound and music journey reflected L.A., because he was L.A.

I had a lot of good times with Jack Nitzsche, particularly when his partner, record producer, and music manager, Denny Bruce, was with him. They were like L.A. Dodgers baseball pitchers, Sandy Koufax and Don Drysdale together. We watched a lot of boxing matches and football games on the tube, ate dinners on their heavy plastic, went to concerts. There was a constant flow of education on rock and R&B music, plus life lessons from the both of them that I still apply to daily survival. Denny was a close friend of Jack for over a third of a century. He was the one who introduced Nitzsche to Neil Young during Neil's Buffalo Springfield days. And when Jack and Denny discussed records, and girls, you listened.

Somehow, the lentil soup and side of spinach at the Indian restaurant Paru doesn't taste the same since Jack died.

Years ago, it seemed that Nitzsche, L.A. DJ Rodney Bingenheimer and I were the only guys who lived in Hollywood who still drove Cadillacs. My ride then was a 1959 with big fins. Things have really changed.

As Jack enters his front room carrying a couple of Hansen juices—*man*, have things changed, upstairs a cable television channel is airing a home improvement show, "Gimme Shelter." Think about that.

The first interview I formally conducted with Jack was mainly about his career with Phil Spector, and was partially utilized in a *Goldmine* cover story, below, in 1988.

Q: How did you meet Phil Spector?
A: I had heard about Phil for a long time. In 1962 I used to hang out at Lester Sill's office on Sunset Blvd., when Lester and Lee Hazlewood were partners. One day, Lester came downstairs and said Phil Spector was in town and needed an arranger. He played me the demo of "He's a Rebel." We went to a rehearsal with the Blossoms. I introduced Phil to the Blossoms. I had been working with them for years.

I didn't have to do a lead-sheet for "He's a Rebel," just the arrangement. I put the band together for the session, a lot of the same guys I had been working with for years. Phil didn't know a lot of these people; he had been in New York in 1960–1962. Leon Russell, Harold Battiste, Earl Palmer, Don Randi, Hal Blaine, Glen Campbell. A lot of the players came out of my phone book. Phil knew Barney Kessel. At one time he had taken guitar lessons from Barney, years before.

Q: Why was Phil different from most of the music people and record producers you worked for in the late 1950s and well into the 1960s?

A: Phil was different from the A&R men and the record company people I had been working with. In those days, A&R men would hire me to do an arrangement or arrange for a three-hour session, and no matter what, we had to get it done before the three hours were over. Phil Spector was the first one to go into the studio with one song, and if it needed two sessions to do the rhythm section, that's the way it happened.

Phil understood the teenage record market. He could relate to their feelings and buying impulses. He was a kid. He would call me up at four A.M. and want to go out for ice cream. Phil's great.

Phil cared about people, outlaws, like Lenny Bruce. I met the songwriters. I heard the tunes in advance that we were gonna cut. Sometimes Phil played them for me at the piano, or I would hear the demos. There were a lot of visits to his house, and he would come over to my house to work on songs. In the beginning he stayed in hotels and came to my house. We became friends real fast. We had a lot of laughs together. I always liked the tunes he played. Everything he played always sounded like a hit.

Q: How was the "Wall of Sound" developed?

A: It happened over a period of time. I don't know who coined the term. The sound just got bigger and bigger. One time we cut the Crystals' "Little Girl." Sonny Bono was the percussionist on the date. He came into the booth, and said it had more echo than usual, and it wouldn't get played on the radio. The echo was turned way up high. Phil said, "What's too much echo? What does that mean?" Phil was smart enough to say, "Wait a minute! Listen to this." If you notice, there's more echo on each song we cut. It hadn't been done like this before. People on the business side, the promotional side of the record industry, felt it was different. He didn't listen to them.

The musicians all played at once. Before that, I was working with compact rhythm sections and three or four players. This was groundbreaking for me.

I had met Don Randi, one of the piano players, a long time ago. He was a pianist at a jazz club on La Cienega. He was cool. He looked like a beatnik. His hair was right. He had the attitude. He didn't smile when he played.

Q: Tell me about the rest of the Spector team.

A: Hal Blaine [drummer]. I liked his work, but sometimes felt he overplayed. That's just the way he plays. A lot of fills. As it turned out, Phil and the people loved the breaks Hal took, especially at the end of the tunes, the fades. Hal had a big kit. I liked the fills.

Earl Palmer was the other drummer on the records. He's the best. Like a rock. A real good New Orleans drummer. Harold Battiste, Mac Rebennack, these New Orleans guys were on the dates, so you had a good mixture of jazz guys, West Coast studio cats, and New Orleans players.

Leon Russell. I met him with Jackie DeShannon; she introduced me. Leon, at the time, was playing piano in a bar in Covina. He was an innovative piano player. He was good. I heard him on a Jackie DeShannon record. In those days it was real hard to find rock-'n'-roll piano players who didn't play too much. Leon talked the same language. You could really hear Leon play in the "Shindig" TV band. I put him in the "T.A.M.I. Show" band, and he's all over the soundtrack.

During the Spector sessions, a lot of the time we had two or three piano players going at once. I played piano as well. Phil knew the way he wanted the keyboards played. It wasn't much of a problem who played. Leon was there for the solos and the fancy stuff, rolling pianos. Al DeLory, Nino Tempo. The pianos would interlock and things would sound cohesive. I knew Leon would emerge as a band-leader.

I knew all the horn players. Steve Douglas on tenor, Jay Migliori on baritone, other horn players as well. I had met Steve through Lester Sill. We were friends for a long time. Phil had an idea about horns. It started on "He's a Rebel." Remember the horns on "Duke of Earl"? Phil wanted something like that. The horns always had to figure out this thing. The thing that came out of it was the voicing. The trumpet was voiced real low, and the voicing of those horns made a big thing happen. The horn section would play quiet behind the rhythm section. Phil sure knew what he wanted. He had all the bases covered.

Percussion. Well, Sonny Bono. I love Sonny. He helped me get into the business. Julius Wechter, later of the Baja Marimba Band, was on a lot of the dates. Frank Capp was on a lot of sessions. He was a jazz drummer who used to play with Stan Kenton. Phil would dream these percussion parts up at the session. They were his ideas. There were no formulas. I played percussion, chimes, orchestra bells. They weren't mixed way in the back.

Guitarists. A lot of the guitarists were jazz players and weren't rock-'n'-roll players, like Howard Roberts, Joe Pass, Herb Ellis, Tommy Tedesco, Barney Kessel, Dennis Budimir. A lot of the guitarists were good and well-known session players: Carol Kaye, Glen Campbell, Bill Pitman. Most of the guitarists had to play eighth notes on Phil's records. There was a lot of acoustic guitar on the songs. Phil used to walk around to the players just before he rolled tape and would whisper in their ears. "Dumb. Don't do anything. Just play eighth notes." It was hard for any of the guitarists to breathe or stretch out on the records.

I was amazed how big Glen Campbell made it as a total entertainer. I knew he was a great guitarist. I never knew he would show up as a singer later. Billy Strange was good, too. I became aware of the twelve-string guitar during the last Phil years. It was a new sound, and a new toy to play with.

Bass players. Jimmy Bond and Red Callender were on most of the dates. Ray Pohlman and Ray Brown as well. The bass parts were written out and the players had to stick right with them. They were mixed way low in the back, almost a suggestive element to the song. No one really had a lot of room with those sessions. Really, only the drummer had any sort of freedom. They weren't R&B records.

Vocalists. It would last all night. Background groups doubling and tripling, so it would sound like two or three dozen voices. Phil would spend a lot of time with the singers. I would split and he'd still be working on lines with the singers. The rhythm section and the horns were done together. Vocals and string parts were overdubbed later.

We did most of the sessions at Gold Star studios in Hollywood. I loved the rooms, but it was always too small for all the people.

Q: Phil was on his game all the time.

A: I didn't realize it at the time. Phil was doing business, even when he was producing a session. What was really unique was that Phil owned most or all of the record. That was different. I think Phil knew what was going on in the record business. He made use of distributors and publishers. He understood the music and the heritage, as well as the people before him who were great producers. Phil was tenacious. He sure learned a lot in New York. Leiber and Stoller must have been good for him. Phil carried the torch for rock-'n'-roll. His attitude upset the industry. Phil plugged into the youth. He knew a lot. He had social feelings.

I never thought about the money. I was happy to be working with him. I loved the music. Phil took me around. He showed me the industry. One time in New York he took me up to the *Cash Box* office, and Phil said, "They're talking about us like a team. That's good." That was really fun, 'cause he was the record producer. Phil was doing business. He'd visit trade magazines and play them the record before it was even pressed, trying to get his groups work.

Q: Tell me about some of the classic records he produced that you worked on.
A: "Be My Baby." Ronnie Spector's voice. Wow! I was amazed at her vibrato. It got bigger and bigger with each record. That was her strong point. When that tune was finished, the speakers were turned so high in the booth, people had to leave the room. It was loud.

The Righteous Brothers. I wrote a song for them during their Moonglow Records period. Sonny Bono also wrote "Ko Ko Joe" under the name Don Christy as well. I did a session with them. I didn't arrange "You've Lost That Lovin' Feelin'," 'cause I was working as musical director for the "T.A.M.I. Show." Gene Page did it. The Righteous Brothers could sing. Bill Medley had energy. They were the first white guys around L.A. that sounded black. They tried hard, and with Phil, had great, powerful songs to work with.

I arranged the Christmas album. We had a lot of fun. Darlene Love singing "Christmas (Baby Please Come Home)" blew my mind. I got chills. Powerful. She could always sing. Sonny always made everyone laugh. The album never really took off. I think some of that had to do with the world after the Kennedy assassination. It affected the public. No one wanted to celebrate Christmas in December 1963.

Q: And then there was "River Deep, Mountain High," done with Tina Turner.
A: Phil was the co-writer on the song. Phil embellished the song and was the producer. I've talked to Gerry Goffin about that a lot: Phil co-writing songs that he would produce. Phil would always have the writers come over and write in the room with him, and I knew he directed it. They all say the same thing: without Phil Spector in the room that song wouldn't have been that way. He helped. He knew what he wanted it to be. I know Phil Spector helped write "River Deep, Mountain High." When Phil played it to me on the piano, I knew it was a great song. We did the rhythm track in two different three-hour sessions. It was amazing to watch the session.

Later, when I did film scores and started to bring in exotic instruments, I wanted to make the sound different and wanted room to experiment.

Jack Nitzsche was also a storyteller. And he was a "Bad Boy." He must have led the league in rehab stints; he even had one hassle that ended up being filmed for an episode of the TV program, "Cops."

In 1998, an editor at *New Times,* Keven McAlester, asked me to write a feature profile on Nitzsche that concentrated on his life as a film composer. For *New Times,* I obtained some statements from a couple of younger musicians and composers influenced by Nitzsche's melodies and methods. Jack's scores were evocative and atypical, the work of an innovative, talented maverick—in many instances garnering far better reviews than the films themselves. And, together with his orchestral work on rock records, his scores and arrangements have quietly become something of a paradigm among the next generation.

"I'm always delighted when I see his name in the credits of a film," says Darian Sahanaja, songwriter-keyboardist and vocalist for L.A.'s Wondermints, who has also toured and arranged for Brian Wilson the last couple of years. "Nitzsche had an ability to take tunes somewhere else for the good of the song. One of my favorite soundtracks he did was 'Village of the Giants,' his first score from 1965, maybe the first heavily-orchestrated teen soundtrack. Like Brian Wilson, he could utilize instruments and voicings that would complement each other, especially in the way he paired strings and percussion."

"In high school, one of my favorite directors was, and still is, Nicolas Roeg," says Jim O'Rourke, the art-rock avatar, guitarist, and producer of everyone from John Fahey to Faust to the Jesus Lizard. "There is a sequence in "Performance" where Nitzsche's lush, melodic music is playing through a Muzak machine in the office of Harry Flowers, and as the scene turns to a sweaty, clammy uncomfortableness, the music begins to pass through some heavy filtering. It took me to a place I'd never been before . . . I can pinpoint my love of resonant filters to this very scene.

"Nitzsche's soundtrack for 'One Flew Over The Cuckoo's Nest' is a perfect example of the sound that was such an influence on me, first in working as an arranger for others, then on my own albums. My record, 'Bad Timing,' was heavily indebted to Nitzsche, the transparency of his arrangements, how they are based more in interweaving melodic lines and variation, instead of voice-leading/counterpoint. Although there is plenty of counterpoint in his writing, it's the transparency of his orchestrations that allows these lines to function as more than just harmonic movement. His 'sound' was such a clearer vision of the whole mid to late '60s L.A. aesthetic. He's an insanely under-acknowledged genius."

Nitzsche used an electric saw instrument on "One Flew Over The Cuckoo's Nest." Kids today are still trying to sample it. I also really like the saxophone parts in the soundtrack to "Heart Beat."

Rent some of the movies Jack Nitzsche scored and hear his sounds around the celluloid.

This raw, unedited Q and A transcript is culled from our last 1998 interview. In our first interview we discussed his work with Phil Spector. In the most recent interaction, I had a specific agenda to discuss: "Performance," Sonny Bono, Neil Young, Little Richard, his "Hot Spot" work with Miles Davis, Howlin' Wolf, the composer as an artist, and Nitzsche's movie soundtrack scores and collaborations.

Q: Let's talk about the film, "Performance." Your soundtrack is still popular and was ground-breaking in terms of music mergers. Blues, rap, and electronic score, all in one package. And Mick Jagger in a film role.

A: The Rolling Stones had nothing to do with it. It was Mick who came to me about doing the soundtrack. In fact, Keith and Mick weren't even talking to each other during those days. Christian Marquand, who directed the film "Candy" came to them to make a movie. (Director) Donald Cammell was close to the Stones. He knew who I was from the beginning, and they didn't have time to score the film. Nor did they want to. So, I went to London for some reason, and saw the film during that time. They were doing "Let It Bleed." The movie blew my mind the first time I saw it. Jesus Christ . . . I saw it without music. It's very tame without music. It doesn't take you to that crazy place. This is the only movie I have ever done where nobody interfered. Nobody. Donald Cammell would drop by the studio once in a while. He let me do whatever I wanted. I did the soundtrack at Western, here in Hollywood. When I was in London, the apartment they got me was right around the corner from where Keith was living with Anita (Pallenberg).

I thought "Memo from Turner" had a clever lyric. I felt Mick was going in another direction from the band. With the film music I was allowed to do musically whatever I wanted to do. No instructions from the director. Nobody telling me yes or no. Anything I wanted to do I could do. So that's what I did. You know, made up things in the studio. It was amazing. I like both the vinyl and the CD. I have a thing for vinyl, but I like what CD does too. Anita on the screen. God-damn. You saw the film. I would want to see the film again. I want to see what's holding that film up. To this day, I'll be in a restaurant, or walking down a street, or leaving a screening on a lot somewhere like at Paramount, and someone will yell out, "Performance!" Recently, (director) Billy Friedkin saw me walking, and across the street yelled, "Performance!—The greatest use of music in a motion picture ever!" That was nice. I co-wrote "Gone Dead Train," which Randy Newman did on the soundtrack. Didn't you tell me Madonna's new producer covered one of the songs?

Q: Yeah. William Orbit did a version of "The Harry Flowers Theme" a while back. Dramarama did "Memo from Turner." Patti Palladin did it. Apparently the trip hop trio Morcheeba did it too. Do you have fond memories of the "Let It Bleed" sessions?

A: There's some pleasant moments, but not many because of what they were doing to Brian (Jones). I met the Stones in 1964. Andrew Loog Oldham called me up. He and the group had met Phil Spector and wanted to meet me. Brian Jones was in a three-piece suit and tie. It was at RCA Studios and I was working with Edna Wright, Darlene Love's sister. A little later, the Stones started working at RCA and it had a big impact on me. A whole new way of approaching records. I was used to a three-hour record date, and they were block-booking twenty-four hours a day for two weeks, and doing what they wanted. I liked going to the Hollywood Ranch Market with Keith when he was in town.

I got them into the "T.A.M.I. Show." I put the band together and did all the arrangements. I was the musical director. I had told the producer, Bill Sargent, the Stones were going to be big. I felt the Stones could close the show (following the Beach Boys and James Brown). Bill said, "James Brown is going to close the show." We all stood at the side of the stage watching James Brown do his act. People were standing and screaming for James. (Legend has it that James told the Stones, "You'll never be able to follow this.") Then the Stones came out and all the girls started crying. It was a whole new emotion!

Q: In 1965, you arranged a gorgeous song, "Love Her," for the Walker Brothers, just before the local group moved to England and ruled the U.K. for a year.

A: I did the session with the Walker Brothers at RCA Studios. Nik Venet produced it. I knew them when they were on the "Hollywood A Go-Go" TV show. "Love Her" was a Barry Mann song. People who hired me then wanted their sound to be like Phil's. Of course, no one could sound exactly like a Phil Spector record.

Q: I just saw Sean Penn's "Indian Runner" film. You did the music.

A: I always have a good time with him. I also did "The Crossing Guard," which he directed. I don't know how he came about choosing me for his first film. I'm a big fan of his work. He called and had me come in and watch the movie. I loved it. He said, "Let's go." He lets me go, too. "Do what you want." But he has a little more input than Donald Cammell did. Donald just trusted me and let me go. He gave me his movie. "Here, put music to it." For every movie that's ever made, that's what should happen.

With Sean, I enjoy his company. He's smart and funny. He's incredibly shy. He was great to work with. I gave him a lot of shit. [Laughs]

I made things difficult for him, I'm sure. With "Crossing Guard," I did the first movie and he was pleased, and asked me to do a second one.

Q: I dig the soundtrack to "One Flew Over The Cuckoo's Nest." Total freedom?

A: Pretty much. Yes. Milos Forman. These are the people. That's when the scores turn out best. But nobody ever knows that. British directors that are fairly hip like Tony Scott, Ridley Scott, Adrian Lyne. Adrian and Tony, I've worked with them and when they come to me to do their score they've got the [temp] track full of "Performance" and "Cuckoo's Nest." The "British invaders," and a lot of other people, who are all good, they are real good at what they do, but when it comes to music there's something all in common. They all steer me towards "Performance." Free reign and musical experiments of anything I want to try. Sometimes it scares people when they hear music like "Performance." And the use of songs in "Performance," I wasn't thinking of publishing. I wanted to get the best score that anyone has ever heard. And I felt like I got it. [Smiles] The Last Poets . . .

Q: I liked the music and participants for the film, "Cruisin'." Some aggressive disco, punk rock, synthesizers. Willy DeVille.

A: An underrated film score. Directed by Billy Friedkin. I think they wanted a score that was action and adventure. Scary suspense and all that shit. And I said, "Fuck that. Let's put some songs in here." So, when it came to the songs, Columbia came up with a roster of "Here's who we have for you." And I said to Billy Friedkin, "You don't have anything for me. I've already got my people picked out." Oh boy. Big meeting on that one . . . The producer and Friedkin wanted a score they thought would sell but would be right for the movie. I love Bill Friedkin. I have a lot of scores that have never been put out.

"Revenge" is my favorite score now that I've ever done. I wrote a real melodic, dramatic love score, which I always wanted to do. I think I wrote some of the most beautiful melodies I've ever heard. "Revenge" (with Kevin Costner) was not a big picture. This happens to me all the time. [Grins] Was "Cutter's Way" a good movie? I think so. I think it was great and the score was another one of those like you've never heard anything like that. The joke lately amongst some people in this town, they say, is, "If you don't get back to work soon, these composers out here are not gonna have anything to write." [Laughs] I hear "Performance" in some films . . . At the time I did "Performance," there were no synthesizers on the market. I was disappointed in the Moog. I thought it was limited. It had to be used in a different way. It couldn't be used as a musical instrument because there wasn't that kind of control yet. It was a proto-type. I knew Paul Beaver. I put all kinds of weird shit in that score. Even though I still had to play with one finger.

Q: I just interviewed the director Jim Jarmusch on his Neil Young movie, "Year of the Horse," about Neil Young and Crazy Horse on tour. It covers their twenty-five-year relationship, and your tenure with Neil and the band as a player, arranger, and producer is covered in photos and collage.

A: "Expecting to Fly" with Neil was the beginning of art rock for me . . . You know, when I was part of the band, it wasn't Crazy Horse. I sort of took over and became the producer and made them sound much better than they actually were. "Gone Dead Train" was done, but I prefer the version done on "Performance" by Randy Newman. Someday, somebody will stop and listen to the lyrics to that song. I wrote 'em at my house on Yucca Trail.

Q: Sonny Bono co-wrote "Needles and Pins" with you. I know he was one of the first people in the music business that was helpful to you.

A: The first guy I worked with on records was Sonny Bono, when he was in A&R at Specialty on Sunset Blvd. He'd let me hang out. I'd play him my first songs and he'd say things like, "You're almost there. Not quite." I did lead-sheets for him at $3.00 each. On onion-skin paper. Don & Dewey. Sonny was receptive to talent. Sonny put me in the record business. He listened to my songs all the way through while I was there. "You got something. You gotta continue writing. You're right on the borderline to write hit records." There were characters at Specialty. Great ones. Larry Williams. I did voices for Johnnie Morisette. The office was right next to the Sea Witch. I saw Little Richard there. It blew my mind. I was with Lee Hazlewood. Can't I save some of this stuff for a book I'm doing?

Q: Keep going.

A: It's fun to talk about this stuff with you because you really know L.A. It was at Lee Hazlewood's office. He was starting a record company after he left Lester Sill. Back to Sonny for a bit. On "Needles and Pins," we used a twelve-string guitar when we put it together as a demo. I've got the tape. And Sonny said, "Thanks, you showed me a whole new way of writing." It was in 1963. He was on the Phil sessions. Recently, before he died, we talked through his daughter Christy—from his first marriage to Donna—about possibly doing some work together. A lot of music people had offices in this building. 6515 Sunset Blvd. I don't know why. It was an ugly piece of shit. It probably was cheap. I don't know.

But anyway, Lee Hazlewood came up with this black singer who was

Jack Nitzsche
(bottom right)
with Neil Young
and Crazy Horse.
Photo by
Henry Diltz.

manic, but he could sing his ass off. He was really good. Anyway, he called himself Little Joe. So Little Richard came up to get Little Joe, who was supposed to be in our office, but he was gone. So, there was Richard up in the office with me. I had my mouth open. I couldn't believe it! There was Little Richard. And he made it easy to talk to him. He was a butterfly all around me. So, it was great. It was during that period where he was supposed to be in retirement, or in religion. I said, "I know that means a lot to you. I won't put that down. But, boy, I sure miss your music. I really wish I could buy a new Little Richard record." And he said, "You want to hear one now?" "Yeah. Of course." He went in another room, the rehearsal room, with me, and there was an upright piano, and a piano bench. And he sat down at the piano bench, playing a couple of fast things. And then he said, "You come down and sit right next to me."

I sat down next to Little Richard on the piano bench and he did literally every God-damn hit he ever made. Oh . . . Jesus Christ . . . And then, after he had finished all that, he said, "Oh my goodness . . . I forgot, I've got lessons. My driveway must be filled . . ." I said, "Lessons? What kind of lessons do you give?" And he said, "Oh. I give lessons in soul. You should come to where I'm teaching. Do you like beautiful blondes?" I replied, "I guess so." And then he said, "There's one I want you to meet that's at my house right now, and I think you two . . ." You know, he liked to watch. It's in his book. But I didn't do it . . .

Q: You turned me on to Charles Ives years ago, and Denny Bruce earlier introduced me to the composer, Jon Hassell, with that album on Jem, and I know you really dig his work.

A: Jon Hassell is the most innovative, important composer alive. He's American. He has lots of records out. He has invented a new kind of music. I mean, way beyond Philip Glass. Jon Hassell. He's so . . . It's on the level of "Performance," but beyond that.

Q: Is it one of those things, a sound, or one of his recordings, that makes you look at the world differently or question yourself?

A: Let's see. After marrying Buffy [Sainte-Marie years ago], I took Hassell's tape along on our honeymoon. And I wasn't trying to do any numbers, or anything. Wherever we'd end up, somewhere in Mexico, Cabo, or wherever—we drove all over Mexico, I'd put that tape on when we'd get in our room. And I didn't make any comments about it 'cause I had been listening to it over and over and over. And about the third day into the honeymoon, she said, "What is that record you keep playing?" And I said to her, "Jon Hassell." And then she really started listening. She heard. She got it. He's mixed third-world-type music, a certain kind of drum, and drum sound, several . . . I gave my top ten list of albums to *MIX*, which you saw, and I mentioned him as number one and two. He saw it and we went to dinner at Paru. Start with the first record, "Possible Musics."

Q: I remember when they took your score off the movie, "Candy."

A: That's right.

Q: Did it bother you then?

A: You bet!

Q: What is it like when a score is dumped? Does it help at all that you've at least been paid for work not used?

A: No. You want to know why. What is it about the score that bothers you that much? On "Candy," they told me, "This turns into a horror film. People will be walking out in droves, frightened." And I said, "So, that sounds good to me."

Q: Are there any survival tips you can give about the music business?
A: No.

Q: I have a poet/writer/guitarist pal in Detroit, Mick Vranich, who digs your "Blue Collar" soundtrack as well as the "Hot Spot" soundtrack you did. Both seem so many miles away from most of the soundtracks released in the '90s. I mean, on "Blue Collar," you could hear Captain Beefheart and Howlin' Wolf.
A: The music fit like a glove. There was nothing to bitch about.

Q: What impressed you the most about Captain Beefheart?
A: The thing that always has about Beefheart: That voice. Howlin' Wolf, man.

Q: Did you ever meet Howlin' Wolf?
A: I spent a day with him on the set of "Shindig." I went down there with the Stones, and Sonny & Cher were there, too. So Sonny introduced me to Howlin' Wolf, and I was speechless. He was imposing. There was a sweetness in there you could see. And anyway, we were sitting there for a long time and he was sitting next to me, and he had a friend with him, who was a little older, and strange. He wore a cowboy hat, boots, and a bolo tie. Western attire. We sat together and I was content just to sit and not even speak. Just to be in the man's presence, ya know. So, after a while, we got to talking and he became more comfortable. So did I. He said, "I didn't introduce you to my friend. Jack, this is Son House . . ." I'm sitting with Wolf and Son House.

I saw the Stones sitting around Howlin' Wolf when he performed. You should have seen the take they stopped . . . They made him stop in the midst of a take. 'Cause he was, like, 300 pounds. Huge, and he had a toy harmonica, a tiny harmonica that he would put in his mouth. He could hold it between his lips. Oh man . . . So he got up there on stage to do his set, and he put that little harmonica in his mouth. That was the surprise. The band was playing, and it came time for the instrumental, and he was kinda dancin' around, when he came up again for air, he was playing harmonica and holding the microphone. It was theatrical, and funny stuff for the fish fry. I had to use a Wolf track on "Blue Collar."

Q: I remember when you did "The Hot Spot," that Dennis Hopper directed. Break down Miles Davis in the studio.

A: We did it at Ocean Way. I said to Dennis, "Let's go with the blues. John Lee Hooker, Taj Mahal." Dennis said, "And Miles Davis." And I said, "You motherfucker. It had to be you that said it. I was going to say it. I wanted to be the one to come up with that." And he said, "Don't worry, you did." [Laughs] So I made the calls. I got Miles. I read that book, *Miles: The Autobiography*, with Quincy Troupe, whom you recorded. I'd never met Miles before. But I was on tour with him years ago, with Neil Young and Crazy Horse. They opened for us. I thought it was an insult to Miles. Fillmore East. Anyway, the deal got made for the soundtrack, and Dennis said, "By the way, you have to call Miles tonight and talk to him about this score." I was afraid. And I'd heard he didn't like white people. But God-damn, he knew who I was. I couldn't get over it. Because I was one of Gil Evans' favorite arrangers and Gil had said to Miles many times he should listen to me. So it was like, "How ya doin', man? What's goin' on?"

So I told him the movie was sort of an experiment. "I'm supposed to talk to you about what I want from you and I feel strange doing that. I feel like giving it to you and letting you play where you want." I thought, "Oh, is he gonna get me." And he said, "Why you scared of this?" And I said, "It's definitely an experiment to put you with John Lee Hooker, who knows maybe two chords." I (planned to have) them in the room together, with Taj and

Composer Jack Nitzsche in session. Photo by Peter Berman, courtesy of Jack Nitzsche Jr.

(drummer) Earl Palmer. Then Miles said on the phone, "Well, wait a minute. Let's see. Is it gonna be blues? You're doin' it, right? You're doin' the score." I said, "Yeah, it's written already. It called for solos." He said, "You're doin' the film and I'm playin' on it, right?" "Right." And he said, "You're writing and I'm playing . . . How can that be bad? How can that be experimental? We've already been through that." I couldn't catch my breath. Miles Davis was talking to me with that kind of respect.

Later, I was in the studio when he walked in the door. He was wearing a pair of sandals, no socks, nice leather sandals. The pants tied at the ankle. He wore a shirt, blouse out. And that body. He would look good in anything. He had the most beautiful skin you'll ever see. He had an aura around him. I can't remember, but I think he embraced me. The session was fine. Can't I save this for my own book?

Q: We're almost done.

A: I gotta tell you that I had written one piece of music that was not for this movie, really . . . Just a piece I had written, like a composer will write at home, or somethin'. It wasn't anything special. But I pulled it out. It was so experimental that I couldn't find chord symbols to go over some of the bars. The notes were so . . . It was really well written . . . That's all I can tell you. And Miles started playing that and said he loved ballads. And this was one. And I said, "I'll wait." And the moment came where there weren't chords to play and all of a sudden he was lost. He didn't know what to play, and he didn't know where to play. I really got him. [Laughs] He said, "Wait a minute. What chord do we play here?" And I said, "Miles, I'm sorry, I can't come up with a chord for this. I mean, a chord even if it changes on the down beat or upbeat, I don't care. Tell me what chord to put where. You can put it in. I can't find a chord itself that will work. You gotta hear the melody and just go with it." And he got off the stool in the dark, with his dark glasses and came over and said, "Let me see that score." Uh-oh. So I handed him the score. So he had the score in front of him and he stood at the piano, looked at the score, and he very slowly played the piano and everybody was quiet as can be while he was playing and getting the feel of everybody else.

And finally he just dropped his hands and put his head down and lifted it up and said, "Man, that is good shit." It's one of my best stories. That's one of the highlights of my life. Really. It hurt when he died. I was looking for the day . . . I think it was Earl Palmer at the session who said, "I've never seen Miles get along with a white guy so well. I know what's next." "What?" "I would imagine within the next year you're gonna see 'Miles Davis produced by Jack Nitzsche.'" "Do you really think he'll ask me?" "That's the way it looks to me." But he didn't live long enough.

Chrissie Hynde:

"Message of Love"

When I interviewed her, Chrissie Hynde and the Pretenders had just finished a fall 2000 U.S. tour, opening for Neil Young.

"Viva El Amor," the most recent Pretenders album, released during 1999, was the band's first studio offering in five years. The dozen new tracks—ten were written by Chrissie Hynde, some with co-writers Billy Steinberg and Tom Kelly—feature production work by Stephen Street (Blue, Cranberries), Stephen Hague (New Order, Pet Shop Boys), and Tin Tin Out (The Corrs). A single from "Viva El Amor," "Popstar," is backed with a studio version of "The Needle and the Damage Done."

The cover artwork photo portrait of Hynde on the album was taken by her friend Linda McCartney. In 1999, Hynde and Paul McCartney performed at the famed Paramount Studios in Hollywood at a fundraiser for PETA (People for the Ethical Treatment of Animals). In 2000, Hynde also attended the twentieth anniversary party for PETA while on tour, and has been very active in the organization.

For over twenty years, Chrissie Hynde has been the voice, face, and foundation of the Pretenders, whose catalog of popularly acclaimed releases has sold over ten million albums worldwide. Drummer Martin Chambers rejoined six years ago, guitarist Adam Seymour and bassist Andy Hobson have been in the band since 1994. Guitarist Jeff Beck guests on the song "Legalise Me," and the Steinberg/Kelly/Hynde songwriting team delivers some strong musical statements. The trio builds on their previous collaborations like "Night in My Veins" and "I'll Stand by You," from the stirring "Last of the

Chrissie Hynde of the Pretenders at the House of Blues, Hollywood, California, June 12, 1994. Photo by Heather Harris.

Independents" collection that was released before a live effort, "The Isle of View," done in 1995. One of the current "Viva El Amor" selections, "Human," was the theme to TV's "Cupid" series.

A very perceptive writer and a real talker, Hynde has also been busy the last couple of years doing some benefit work, and recording and appearing on some choice special events and programs.

She is heard in a duet with Emmylou Harris on the song "She," about Janis Joplin, on the Gram Parsons "Return of the Grievous Angel" album, and in 1998 was part of the New York televised salute to Burt Bacharach, where she sang two of his songs written with Hal David, "Baby, It's You" and "A Message to Michael." Chrissie Hynde also performed on the TBS cable TV show, "One Love," a reggae concert tribute to Bob Marley and did a version of "Waiting in Vain." In addition, Hynde appeared with Sheryl Crow at her recent Central Park concert in New York, during which she and Sheryl backed Keith Richards on a live version of "Happy" from the Rolling Stones' "Exile on Main Street."

A print interview Chrissie Hynde had conducted with Tim Buckley when she was a rock critic for *New Musical Express* in 1974 is cited in the 2002 book, *Urban Spacemen and Wayfaring Strangers,* by Richie Unterberger. A little while ago she wrote an appreciation on Buckley for *MOJO* magazine in the U.K., in a larger Buckley feature story. And in 2001 she contributed a liner reflection to a Janis Joplin package that Legacy/Sony Music released. You can even find her singing some backup vocals, circa 1977, on the just-out CD, "Black Tracks of Mick Farren's The Deviants 1967–96."

I first heard the Pretenders on an advance white label acetate pressing that my good pal and KROQ-FM DJ, Rodney Bingenheimer, played for me around 1978. I then saw the Pretenders' debut U.S. tour in 1980 at the Santa Monica Civic Auditorium. Their records came to life, the gig was a little loud, she sang well, and I liked the way she danced, too. Before the show, I was walking down Sunset Blvd. in Hollywood and eventually shared an elevator ride with Hynde and her group members when they were departing from a radio interview on KWST-FM.

One time at Perkins Palace in Pasadena in the early '80s, I caught the Pretenders again, and Bruce Springsteen joined Hynde and the band for an encore. It wasn't, you know, Otis Redding and Carla Thomas . . . but it was *pretty* hot.

I've also heard her sing solo in a rather unique venue. A few years back, one late afternoon in Beverly Hills, I took my longtime friend, Ellen Berman, to her nail appointment at Sandy's Nails. In strolled Chrissie Hynde and her close friend, actress Rosanna Arquette. I was waiting around for Ellen to have her fingers done (believe me, I don't do this sort of thing ever), and then

Chrissie started belting out a rendition of the Rodgers and Hammerstein classic, "I Enjoy Being a Girl," that Nancy Kwan made famous in the play and movie musical, "Flower Drum Song." I was most impressed. Ellen was blown away and even paid for dinner later that day. Berman asked that I take her to the next Pretenders concert so she could see Hynde once with a band. And I did.

I still put the Pretenders' "Cuban Slide" on some of my mix tapes.

An edited version of this interview first appeared in *HITS*. It started with a phone call as I was viewing a cable TV documentary on singer Patsy Cline one late afternoon. Sometimes the writing gigs just happen. "Kubernik . . . I need a piece on Chrissie Hynde. Get it to me in a week," barked Roy Trakin at *HITS*, sounding more like *Daily Planet* editor Perry White in an old TV episode of "Superman."

Liz Rosenberg of Warner Bros. Records arranged for me to interview Chrissie Hynde over the telephone from her office in New York. Chrissie and I ruminated about her recent "Viva El Amor" album writing endeavors with Steinberg and Kelly and covered some additional territory as well.

After *HITS* was published, *Goldmine* requested a more detailed Chrissie Hynde interview for a cover story later published that gave us the forum to discuss the Gram Parsons tribute album, and her involvement with the Burt Bacharach salute. Hynde gave me some insights into her own vocal recording techniques, and, ever the fan of legendary rock veterans like Bob Dylan and the Rolling Stones, why their "Time Out of Mind" and "Exile on Main Street" albums, respectively, would be on her own desert island disc list.

I later heard from someone at her Warner Bros. label that Hynde was very pleased with our interview, particularly that I concentrated on the music and her songwriting process, not an '80s memory trip or a ride through some of the chaos and madness that has permeated her life within the Pretenders.

I sent Chrissie the "Jack Kerouac Box Set" that I was the production coordinator on, and she sent me back a nice thank you note. Coolness.

Q: On the new "Viva El Amor" album, you've continued co-writing with songwriters Billy Steinberg and Tom Kelly on some of the tunes. On the last studio album, "Last of the Independents," you teamed up with them for a few tracks, including "Night in My Veins" and "I'll Stand by You." Can you discuss working with them on songs, and besides the things you write by yourself?

A: Someone that Billy knew, so he says, maybe it was Billy all along [Laughs], sent a letter to my manager saying they would be interested in collaborating, or trying to do something. This was probably five or six years ago.

I hadn't ever collaborated with anyone, and I really had never thought about it. But I looked at this letter and thought, "Hey, that would be kinda cool, just to go to L.A. for a week or so." I was very much in my sort of "domestic *schtick*," and it just seemed like fun to go out there on my own for a week or two, and this idea of writing with other people was kinda scary, 'cause I hadn't done it. I'm much more of an "introverted-girl-with-her-guitar" songwriter. But I thought it sounded interesting, and what appealed to me was that it sounded disciplined—you know, with two other people, we were bound to get something done.

So I went out there, and I met Tom and Billy and we started, and what, for me, has become one of the most fun parts of everything I do, as if I'm gonna go out with Tom and Billy. Because Billy writes a lyric and gives it to Tom, and Tom puts it to music. I don't understand how it works, how they do it. I couldn't write just a lyric on its own. And I couldn't put it to music. That's what they do. It works beautifully for them.

Photo by Linda McCartney, courtesy of Warner Bros. Records.

What I do is that I go right in the middle of it and fuck the whole thing up. Turn it, meld it into my own song. What has happened, they naturally know, if we are going to do something together, Billy writes a lyric, or he'll pull out a lyric that he thinks is something that I would sing. Or he might even write with me in mind a little bit. And he's the only lyricist I've ever done anything with. And then, chances are, he fires me up and I will change the lyric to suit myself. He gets me off the starting block. I'll take his lyrics, which sometimes I think are earnest, and I'll make them sound more irreverent. Also, Tom, like, he'll write "Night in My Veins"—it sounded so much like a Pretenders song. And then, once again, I can alter it just enough. I mean, Tom is very musical. That's why I got him to play on half of the album and go over to England. 'Cause I wanted him to play on all the songs that we "demo'd" together, to keep the original feel.

And Tom, who is probably about forty-nine years old now, he grew up with the same musical influences as me, and had the same musical background. He was a bass player, and I think he probably stopped playing in bands maybe in the early '70s. He had exactly the right sensibility of what I like. He kind of had this arrested development and he still plays like one of the guys on the first Moby Grape album. That's how he plays, you know, like Bob Mosley or something. And he just has that sensibility. And for me, it's just fantastic.

That really fired the band up. I got him in to play on some stuff 'cause he's very distinctive. And he plays on "One More Time," another song on there, which has a very live band sound. He's a great singer, too. He sings a lot of background vocals and I like that, because it adds a bit of Americana to this otherwise mainly English pop thing, and that is the vital ingredient.

Basically and musically, they are extremely particular and very fastidious. Nothing is by accident with those guys. They really do think about it. And if they want to do a particular thing—like on "Last of the Independents," there's a song, "977." I had the initial idea for this couplet, "He hit me with his belt, but his tears were all I felt, when I saw my baby crying, knew that he loved me." Then Tom will sit down and put this "John Lennonesque" feel to it. And Billy sits there and makes some other suggestions. It's the three of us trying to find the direction. But mainly, they're the ones who start with the initial idea and then I come in, 'cause they're so used to working together they might have prepared a few things before I get there. It is a lot of fun, and I think I've gotten some great songs with them.

People think that Tom and Billy are these professional songwriters that have all these hits. And it's true that they have a bunch of hits, but people forget that I'm also a professional songwriter and just because I write my songs for myself and my band while Tom and Billy sort of farm theirs out to other people, I don't think that lessens them as songwriters. We have two or three songs that didn't make the album, which we still might do later. We're pretty prolific when we get together. We also try and do other stuff over the phone. Tom will call me on the phone just because of one note I sang, and he'll say, "Can't you do it the way we talked about it?" Billy will call and say, "Chrissie, I got some lyrics I want you to look at." He sent me a song recently that I just haven't had the time to listen to. I feel with them, in the past, they've written with some other people, but I think it's mainly them, and they'll write for an artist who might make a couple of suggestions. But with me, it's really a collaboration, and the reason I feel very, very fortunate in having them is because I feel I have this "guest of honor" position with them and we get great tunes. They've said, "Chrissie, whenever you want to write, we'll drop everything. Just give us two weeks notice and we'll be there."

Q: How do you traditionally write songs?

A: There's no real set formula, but one thing is for sure. Number one, I sit down with a guitar. Number two, I have a pen and a pad of paper. I don't use anything else. That's all I do. If I get an idea, I write it down. And then the next time I sit down with a guitar, and if I remember it then, well lucky me. If I don't, then that was a waste of time. But I don't have much more structure than that to it. Tom and Billy record absolutely everything. They record everything, they go over everything. They are real meticulous. "What was that note yesterday?" "Let's listen to that." And it's all on tape and Billy can find it on the tape. It would take me forty minutes just to get it, between fast forward and rewind. I'd be in tears trying to find something.

Q: Do you title the songs before or after they are written?

A: It can go either way, really. For example, Billy had an idea about a song called "California." He wrote a whole set of lyrics and I loved having this definitive song about California, and that really appealed to me. I looked at his lyrics, and Tom had written some beautiful melody ideas around it and I just took it home and re-wrote the whole song with my lyrics. But I would still call that a Steinberg/Kelly/Hynde collaboration, 'cause the song would not have existed if he hadn't had this idea to write a song called "California."

And that doesn't mean that just anyone could write me a letter and say, "Hey, how 'bout a song called 'California'" and we're in a songwriter team. When we go into a studio we pretty much stay true to the original vision of the song.

Q: On "Viva El Amor" you do a version of "Rabo De Nube" written by Silvio Rodriguez. Who is he and where did the song come from?

A: He's a Cuban songwriter, and my husband was playing one of his records and I thought that was such a beautiful melody. And I asked him what it meant. And it's a song about the hope of the people. And I thought it had a real beautiful poetic message. And then my husband reckoned that he was considered sort of a Bob Dylan figure in South America. I thought that was pretty cool.

Q: Jeff Beck plays on "Legalise Me." Describe the session.

A: Well, I've known Jeff for some years and he's someone who is my guitar hero. Meeting him was such a huge thrill for me. We were going to do some charity work over ten years ago and since then we've remained very friendly. And I sort of introduced him to a guy who has become one of his best friends, so that was always good, and the three of us go out together and do things. We've always had different schedules and been working on other projects. But when I heard "Legalise Me". . . I'm just such a fan of his rock guitar playing, because he's the greatest rock guitar player. And in his own stuff he's done the last twenty years, he certainly has gone on to Planet Beck. Where no other guitar player has ever gone. And he doesn't use a pick. What I always wanted to do was pull him down to Planet Earth and get him to play rock guitar. For him that might be a little elementary, but for me that's where my head is at. So when we did "Legalise Me," I thought, "Maybe I can get Jeff in to play the solo."

So I called him and told him I had a rock track—"Do you want to come down?" "Yeah." So I sort of cleared the studio out, 'cause I didn't want him to feel in any way any kind of scrutiny by people who were like crying and stuff, because he's so fuckin' amazing. I just had Stephen Hague and the engineer, Richard Norris, who works with Stephen. And Jeff pulls up in his Corvette, in this English studio, RAK Studio, where he probably recorded "Hi Ho Silver Lining" (with Mickey Most), and he walked into the studio. Everyone was very calm, great, "Thanks for coming." We played the track four times and he had a couple of passes on it and got into it a bit. Once he started playing, I thought, "This is great. I'm gonna have him sit right next to me so I can watch him play." But I couldn't lift my eyes. I couldn't look up. I was so in awe. It was so absolutely stupendous when he was playing, I was sort of immobilized. At one point, I caught Stephen Hague's glance from across the room and he too had this sort of stunned expression. You know, Jeff did about five takes. We said, "I guess

we've got it" when he finished playing. "Great. Thanks for coming down."
He said, "O.K. Talk to you later." And as soon as the studio door shut, we
all yelled, "Fuck! Oh My God!" We were screaming. The engineer had
never heard anything like it. We were shaking in disbelief, but when Jeff
was there . . . "O.K., Jeff. Thanks for coming in . . . Talk to you later. . ."
And, not to mention, I also have David Johansen on the song, "Popstar."

Q: Drummer Martin Chambers rejoined the Pretenders five years ago. What
has it been like to record with him in the studio again and play gigs over
the last half-decade, after not working with him for a period of time?

A: Martin is playing better than ever because we had some down time. I
think the trauma of losing Pete and Jimmy kind of did our heads in a
lot. And neither of us were playing any good.

In the Pretenders, no one expects me to play very good, but you know,
that's just how I play. But I expect excellence out of all the other players
or . . . I can't have everyone play like me. Martin's timing is impeccable. I
think in the early band that was down to the other players, too.

Like I said, there were some traumas. He lost his two best friends
when Pete and Jimmy died. And I desperately needed some other inspiration to keep myself alive too, because I was sinking after that, because
that was a big kick in the teeth for us.

So I played with a couple of other guys, and worked with other producers, went out into the wilderness on my own to kind of re-discover
what the fuck it was that I did. Suddenly I had Chris Thomas, the
Pretenders, and there was this great formula. And one day it was gone.
So I felt I had to go out and find my feet again. But what I missed about
Martin, his real *forte*, is that no one plays those mid-tempo Pretenders
songs the way Martin does. He has a particular "lolloping" feel that also
includes a sort of shuffle beat that he's really good at. And these days,
he plays on stuff like "One More Time" on this album, the more sort of
conventional R&B-based stuff, which at one time I thought he wasn't
very good at. Again, when we were going through our traumatic period,
we were losing our feel a bit. But he's come back so strong, it's fright-
ening. And he's the most entertaining drummer to watch, which I always
thought was probably the funniest part of watching a band, apart from
the guitar player, of course. If the guitar player is great, you can't replace
that. An entertaining drummer is just a joy to watch.

I don't ever like to turn my back to the audience when I'm playing, but
these days I just can't resist watching Martin because he's just such a
fuckin' riot. If I watch him, he shows off to me and he's even funnier. We
now have Martin play behind a screen so there's a lot of separation in the
sound. That gives our sound mixer a lot more flexibility, and Martin

Chrissie Hynde on stage at Universal Amphitheater, Universal City, California, 2000. Photo by Harold Sherrick.

doesn't have any spillage into the vocal mikes. And also he's not playing right behind my head, which I find a tremendous distraction as a singer. So he can really play out more. Consequently, he has to use headphones, otherwise the cymbal sound would be so loud that he'd be deaf. So I insist he use headphones at all times. Because the sound comes right back at him. But that's also why anyone who goes to see a Pretenders show always walks out and says, "That's the best sound I've heard in that hall." And it's down to the fact that we play minimum volume on stage, and we always use the screen, and we're very careful about our onstage sound to make sure, because that's the most important thing. It's the unseen factor of a show that ordinary people probably wouldn't really notice, but the sound can ruin the whole show. If the sound isn't excellent, it will ruin the show.

Q: You participated in the tribute to Burt Bacharach, "One Amazing Night" video and audio compilation, and "Return of the Grievous Angel," which is a "Various Artists" homage to Gram Parsons. You do a rendition of "She." Can we talk about the Bacharach and Parsons appearances?

A: I knew Gram Parsons' "Grievous Angel" album when it came out in 1973 and loved it. And meeting Emmylou Harris has been such a fantastic thing for me, 'cause I think she has one of the greatest voices of all time. I've crossed paths with her a couple of times. Her long-time road manager (and Parsons pal) Phil Kaufman was a biker who had a Harley Davidson in a garage where I used to have a squat in London, and I used to walk by there and read his *Easy Rider* magazines—this is way before I was in the Pretenders. I met Emmylou, we both did something for the Neil Young Bridge Concert one year. And I was enthralled being on the same bill with her. Then we met and had a few conversations on the phone and she said she was putting together this album. I told her, "You ask me to do something and I'll do it. I don't even have to know what it is." So she came up with the idea to do "She." That was the first song actually that she recorded for this tribute album.

Q: Years ago you did a cover of the Burt Bacharach and Hal David tune, "Windows of the World," for the film, "1969." In 1998 you sang their medley, "Baby, It's You"/"A Message to Michael," at the Bacharach event. Were you always an admirer of Burt's music and the work with Hal David?

A: The Bacharach and David team. I was always a fan ever since I first heard them. Dionne Warwick was always one of my favorite singers so, naturally, those were the songs of the late '60s. They were like the great melodic songs, they weren't just records. I got to take my pick of what was available for the show and I mentioned those two and they said, "You could do half of each."

Q: Is your mindset or approach to "covering" a song different, when you perform it, from a song that you wrote yourself and later sang?

A: Not particularly. In some ways it's fun because it's different and I can interpret one of my favorite songs, which is great. It's like a freebie. There are hundreds of fantastic songs out there and we can do any of them and we're free to do whatever we want. That's a great thing. Obviously, singing my own songs I'm expressing myself, but I would only sing a song that I feel. Anyone who can relate to a song will enjoy singing it. To interpret it my own way—I would never cover a song and do it if I didn't think I could give it a "Pretenders-esque" twist, or lend something to the song.

Q: On an earlier Pretenders album, you did a wonderful version of Bob Dylan's "Forever Young."

A: It's got such a beautiful lyric. I just love it. He's the pride of our generation. The song is genius. I'll tell you another great Dylan album, that was not one of his most popular ones, was "Shot Of Love." The song, "Lenny Bruce."

Q: And I know in a recent issue of the U.K. music magazine, *Q*, you really endorsed Dylan's "Time Out of Mind." I heard Dylan's office sent you an advance copy of the CD.

A: It's one of his best albums. He just sings magnificently, for a start. They're just great songs. Bob always writes impeccable songs, but my suspicion is that he's a little impatient in the studio. On this one, he really stuck it out and got gorgeous vocals. The singing is fantastic. The songs are so well crafted and they just got the great sound for each song. You don't feel like he just got a band in, wheeled them in, and played all the songs and left. Each song is very carefully thought out. Obviously that's a lot in the production and I'm sure that's Danny Lanois who masterminded that.

Q: Jim Keltner said some of the same things to me, and he played drums on "Time Out of Mind."

A: Jim Keltner is the perfect drummer for any band, if you ask me. He's great with Bob Dylan. Keltner is a genius drummer. I love that guy. And the Booker T. band is the best band in the world.

Q: Al Green autographed a CD for me last night!

A: That's awesome.

Q: By the way, I've been reading the PETA literature and vegetarian materials at your concerts for a while, and proud to say, for me ten years no meat or chicken.

A: That's a start . . .

Q: Getting back to that *Q* Chrissie Hynde Record Collection article, you mention the Rolling Stones' "Exile on Main Street" as "the definitive rock album." Why does it hold up so well?

A: It's just one of those great records and had a great resonance in the time it was made. The band was really hot. I still play it. Another thing about "Exile" was that it was a double album. And double albums don't digest very easily 'cause there's so much information on them. Nowadays I think people make the mistake of putting too much information on a CD because you can afford to, time-wise. But "Exile" was a slow, slow thing. It wasn't as immediate as albums characteristically were in those days, 'cause there were two albums. I think another thing with "Exile"—now that I think about it—yeah . . . It was a very "Keith-spirited-by-Keith" album.

Ravi Shankar:

"East-West"

He was born Robindra Shankar, in Benares, United Provinces, on April 7, 1920. He has brought you the sound of the sitar. When I did this interview in 1996, Ravi Shankar had just released a new album, "Chants of India," via Angel Records, produced by his longtime friend and musical collaborator, George Harrison. "Chants of India" is based on prayers and ancient chants of Shankar's native India. The session musicians included Harrison, tabla player Bikram Ghosh, and Shankar's then fifteen-year-old daughter, Anoushka, who helped assist and conduct and is now quietly gaining her own reputation as a dazzling sitar player in the shows she shares with her father.

In 1996, Angel Records issued the acclaimed four-CD retrospective of Shankar's career, "Ravi: In Celebration." This compilation was produced by George Harrison and Alan Kozlowski in association with Ravi Shankar, and according to Harrison, "The idea behind this four disc set is to show the different aspects of Ravi's music." The discs were arranged into Classical Sitar Music, Orchestral Indian/Ensembles, East/West Collaborations and Vocals, and Experimental.

Ravi Shankar continues to perform around the world, and has recorded dozens of albums in his stellar career. He has just published his autobiography, *Raga Mala*. He has continued to provide well-received soundtracks in both East and West, including "Kabuliwala" in 1956, for which he was named Best Film Music Director at the 1957 Berlin Film Festival. He also contributed to Ralph Nelson's Oscar-winning "Charly" in 1968 and, later, Shankar received an Academy Award nomination for his music in Richard

Ravi Shankar and George Harrison. Photo by Carolyn Jones, courtesy of Angel Records.

Attenborough's "Gandhi." He has also recorded with conductors Andre Previn and Zubin Mehta.

In 1966, he played the first sitar-violin duet with Yehudi Menuhin at the Bath Festival and, the following year, he reprised the collaboration at the United Nations as a centerpiece of the Human Rights Day celebrations. It was also in 1966 that Shankar first met George Harrison. Harrison had first heard the sitar on the set of the Beatles' movie, "Help!" Later that same year, he would record with the instrument on John Lennon's "Norwegian Wood (This Bird Has Flown)." Subsequently, Harrison integrated the sitar into his own composition, "Love You To," from the Beatles' "Revolver" album, as well as fusing sitar and Indian influences on his selection, "Within You Without You," on the influential "Sgt. Pepper's Lonely Hearts Club Band" album, and also on "The Inner Light," the obscure B-side to the "Lady Madonna" single.

In a brief, separate interview I conducted with George Harrison from New York, George discussed meeting Shankar at a dinner party for the North London Asian Music Circle, all those years ago. "His music was the reason I wanted to meet him. I liked it immediately, it intrigued me. I don't know why I was so into it—I heard it, I liked it, and I had a gut feeling that I would meet him. Eventually a man from the Asian Music Circle in London arranged a meeting between Ravi and myself. Our meeting has made all the difference in my life." Harrison further elaborated on his own sitar playing. "I'm not a very good one, I'm afraid. The sitar is an instrument I've loved for a long time. For three or four years I practiced on it every day. But it's a very difficult instrument, and one that takes a toll on you physically. It even takes a year to just learn how to properly hold it. But I enjoyed playing it, even the punishing side of it, because it disciplined me so much, which was something I hadn't really experienced to a great extent before." Harrison went on to describe his earliest attempt at playing the sitar with the Beatles: "Very rudimentary. I didn't know how to tune it properly, and it was a very cheap sitar to begin with. So 'Norwegian Wood' was very much an early experiment. By the time we recorded 'Love You To,' I had made some strides." Harrison put his sitar experiments with the Beatles in perspective: "That was the environment in the band, everybody was very open to bringing in new ideas. We were listening to all sorts of things, Stockhausen, avante-garde music, whatever, and most of it made its way onto our records."

Harrison traveled to Bombay in September, 1966, and became one of Shankar's students. Harrison and Shankar remained friends for over thirty years, and George continued as Shankar's recording producer. Harrison laid out how he first became involved with the new record: "Steve Murphy, the president of Angel Records, had heard some songs that were similar to material on 'In Celebration,' a Ravi retrospective that I had helped assemble last year. He suggested we go into the studio to record more. This music, which is based on ancient Vedic chanting, I very much enjoy. And, of course, it gave me an opportunity to work with Ravi, so it made perfect sense." Harrison's role on the record went beyond simply producing. "I organized the recording of the album, and during the recording I sang and played on a couple of songs. Bass guitar, acoustic guitar, and a few other things—vibraphone, glockenspiel, autoharp. The main thing was organizing—finding the right musicians, busing everybody out to my studio, and making certain everyone was properly fed. Finding the right engineer, John Etchells, was also key."

When asked, in 1996, why it was then the right time to release "Chants of India" to the world, Harrison was eager to explain his motivation. "In a way, it represents the accumulation of our ideas and experiences throughout our thirty-year relationship. But to put it into a slightly more commercial aspect, the record label asked us to do this, and that would never have happened fifteen years ago. Because multiculturalism has become more accepted, and more people are interested in what this music offers, this project has become more commercially viable. And this music is very close to me, this is something I very much wanted to do. I actively read the Vedic scriptures and I'm happy to spread the word about what this project is all about. People also need an alternative to all the clatter in their lives, and this music provides that. Whether it's Benedictine monks chanting or ancient Vedic chants, people are searching for something to cut through all the clatter and ease stress."

In Los Angeles, Ray Manzarek, keyboardist and co-founder of the Doors, gave me his take on Shankar's talent: "The genius. The master. He opened the door to the East. The vibrations, the inner spirit of music."

Manzarek, then in the band Rick and the Ravens, a pre-Doors R&B rock band, was introduced to the music of Shankar in 1965—before it was fashionable—by Richard Bock of the influential World Pacific Records label. Bock spun Shankar's albums in his office for young Manzarek, and then Rick and the Ravens cut a few singles and "demonstration" tapes for World Pacific's Aura Records label. Those acetates eventually became the Doors' calling card to other prospective employers.

Shankar's first book, *My Music, My Life*, was the subject of the film "Raga," which documented his musical roots and his impact in America. He has been a visiting professor at City College in New York (1968). With countless honors to his credit, he is viewed as India's unofficial cultural ambassador.

Ravi Shankar is now eighty-two years old. He resides in the beach community of Encinitas, near San Diego, where he lives with his second wife, Sukanya, and his daughter and protégé, Anoushka.

In the late '60s, Ravi Shankar had a house in Los Angeles on Highland Avenue, near our school, and half the kids in my eleventh-grade homeroom had a *very good time* at his unforgettable Hollywood Bowl concert. We all wore our Bombay Buckles from Thom McAn Shoes, which was next door to radio station KFWB on Hollywood Boulevard.

I once did a term paper on Ravi Shankar at Fairfax High School. An old friend of mine, songwriter Tom Johnson, always thought that was the *coolest* thing, and years later gave me a birthday present of a Ravi Shankar album, on 8-track cartridge, that he found in a thrift shop on Western Avenue. Tom used to live down the block from Charles Bukowski. But that's a whole other movie . . .

Over the subsequent years, I'd sometimes do my work and transcribe interview tapes to the sound of Shankar's music. I am always amazed that people don't realize how much of a staple Shankar was on late 1960s L.A. FM rock radio free-form playlists, on KPPC, KPFK, KMET. Sometimes worming in on the KBLA and KRLA AM airwaves, as well as rotation on KBCA-FM, the jazz channel.

Shankar was literally recording around the block from my parents' Fairfax District house in the early 1960s, at the famed World Pacific Studios,

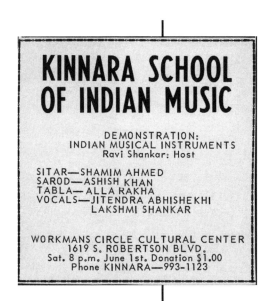

Advertisement from the L.A. Free Press, courtesy of the Harvey Kubernik Collection.

and always had a following in the Southern California area, before the Byrds and the Beatles picked up on his musicianship. Musician Chris Darrow remembers Ravi playing colleges around town and the Ash Grove club in the last part of the 1950s. Shankar also hosted the Kinnara School Of Indian Music on Robertson Blvd. An Indian restaurant near Irving and Melrose presented his debut L.A. recital.

Originally, I was slated to chat with Shankar over the telephone for *HITS* magazine, and then at the last minute, he requested, after talking to a close friend,— I was later to learn it was George Harrison—that I come down to his home for "a proper visit." So, I asked Tom Johnson to pick me up at the Bodhi Tree—where else?—and join me, and we hopped in his car and made it to the San Diego area in ninety minutes. I bought the most expensive cassette tapes I could find at Tower Records to record Ravi. It was such a mellow and happy experience. The record label was cooperative, the publicist was so professional, and George Harrison was delighted to be involved as well.

At the conclusion of our two hours, daughter Anoushka walked in from school, and Ravi comically shrugged his shoulders and whispered to me, "Boys are calling on the telephone." I reassured him that his daughter would be able to handle it, and she would not be putting down her "axe" for anyone. He seemed thankful for the pseudo-parental feedback. Shortly thereafter, Tom and I went to see Ravi and Anoushka perform at Pasadena City College. I used to work at the school's campus radio station in the late 1980s. At PCC, Ravi still had the goods, and Anoushka radiated like "Glittering Girl" in the Pete Townshend Who song. I later went to see a benefit recital by Anoushka and Ravi in L.A. at UCLA's Royce Hall venue, to help establish the Ravi Shankar Center.

In our conversation, Ravi was eager to discuss his new "Chants of India" CD, the 1996 "Ravi: In Celebration" box set, his friendship with George Harrison, producer Richard Bock, the Monterey Pop Festival, Woodstock, the Concert for Bangladesh, and many other topics, including his recording collaborations with jazz musicians and his series of meetings and talks with the legendary John Coltrane. Ravi's music lives on even in this MTV-saturated culture. In May of 2000, VH1 aired D.A. Pennebaker's "Monterey Pop" documentary (now out on DVD), which featured a set by Shankar, and the legendary "Concert For Bangladesh" video still does brisk video store rental business.

We took our shoes off and started to roll tape for two hours. The findings . . .

Q: Your new CD, "Chants of India," is produced by George Harrison. Can you discuss your relationship with George? You've been friendly for nearly a third of a century, and he's always managed to help support your artistic desires and subsequent recordings.

A: He's a very rare person . . . It is something so special. There are many other people who could do what George does, but they don't have that depth. He's so unusual. What has clicked between him and me, what he gets from me, and what I get from him, that love and that respect and understanding from music and everything, is really the most important thing. It's not the money, or him helping me to record, that's not the main thing. But it's the very special bond between both of us. The idea for

"Chants of India" was suggested by Steve Murphy (president of Angel Records). He mentioned the success of those Spanish monks. George was very enthusiastic after the idea was given. I was very much attracted to the whole idea, and so was George, as we have already said. I found, going deeper into it, what a difficult job it was, because, you know, when you deal with something very traditional, as those few thousand year old things, the concept and the oral tradition that has been handed down by the family who chants . . .

Also consider that there have been so many recordings already done in different ways, from very pure to very raw. Very sophisticated, from classical musicians singing the classical style of our ragas and melody forms, and also done by a lot of commercial people in very strange modern concepts. To make something so different from all these was a great job for me and a lot of responsibility. I had to keep it traditional, as well as be different. So that's how it took me some time to study a lot, to hear a lot and change my ideas again and again, to finally do what we did.

[In a recent interview in the *Los Angeles Times* with writer Don Heckman Shankar acknowledged translating the ancient, sacred material into a commercial recording medium: "The Vedas actually have been done over and over again, in every manner. In India, you wouldn't believe the number of ways in which they have been interpreted by famous singers in the classical manner, with simple tambura drones, with synthesizers and saxophones, every way imaginable. What I wanted to do was to maintain a respect for the tradition without making it sound strange for the listeners—to give it a celestial, very spiritual sound."]

The recording was done in different time periods and different places. Twice we did it in Madras, of course. Madras is in the southern part of India and a lot of tradition remains intact, you know. I took the help of traditional chanters who for centuries, their families have been keeping it intact. But I gave it a background of holding drone instruments like cello and the Indian instrument tambura and also some big bamboo flutes, doing very slow passages, taking a particular raga. I didn't play the sitar, but I strummed the sympathetic strings which are underdiminished strings. All of that made it sound so different, but at the same time it did not sound so foreign.

Q: In *Billboard*, in May 1997, in an article written by Bradley Bambarger, you said, "There is so much turmoil, so much discord in the papers and on TV. Music is the greatest medium for peace, and like Western plainsong, the Indian chants can offer solace. They are prayers for shanti, or well-being. But whether texts are in Latin or Sanskrit, the feelings in this kind of music are universal." And George Harrison added, "It's a mad world we live in. And there's so much music out there that is, well, aggravating. This is our effort to achieve some semblance of balance. People everywhere are looking for something, they always have been, but maybe now more than ever."

A: The main intention, to tell the truth, because I have been very much disturbed by things that have been happening. You know, I could have done these chants in an entirely ritualistic, fundamentalist approach also, which any religion can do. But I was very conscious of this and wanted to make this so international and universal that this whole spiritual feeling comes out, even if you don't know the meaning of the words. And we have done our best to keep the words with translations and everything, so that it helps and you will know that the mantras selected from traditional Vedic and Upanishad (ancient Indian spiritual texts) pertain to peace, love, happiness, well-being, health, mental health, spiritual health, and the goodness and prayers for nature and the planet.

I chose the special prayers, what we call mantras, which focus more on ecology, the atmosphere, or whatever. What I did, I added the music into such a proportion that it does not overpower it, and the same time it helps in the background. Not making it Westernized, to make it palatable for Western people. But I did take help of cello, harp, violin, autoharp, things that have a very celestial sound, along with the Indian bamboo flute and the tambura. But I didn't use the sitar or the sarod, which I've done in the past in many of my recordings. These I avoided, I wanted to be completely different.

Q: Was it hard for you to make a recording without it being "sitar-driven?"

A: No. [Laughs] It was not. Because I have done lots of recordings and have made others playing the sitar and used other Indian instruments like the sarod. In this one, I avoided those and kept in the background something which is hypnotic and repetitive, mantras, along with what I call the three mystical and magical notes, which are the tonic, the lower note and the raised note. Which are the traditional system. And that has shifted into different pitches in the background, corresponding to the raga which fit those notes. That's the only way I used the instruments.

Q: Why is the repetitive nature of mantras so powerful?

A: That's what it is, you know . . . The power of the mantras has always been because of the repetition. It has been scientifically explained by many people, which I cannot do. I achieve through the particular vibrations of those sound syllables, the repetition has tremendous effect and monotony always gives that high feeling, even if you listen to folk music, they go on repeating passages and sometimes it gets in a trance. So, mantras have tremendous power and even if people don't understand it, they do. When you say "Ohm . . ." Close your mouth. "Ohm . . ." When you close the lips and put the sound louder, "Ohm . . ." Keep it as long as you can and feel the buzz! It does something to you . . . It has been proven to be very strong. Ohm is something that can be practiced by anyone. The word Veda. There are four principal Vedas and later came many books which tried to explain each of these mantras and scriptures. They all tried to make interpretations, because it's a very old language. The main four Vedas have been explained through all the letter scriptures. First, oral tradition, then written on scrolls and given to the families. It was a very closely-guarded secret, but now everything is open and published, read, and people take it very lightly and think they know a lot, but it's something very deep.

When I had the chance to do this recording, it was not difficult to get into it, but what was difficult was to choose exactly the right scriptures. What I have done for years is offer harmony and clarity, but through sound, not words, you know. What we play on sitar and the origin of our music is all the same root. The sound is God. Whether we have the word planted into it or not, we bring out the music with the same feeling, with the love and devotion, and it goes deep. Whether you like it or not, I am not concerned. This is from the depth of my life. I am a vessel and a translator for the audience, as you said earlier. During the pre-production and the music itself on this new recording, before we started, I tried to hear in my mind what I was wanting to do, and sometimes experimented with a few of my students. I had the whole plan and the choice of the things I did.

It was then that George came into the studio, while we were recording. His help started from then on in balancing, giving bass to particular things and mostly afterwards in the mixing. He was also very involved when we were in his studio at his home. On many of the numbers, I asked him to strum acoustic guitars, along with other instruments. It's so subdued. He played some additional instruments and even joined the chorus, giving his voice. He was all the time there, that was one of the most beautiful things and very helpful in the mixing. We had such a fantastic experience. He does not impose his ego into the music. He never does that. That's such a wonderful thing. He gives some suggestions like, "Use that particular voice a little louder than this one." When I felt he was right, I said "Yes." When I didn't feel right, I said "No." No problem of ego at all. He gave fantastic suggestions, especially when it came to the volume and the combination of cello and violins. We were together.

Q: Is there a difference, recording in India and then in England?

A: To tell the truth, I feel happier in India. But, unfortunately, this time I wasn't. Because cities like Madras and Bombay have become strongholds for film, Indian films. India makes twice as many films as America does. In all different languages. So the studios are booked for two years in advance. Can you believe? So we had to get the studio time through the biggest influence. They are working twenty-four hours a day. We had to use all our influence to get this chance of recording. Here I am in India, doing Vedic things . . . It was much worse that I had expected in getting a studio. But, once we got started, we had fantastic musicians and singers. When we recorded it was fantastic. In Henley, at George's studio, there was no problem. There's no pressure when I go to his home and into his studio! It is so relaxed. No "Finish this at this time!" We had a wonderful engineer, John Etchells, who was calm and beautiful. The musicians that we got in London were very good, and I had known some of them earlier from the schools. My wife and George's wife Olivia were so helpful, my daughter was helping me, writing, conducting and talking to the musicians. There was no tension, like in Madras, you know, which was unfortunately so commercial. That was a big difference. My daughter is extremely talented and I was training her with this recording.

Q: Keep her away from Hollywood!

A: [Laughs] I know! I know! I'm trying my best [Laughs]. I see the growth and commitment in her studies. My daughter does Indian notation and she knows Western notation, because she is learning piano. This is how she started. She's very fond of rock-'n'-roll. You name it. MTV. She's all around it. She's out of this world from that point of it. A teenage magazine came for a modeling thing from India. Anoushka is the best student I have had for a long time. George adores her. He's Uncle George. She is the right person to whom the sitar music must be passed. Before, the destiny of women (in our culture) was to get married and to bear children, so naturally, they could not pursue music. But now they are pursuing, even if they get married, even if they have children, they are much more serious and the standard is very high.

Q: I know you are extremely involved in the sequencing of selections when you record. Is that the same way you did "Chants of India?"

A: That's one thing, one area, you know, without praising myself . . . I have done so much programming in my life, starting from my early days in All India Radio, being a director there, that the psychology of programming, or sequencing, as you call it, comes very easily for me. You

---

East–West

know, give them a bang, then after that you pull them, build it up. That sort of natural tendency I learned from my brother, who was a great dancer and had great stage craft, which I learned from my childhood. George went through the sequencing with me and agreed with what I made from the buildup when I did the programming.

Q: In June, it will be the thirtieth anniversary of the Monterey Pop Festival, and Rhino Records will be releasing a special thirtieth celebration four-CD box set, which includes your performance from the festival. What are some of your memories of the event? How did you get the booking?

A: Dick Bock, of World Pacific Records, called Lou Adler. I was recording for World Pacific. Some of my recordings with jazz musicians are on that label. Dick was a wonderful person. Anyway, Monterey to me was like a revelation. Completely new. I had met George before that, and that started the whole big hullabaloo, as you know. And I saw the whole folk movement that started in England. That's when I started seeing all the strange dress and the smell of patchouli oil, the hash, and LSD. To me, it was a new world. Anyway, I had been performing in the United States since 1956. Carnegie Hall. My first fans were jazz buffs and jazz musicians and average American people. So, a decade later, I arrive in Monterey and see butterflies and colors and flowers with peace and love. It was fantastic. I was impressed, but everyone was stoned. But that was alright and I was meeting all these beautiful people. Fine. It was one day before my concert and I went to hear the whole thing. That to me was the real experience. One night, I really heard Otis Redding. He was fantastic. One of the best, I remember. I really like the Mamas & the Papas. Lyrical, harmony, and good choruses and harpsichord. Then, you know, came the hard rock. The Jefferson Airplane. The Grateful Dead. To me it was difficult in a very loud, hurtful in-my-ear way. And Janis Joplin. I had heard of her, but there was something so gutsy about her. Like some of those fantastic jazz ladies like Billie Holiday. That sort of feeling, so I was very impressed by her. Then, some others and what really disturbed me was the hard rock. The worst was to come. I had heard so much about Jimi Hendrix. Everyone was talking about him. When he started playing . . . I was amazed . . . the dexterity in his guitar playing. But after two, three items, he started his antics. Making love to the guitar, I felt that was quite enough. Then, all of a sudden he puts petrol on his guitar and burns it. That was the leaving point. Sacrilegious. I knew it was a gimmick. Then the Who followed, started kicking the drums and breaking their instruments. I was very hurt and ran away from there along with the others who play with me. My feelings were hurt deeply, as well as my respect for music and the instruments. We ran away from the festival. I said at the time, "Please. There is a

Ravi Shankar at the Monterey International Pop Festival, California, June 1967. Photo by Henry Diltz.

contract, and whatever you want to fine me, I won't play. I definitely will not play in between any of these items tomorrow." So, there were talks and meetings between Dick Bock and the festival people. The next day, in the afternoon, we set up a special section between 1:00 and 3:00 P.M., where there would be no one in front of me and after me.

It was cloudy, cool, it had rained a little and that's when I played, and it was like magic. Jimi Hendrix was sitting there. (Jerry) Garcia was there. I remember a few names. All of them were there and you can see on the film what magic it had. I was so impressed, and it is one of my memorable performances. I didn't plan for this. I was grateful to God that I was sitting in the atmosphere without anyone disturbing me. It drizzled for a few minutes and then it stopped. So it was cloudy and there were flowers from Hawaii and you know, what atmosphere! After my set, it was crazy. I have never felt such a commotion of this sort. I was so pure, in spite of the fact that there were many people who were also strong. But it didn't matter, because the whole atmosphere was so clean and beautiful and I could give my best. That's all I can say.

Q: I know you weren't in the Woodstock Festival movie, but I recall a live album from your appearance at Woodstock, right?

A: Yes. I have always said that if Monterey was the beginning of this beautiful peace, of love, flowers, and all that, then Woodstock was the end of it. Because it was so big. Half a million people. Rain so much that there was mud all over. You couldn't see the people or look into their faces. Such a distance and such a vast multitude. And it looked like a big parking place. We came by helicopter and landed behind the stage and it was raining. It was a mess. But, my commitment was so strong, because I couldn't get out of it, so I did my best. And somehow, in that atmosphere, I did my best, but I couldn't feel anything.

Q: Was playing outdoors or at festivals a stressful situation for you or the instruments you were playing? I know after Woodstock you stopped doing pop festivals.

A: For technical reasons, our instruments are so sensitive and delicate and weather affects pitch and completely ruins the sound and it becomes muffled. Out of control, out of tune. Even indoors, we have to be very careful not to have very strong lights. Heat, humidity affects the instruments. Now, all the halls have air conditioning. And we never have big concerts in summer or in the rainy season. The main concerts are all in the winter season, three or four months when it's ideal weather, dry and cool. I don't like playing outside very much, but there have been some wonderful outdoor places and performances, like Tanglewood, because the weather was quite good and the great audience, and a few other places where the weather was just right.

Q: Last night I was at a recording session of the Rolling Stones, and Jim Keltner was adding percussion and playing on some of the tracks. I knew he recorded with you in the 1970s, and the track appears in your four-CD retrospective. He and Ringo Starr were the drummers for the Concert for Bangladesh. Keltner still feels that show really did make a lot of people, especially performers and rockers, socially aware on how music can help and heal. You know what I'm saying. He ran it down to me in the hallway, and the gig was over twenty-five years ago. I also know you had some conflicts after Woodstock and before the Madison Square Garden Bangladesh concert about playing in front of U.S. audiences. You had a problem with people in the audience being stoned and high, correct?

A: It was terrible. My manager (at the time) had me committed to play and I went to clubs to perform. I didn't know. There were tables, they were drinking. I said I will not play until you stop drinking, which they did and they accommodated me. But still the atmosphere . . . and they didn't drink or smoke while I was playing, but they were already . . . I want the *music* to get people high. I had to take drastic steps sometimes. I walked off and left the stage with my sitar a few times where they had booked me. Then, I could not believe one time, people in front of me were masturbating and copulating and that was too much for me and I walked off. Then, they made stage announcements to behave and I came back and it was better. I backed away and stopped performing for a year-and-a-half in the United States, until I got back some classical promoters, because by that time my promoters were either rock or pop or folk. That was where my manager was booking me. So I left that manager and completely stopped performing.

Q: How did the Concert for Bangladesh come about?

A: I told George, and George wanted to help me. The film "Raga" was ready and it needed some finishing, in which George helped. It was released, I believe, in 1972. At the time, I lived in Los Angeles and had a house on Highland Avenue, a beautiful Spanish villa. George was in town, and I was planning to do a benefit concert for Bangladesh, because I was very hurt that this whole thing was going on. To help this refugee problem, I wanted to raise some money. Everybody, every Indian, was thinking about doing that. And then, when I thought about it, I knew I could do more than any other Indian musician. Still, how much can you send? $20,000? $25,000, at the most? At this time of turmoil I was having, George was there. He came to meet me and I was sitting. He saw me. From 1966, whenever he came to town, we would meet. At that time, he was staying in L.A. for a couple of weeks. I told him what I was planning. You know, it's like a drop in the ocean. At the same time, I never wanted to take advantage of him. I did not want to say, "Would you help me?" But, somehow, it came very naturally. He was so sympathetic. "Well . . . let's do something." And you know, that made me feel so happy. What he did, he immediately started phoning and booking things up.

Q: Was he good on the telephone?

A: [Laughs] Very quick. [Laughs] His position naturally makes it quicker. He phoned and got Madison Square Garden [in New York]. Later he contacted Bob Dylan, Eric Clapton, Billy Preston, and a few of his friends. Somehow, it was done [Snaps his fingers], like that. Within three weeks or so, we gave a performance and it was sold out. So they had to schedule a matinee. As you know, the first half was me. I called my guru's son, Ali Akbar Khan, who plays the sarod, and who now has a college in the Bay Area. Alla Rakha now lives in Bombay, and he's running a school for himself. We were the first part. I composed the first lines for the items played as we always do, and we improvised. And then intermission. There was no clapping when we were tuning, which is seen in the film, and the people were so well-behaved. A lot of matches. It went beautifully. It was a young audience, especially because I had this existing audience already, who were mature listeners and who had come to Carnegie Hall. This audience was the same type of audience as Monterey, but they were very attentive and there was no problem at all. After our segment, I went to see the second half. Their program was very complementary, because they chose the numbers that were very soulful in the sense that they weren't hard rock. "My Sweet Lord," "That's The Way God Planned It." Bob Dylan had his harmonica and did ballads. George sang "Here Comes the Sun," and the song he composed, "Bangla Desh." There was harmony and it wasn't so different. It went off beautifully. The soundtrack for the event won a Grammy [for Best Album of 1972].

Q: I know George Harrison played on the album, "Shankar Family and Friends," which came out in 1973, and produced "Music Festival from India" in 1975, which featured soloists from India. You also shared billing on the "Dark Horse" tour of the U.S. and Canada in late 1974.

A: I'm glad you mentioned the "Dark Horse" tour. Again, a wonderful attempt and a wonderful thing that George really planned. Unfortunately, what happened, and we had the first forty-five minutes with fourteen musicians, and believe me, I would safely say there were ten to fifteen percent of the crowd who came especially for us, the Indian crowd, and the American crowd. But, definitely, it was almost eighty to eighty-five percent which were for George and his group. So, it didn't please either of the groups, if you see what I mean. George, unfortunately, had a hoarse voice the whole tour. He had too much strain and he didn't want to sing the old melodies, which people were crying for. What he wanted to do was sing his new numbers, which he was so anxious to do. But it didn't work with his hoarse voice, and because he didn't sing the items that people were shouting and clamoring for. We had sell-out audiences everywhere and no problem. We were so happy in the plane and happy travelling. The food cooked was Indian and it was fantastic. But people were not very happy. Neither the audiences who came for me nor for him. But . . . it was just one of those things, unfortunately.

Q: I know it might be awkward to you, but you have been integrated into the retail record and radio world as a "New Age" artist or in the "World

Beat" category. Especially in the last ten years. I realize it's a marketing handle, but how do you feel about this area?

A: It was never my intent, but I got grouped into it for two reasons. Many people still don't realize I had the fortune, or misfortune, of playing a double role all my life. One, as a very traditional, orthodox, purist sitar player, representing the tradition of India, which connects with the "chants" and everything. Another side, I was exposed during my childhood with my brother, listening to all the symphonies and the best musicians in the world, jazz. I had this creative, inventive mind all the time, even after I went through all the training. So, I turned out to be a composer as well, which in our Indian music was a "no-no," or not usual. So, I had to go through this problem always, being mistaken for these two identities. People thought I was sacrilegious to my music when I was trying out something with Yehudi Menuhin or Jean-Pierre Rampal, or George Harrison becoming my student, or doing music for some film, or writing scores for this symphony orchestra. I've had this problem, always. Leonard Bernstein had this same problem.

See, people like to box everyone, put them into a slot. In 1973–74, I did those two records with George and it went completely above most people's heads. But now, people are saying such beautiful things about them. It all came together during my seventy-fifth year, with concerts in London, New York, and New Delhi. A book will be coming out and the box set is now available. George was so interested in producing [with Alan Kozlowski] and compiling the box set. I had very strong ideas about the concepts of "In Celebration." That they shouldn't mix everything together, so each record was according to the idea, like the classical side, the orchestral and ensembles, the East-West collaboration, and the vocal and experimental.

I revisit the work on this [box set] collection. I listen and hear, "Oh, my God! It could have been a little better if it was like this . . ." I'm never totally one hundred percent satisfied with anything that I have done. I hear some of the items [on the box set] and I think of Dick Bock, or a restaurant on Vermont Ave. That happens a lot. I met such wonderful people when I first came to the U.S. to record in the mid-1950s. Dick was such a lovable character who knew everyone. And everybody loved him. The other person I met, I don't know if you know him, is George Avakian [producer of Louis Armstrong, Johnny Mathis, Charles Lloyd], who was at Columbia Records and took me to all the Miles Davis concerts. These two were my greatest friends. On this collection, without doubt, I missed a few of them [Laughs], which are not included. There are at least four to six other box sets that can be made with all the things that have not been put together.

The [new] package is so beautiful, liner notes, and George was very enthusiastic.

Q: I went back and rediscovered the work you did with jazz musicians: Bud Shank, John Handy, and I know you composed the piece, "Rich a la Rakha," for Buddy Rich and your own tabla accompanist, Alla Rakha. And you gave lessons in Indian music to Don Ellis and John Coltrane.

A: I clicked with jazz musicians, always. From my childhood really, jazz reacted so strongly in me. Because of the rhythms and beats and the freedom to improvise, which we also have. The whole basis is different because we improvise on the ragas and have very strict rules, whereas jazz takes chords, the harmony of Western classical music, and takes a theme, and then they go free, whatever they want. But they don't observe the raga or the complicated rhythmic cycles.

Q: I know John Coltrane was going to formally study with you before he died. He has a son, Ravi Coltrane.

A: He was coming to learn from me. I told him, "John, why do I find so much turmoil and disturbance in your music?" He laughed and said, "That's exactly what I'm trying to find out myself and you can help me." We had three meetings and he came and sat twice, a very long one and a very short one in a New York hotel where I used to stay. And he wrote down many ragas, and I taught him how we improvise and he was asking me, "How do you bring the spiritual quality in your music? How do you do that?" Afterwards, he started using more drones, if you remember. I heard the turmoil in his music. He was like a child. It was a wonderful revelation for me to see this man. Dick Bock always tried to play me as much Coltrane as possible, in the car, or a few records. There I was hearing certain melody qualities that were so wonderful.

Q: Then, there's the Indian Music Circle, a non-profit organization, which has been a force in bringing Indian classical music and dance to Southern California since it was founded by you and Harihar Rao in 1973.

A: It's a society with my disciple, Harihar Rao. I'm so happy. Thanks to him and everyone, it has had such a wonderful impact in different cities, which have formed societies since then. I performed ten days ago at a sold-out house in Chicago. Would you believe, eighty percent of the audience were young people, fifteen to twenty-five years old. It's always been a mixed audience. People who have discovered me, those who stayed are now older, they are still here as well.

Q: What do you want to give the audience when you perform?

A: I can only tell you what I've heard, not once, but a thousand times. It comes from a black man who is a porter at the airport, or the Immigration Officer, and they say one thing, which I always get tears in my eyes: "Thank you for what you gave us through your music." Some go back to the '60s, even 1956 or whatever, and this has always been the case. That's what I want to do through my music. To give them, as much as is possible, love and peace and the feeling of all the different sentiments that we have, starting from romantic to playful, to happiness, to speed, to virtuosity and fun. And finally, something which is most important to me, the spiritual.

On the way home, Tom and I stopped off and had Indian food for dinner.

Marianne Faithfull:

Encounter in Hollywood

I've interviewed Marianne Faithfull a few different times, once right after her album "A Secret Life" came out in the mid-1990s. It's a collaboration with producer/arranger/co-writer Angelo Badalamenti, best known for his score to filmmaker David Lynch's twisted TV series, "Twin Peaks." Island Records has also released "Faithfull: A Collection of Her Best Recordings," including "Broken English," and in 1994, Little, Brown and Company published her memoir, *Faithfull: An Autobiography*, written with David Dalton.

A couple of years back she coaxed longtime pal Keith Richards into producing her version of the Patti Smith–Lenny Kaye song, "Ghost Dance," for an Irish AIDS benefit CD compilation. In the mid-1990s she did a song, "Love Is Teasin'," on the Chieftains album, "Long Black Veil," and Marianne sang "Ruby Tuesday" on the Rolling Stones Symphonic album that Chris Kimsey put together.

In the early '90s, she was made a professor by Allen Ginsberg at the Naropa Poetry Institute in Colorado, where she has taught lyric writing. Her certificate says: "Marianne Faithfull, Professor of Poetics, Jack Kerouac School of Disembodied Poetics."

In 1995, she toured extensively in the U.S. and Europe, performing the music and lyrics of composer Kurt Weill and playwright Bertolt Brecht, in a cabaret show, "An Evening in the Weimar Republic," with pianist Paul Trueblood. In the same decade she also undertook film roles in "When Pigs Fly" and "Moondance."

ABKCO Records has also just issued a collection of Faithfull's songs of the '60s, "Marianne Faithfull's Greatest Hits," a delightful brace of tunes,

Marianne Faithfull, London, 1964. Photo by Gered Mankowitz.

including "As Tears Go By," "Summer Nights," "Come and Stay with Me," "This Little Bird," and "Sister Morphine."

Marianne Faithfull was born in 1946 in Reading, England, daughter of an Austrian baroness and an English academic. At seven, she was sent as a boarder to the local convent school, St. Joseph's.

Faithfull has been one of pop's most endearing and intriguing figures since 1964, when she was discovered by Andrew Loog Oldham, the manager and producer of the Rolling Stones.

Under Oldham's direction, Marianne had some pop chart placements and recorded an international Top Ten single, "As Tears Go By," written by Mick Jagger and Keith Richards. She helped pen the harrowing lyrics to "Sister Morphine." She also introduced Jagger to Mikhail Bulgakov's book, *The Master and Margarita*, which helped birth the classic Stones composition, "Sympathy for the Devil."

It was around 1996 that Faithfull's friend, Allen Ginsberg, encouraged me to look her up the next time she was in Hollywood. Faithfull had just performed at the Henry Fonda Theater on Hollywood Boulevard and was in the city. "Go talk to her and let her talk to you," A.G. suggested. Her PR liaison and Island Records arranged for me to visit her on Sunset Boulevard at the famed Chateau Marmont Hotel and talk about her autobiography and most recent album.

I knocked on the door to her hotel room, and Marianne answered. "Welcome to the poet's corner," she beamed. I responded, "Whatcha readin', luv?"

I looked at her for about thirty seconds.

Marianne was in black. Not punk black, but black blouse, black pants, and black nylons. She was an image out of Hollywood's Jazz City music club, circa 1958. Musician/activist Buddy Collette once described the venue to me, "where a lot of hip and talented musicians went. 'Lady Day' . . . And the girls . . . the hair, in black, smiling . . . And the music in that place . . ."

Marianne Faithfull is now in front of me. I had a picture of her many years ago in my Fairfax High School locker, later replaced by Judy Geeson, and then Julie Christie and Tina Turner. Think about that one . . .

Marianne is wearing no makeup, blonde, long hair, a little *zaftig*, shorter in person than I expected, kind of a Juliette Greco meets latter-day Gloria Grahame visual.

This still-alluring Marianne Faithfull turned out to be a fascinating interview subject. A real *yenta*. She's a lot of fun and never avoided a question during our meeting. I've always liked the sound of her voice, too.

Marianne has a dancer's body. In fact, twice during the two-hour chat, she leaped off the couch onto the rug and sort of did a move, an interpretation of the "sideways pony" dance that Tina Turner once taught Mick

Jagger in the hallway in front of her in 1965 at Colston Hall in Bristol, England. She explained that her mother Eva taught her to dance as a child. I then mentioned that I briefly danced on "American Bandstand" as a teenager, and many years after that, I had interviewed Tina Turner for *Melody Maker*, gave her a kiss on the cheek at Chasens Restaurant (before the comeback), and Tina taught me how to do "The Popcorn." "Hmmm . . . Remind me to give you a kiss and a hug when you leave today, and don't worry if my boobs get in the way," she warned. "No problem," I assured her.

Room service delivered additional Marlboro Lights. I earlier brought her a pack of menthols. She also ordered a vodka martini for our smoky conversation. I had a mineral water. The record label paid.

I then tossed the astrology card. All I had to say was that I'm a Pisces, born February 26th, the day after Beatle George Harrison and before the Rolling Stones' Brian Jones. She quickly responded that her first love, first husband, John Dunbar, is a Pisces, also that her ninety-three-year-old father, Glynn, is a Pisces. She is a Capricorn and left-handed.

As I pushed the button on the cassette machine, I needed to tell her that a mutual friend, Kim Fowley, said hello. "Kim! Give him my love. What a brilliant eccentric character," she chuckled.

He's the one who told me many years ago that Marianne Faithfull was "really a hip Jewish chick." I had read decades ago she was raised Catholic.

I told Marianne, "I said to Fowley it couldn't be true, and knew you went to a Catholic School, St. Joseph's. But Kim went to a Catholic School, and I was born in a Catholic hospital, Queen of Angels, so I guess anything is possible. Right?"

"My dear little Piscean . . . My mother and my grandmother were Jewish," she declares. "My mother came from a line of Austro-Hungarian aristocrats. My mother was a doctor's daughter. She was a Jewess, those great Jews who went out and did it from the Austro-Hungarian Empire. Doctors, writers, sort of like going into Oklahoma. Allen Ginsberg now is my Jewish Mother."

Q: How did your autobiography come together? I know you've been approached over the years to write it.
A: It took a long time. I have great recall.

Q: Why did you do the book?
A: I did it for you. [Laughs] I did. I felt there was something in the story that was very common to everybody. I do believe that the details and the individuals are different, but the emotions and the sort of core thing is very, very connected to all human experience. Therefore, I felt it was a

valid story to tell. And then again, I felt I was very close to some of the greatest people of my time. And I had a lot of help.

David Dalton came to Ireland for two weeks. He's a very shy person. He selected me. Such a strange story. Tony Secunda, who recently died, I dedicated my paperback English edition to him, he had become a literary agent, and he was working with Dalton and he came to Ireland. I didn't want to do this book, really. Much as I care for humanity, I knew it was going to be a really hard thing to do, and it took a lot to get me to do it. Tony came to Ireland first to talk to me. It needed that. He really made me realize that it was very serious to get an offer from Little, Brown publishing, and Michael Joseph is very serious, and this was not the moment that I could do my flauncy, "Oh no. Oh no," sort of thing.

Secunda had managed me for a little while just after "Broken English." I was very fond of Tony. He had not gone through the rehabilitation bit yet, and indeed nor had I. He was fine. Great fun. But he ended up ripping me off. [Laughs] What I realized about Tony coming to Ireland, and it's a very unique thing that happens very rarely, but it happens to me quite a lot, actually. Tony was making amends, and he negotiated for me a book deal you could not believe. To Dalton's fury, and that of his agent, Tony insisted that the deal favor me. We had had this history and he was making up for that. He came out of this very honorably and he suggested David, who I've ended up very close friends with. By then I realized that Tony was on the level.

Q: And he picked David Dalton, who was a big Rolling Stones fan.

A: That was peculiar for me. And my great tease. I would tell David at first, that what I saw in him as a writer was that he was basically a necrophiliac. "You have only written books about dead people." (James Dean, Janis Joplin, Jim Morrison) "How are you going to cope with someone who is not dead and not likely to be dead?"

Q: But I'm sure you also gave a view and observations of your life and art process that were different from the myth and history events captured so far in the Rolling Stones' printed documentation.

A: It took him a long time to believe me. I have to stand up for David because it wasn't as simple as that. Yes, he was a Rolling Stones fan, but that in itself shouldn't be a problem. The interviews went on for hours. It was so dreadful. Those first two weeks, we would start in the morning. David would sit there and ask me. He's kind of conservative, but a loon. He didn't know me at all. He came up with all the preconceptions that everybody else does. It was Ellen Smith, my press agent, who said to me, "Think of him as everyman. He's just coming to you with everybody's preconceptions. Think of him as everyman."

Q: And for once, you had the opportunity and forum to tell your side of the story. The truth you saw and experienced. You were in control.

A: Well, I didn't realize that, ya know. That's what made it so hard for Dalton. He kept saying to me, "This is your book! This is your thing! I will only do what you want." But I didn't believe him. What he did suggest . . . The first two weeks were a nightmare. He would sit there and say, "Marianne, what exactly happened, and what were you doing on March 10, 1965?" Didn't work at all. Then he got into despair. After two weeks, I remember the taxi came to take him away and I said goodbye to him, and it was so typical of the way I am, and Allen (Ginsberg) knows this backwards, as Dalton was leaving my house, after we toured the castles of Ireland and he met my friends, his mind had been completely blown. I had been very funny and told lots of stories. But at the very end, just sorta in my way, "Well David, you do know these are just my 'party pieces.'" And on that, poor bastard, he went back to the States. So he was in despair. So his next thing was that I would take "truth serum." Sodium Pentathol. [Laughs] He had some serious preconceptions. And he thought I was lying. [Laughs] So for three years, two years in, suddenly it all fell into place.

Like I would tell him a story, like "Dylan Redux," and he did not believe it. And then Demelza came up from Cornwall, I hadn't seen her in fifteen years. She walked into my brother's house, she sat down and told him, without even consulting me, exactly the same story. So then Dalton began to realize I was telling the truth. I was there! I ended up adoring David. He's one of my best friends now.

Q: Did photos trigger recall of events?

A: No. I've been carrying this around for a long time. And I had remembered the things that were important to me, which were always the same. It was always very, very clear that what I was really interested in and always had been interested in was motive and psychic position. And why. There were a million things I could not remember, which are not interesting to me. Like most of the time I don't remember what people were wearing. I remember what Allen was wearing, because often, Allen would take his clothes off. So, I would know that and understand that. I would see Allen clothed and unclothed. And that's a very simple situation.

And I remember one thing, I think, is the White Ball and the black dress. So it's only on very clear demarcations like clothed, unclothed, black, white, that I really know exactly. Now Anita [Pallenberg] actually remembers things only through what we were wearing. 'Cause that's what she's interested in. I don't mean that as a put-down. But that's how she remembers things. When I say, "Do you remember such and such a day?" the way back for Anita is, "Oh yeah . . . You were wearing a red velvet . . . and I was wearing . . ." You'd dig her, man.

Just let me say, the best work David and I did was on the telephone, which I think is very fascinating.

Q: Can you be more honest over the telephone?
A: I'll tell you, exactly. Did you ever read *The Art of Memory?*

Q: No.
A: I read it, so I knew that there was a real key to this thing. And eventually, I suggested to David that we would choose a time of day, because we weren't getting anywhere. Around 7:00 P.M. in the evening, my time. I was in Ireland and he was in New York. I went about my day, and I went for my walk, and I had my lunch and I did my little things, nothing major, you know, just my little life. And all day I would be thinking about the time period we were in. Every night at 7 o'clock, I would call Dalton and he would put the little machine on into the phone, and I think that not seeing him, and not having another human being (there), and being on the phone—which is something I learned from being in the program, how to use the phone—and that would really free up a lot of . . . And the fact that all day I had been thinking about it and I knew, as the weeks and the months would go by, I'd always know where we were. I write longhand with pen on legal paper. Helps memory. The real stuff.

Q: Was it hard during the interviews and the collaboration with David Dalton to tell your point of view? I would imagine you had to at times be combative.
A: Yes. I thought it was really good for me and about fuckin' time I learned to do that. I didn't want to. I resisted it, but I had to. I had to. David is married to a very intelligent woman, Coco, and she really worked very closely with him, and I think it had some impact. It was much harder work than David had ever done before. A living person.

I cut out some things about Brian Jones. He went on and on and made him much worse of a person than he was. He could only do that really because he was dead. He couldn't go on and on about Keith (Richards) and Anita, or even me, because I did the classic Buddhist thing: I just did a "drive all blames into one." I made that decision. That is something I learned from Allen. I've had good Naropa training. The galleys were hard to read.

Q: I got from the book you were a poetry-head.

A: Always. That's one of the reasons I love Allen so much. And William Burroughs.

Q: And, needless to say, one of the things that drew you to the music and word work of Bob Dylan. I noticed you were in one of the hotel room scenes in Bob Dylan's "Don't Look Back" film that chronicled his 1965 British tour. In your book, in the "Dylan Redux" chapter, you provide a real cool glimpse of Dylan in action in the mid-'60s and then years later. I thought it was one of the sections where you and David Dalton worked really hard in bringing the moment to the reader.

A: I think that was the bit that David did best. I didn't work the hardest on that, David did. But it was wonderful. I wish he'd written the whole book like that. And all the Bobby Neuwirth stuff was so beautiful.

Q: Had you never seen a rock-'n'-roll person like Dylan or an American like him in 1965?

A: Never. Never seen. Never in my wildest dreams could I have imagined anyone like Bob in 1965. His brain . . . but I was frightened. I didn't know they were probably more scared of me. I don't know. They were all on methedrine. He played me the album, "Bringing It All Back Home," himself on his own. It was just amazing. And I worshipped him anyway. That was where I got very close to Allen 'cause Allen was the only sort of person I could recognize as being somewhat like me.

Q: I really enjoyed the passage in your book when Allen came to London with the Italian poet, Giuseppe Ungaretti. They read at Queen Elizabeth Hall. You had spent some time with Ginsberg during Dylan's "Don't Look Back" tour, and I laughed out loud as you described inviting Allen to the house you shared with Mick Jagger. Until this book, I never knew you were such a Beat Generation poetry fan.

A: [Smiles] I find them very sexy, all those guys. Wonderful. I teased Allen in my book. I adore him. The first time I went to Naropa, Allen was literally by my side, like he is. There was a lot of criticism and, "Who is the woman?" "Why do you (Allen) think she can do this?" And he didn't say anything. "I just do." And then I came back again. We are very good friends. He also represents a lot of things for me that aren't part of our friendship or our relationship. He is the greatest living American poet.

Q: In the book, you write that some of the Rolling Stones' characters, in their songs, came out of acid.

A: Of course they did. I don't think acid is relative or relevant anymore. I wouldn't do it again. But I think that it was important then, and I think it taught us a lot.

Q: I don't want to dwell on recovery, but it's a part of your book. You mention your doctor; you now have a support group, and so many people are happy for you.

A: It's okay. For me, I needed a lot of things. I needed the program. I needed a sponsor. I needed to not drink or do any drugs . . .

Q: I don't want to "boundary-violate."

A: But I'm not in the program. Look at me. I'm having a vodka martini! When my mother died, I decided to leave the program. And I think I did the right thing for me. I had a great shrink, as you know from my book, and he's still there if I need him. I can still go and see him. He's a really great man. I think it was a real bad habit. But I got into it when I was very young. And I was part of the generation that grew up believing in the drug culture. We really did believe it. We made an investment in it. And it nearly killed me. I had to make a really clear decision. That if I wanted to live and do my work, I couldn't use narcotics. I feel really, although I got a lot from the drug culture, it was, in a way, a waste of my time. And that's all I can really say. I think people are beginning to see that. And I think something is changing in the world. Thank God I've never done crack. For those of us who are very sensitive, and that is a lot of us, the minute you take a strong narcotic, you open a door to Hell. In, from that door, come all these unbearable demons.

Q: Are you happy there has been a plethora of books on Brian Jones and kind of a musical re-evaluation of his many instrumental talents?

A: I use Brian. I have a whole lot of friends on the other side that I call up when I need them. I use Brian, Janis, and now I've got Tony Secunda and Denny Cordell. Well, Brian was a genius, but he was a very irritating person. Keith really loved Brian.

Q: In reading your autobiography, I also learned that your first husband, the artist, John Dunbar, played a lot of jazz all the time—John Coltrane, Eric Dolphy, Charles Mingus, Charlie Parker. He was into bebop jazz.

A: Hmmm. Last night, after my gig at a great blues club in San Diego, we drove up the West Coast on the Pacific Coast Highway and discovered your local jazz station, KLON-FM 88.1. It was fantastic driving home and hearing full long cuts by Art Pepper and Cannonball Adderley.

Marianne Faithfull, 2002. Photo by Mary McCartney, courtesy of Virgin Records.

Q: One of Brian Jones' sons is named Julian, after Julian "Cannonball" Adderley. How did it feel, singing and interpreting "Ruby Tuesday" on the recent Rolling Stones symphonic tribute collection?

A: I loved it! I have a feeling Chris Kimsey, the producer, is very close to the Stones. I think Mick and Keith, particularly. Keith said to Chris, "What you should do is 'Ruby Tuesday' with Marianne." 'Cause I was there when it was written. And Chris asked me if I would do two songs. He wanted me to do "As Tears Go By" and "Ruby Tuesday." And then gave me the green light to say, I would not like to do "As Tears Go By" again, I would just like to do "Ruby Tuesday." The point of the Kimsey Symphonic Rolling Stones album was, in a way, a mission to reveal Brian. It's dedicated to Brian. He wasn't as bad as everybody thinks.

I did "Ruby Tuesday" very simply. I think it's the best thing on the record. I'm very proud of it. I know people haven't heard it much, but I'm going to do it in my show when I start working with the band. We need to do "Ruby Tuesday." I've always felt it was about me. I'm sure that's why Keith suggested it to Chris Kimsey. [Laughs] They were all very much in love with me at that time. Not only me, but I was one of the many women they were in love with. Keith and I are still very close. I'm under his wing and I know I will always be under his wing.

I mean, I pushed them away so much. It's my fault. The door is open completely. I had to push them away, I suppose, to find my own spot. Much too much. Mick, too. 'Cause I couldn't stay in that position.

Q: I still dig the band, and always go to see them play, but . . .
A: Don't be too harsh on Mick. [Smiles] You'd really like him and he'd support you. He's a good guy.

Q: Let's talk about your album, "A Secret Life." The recording begins with a spoken word excerpt from Dante's *Divine Comedy* and concludes with a passage from Shakespeare's *The Tempest*.
A: I could tell you and you'd understand, exactly. I had been working with Angelo for maybe a half a year before we finished. I'd come to New York after faxing my lyrics, or fragments, to him in New Jersey. We work very intensely. He works in the city. I was going home for my walks and meditation. And the night before I left, Angelo called me, "Marianne. You are going back to Ireland." He would give me homework missions. "Go back to Ireland and write a manifesto of everything you are, who you are, and what you believe in." I could not. You want me to write a manifesto? He said eight lines. I was devastated. I got home. I tried. I tried to put into eight lines the essence of my life. I just couldn't. So, I turned to Dante. "When in doubt . . ." Then the last thing from *The Tempest*. They are the perfect manifestos of this record.

Q: Throughout all your recording career, you've included speech or narrative aspects to your vocal singing style. You never had a "Motown" voice.
A: [Laughs] It's something I've done all my life. Listen to "Jaberwocky." I've always included the spoken word. The talk. To their credit, really, the music business let me do it.

Q: What about writing lyrics for "A Secret Life?" You also co-wrote the songs, "Sleep" and "The Wedding," with Irish playwright Frank "Someone to Watch over Me" McGuinness.

A: "The Wedding" is a very highly complex lyric. We worked on it. It's a real story and it develops, and in the middle of the song you get references to what happened before and you also get a little bit of what will happen in the end. He's also a great writer. Frank and I both know the cut-up method, but what Angelo wanted was much more fragmented than what we were able to do. To be like that with me is very clever, very bright. It gets me to work much harder. Angelo liked the short-form, cut-up methods. He encouraged fragments. What we were examining was where William Burroughs exists anyway. I think William is the greatest lyrical poet of our time. And his books are that. I wrote lyrics for music to be songs.

Q: In the notes to "A Secret Life," supplied by Island Records, you said, "This record is about love, sex and doubt."

A: It's very clear, and lays it all out very honestly. It's moody and complex. The album deals with a lot of darker themes that I've always explored, but I think it's also got a great sense of hope to it—which I think will be a big surprise to everyone who still thinks that "Broken English" is who I am.

I am very into the craft of my work. The bit I like is when you have the rough stuff down and then you shape it and get it all. We put the vocals down on a rhythm pad and a bit of drum machine. The orchestrations were added later, with the drum machine and the rhythm pad being wiped out. Then he would take my vocals. It was a collaboration, and I trusted him. Real strings. Thank you, Island Records.

[In a recent interview with Tower Records' *Pulse!* magazine, Badalamenti described the project as "a woman's score—it's a conceptual, beautiful story, told in song and recitative, that runs the gamut of a woman's emotional and passionate life. Marianne sent me a number of fragmented ideas which gave me the opportunity to get to see inside this person and these melodies. Marianne and I hit it off together very well."]

Q: And the formal recording process when it came to capturing your vocals?

A: Angelo and I worked together very closely on the writing. But when we had got that, he wanted me to put down these brilliant vocals and he did get good vocals. That's what Angelo is known for in the business. That's how he got the gig with David Lynch. Angelo is known, that if you have a problem with a female vocalist or, in those days, "you know the man for the gig," it's Angelo Badalamenti. Our record went on for three years. It was the same length as the book.

Q: "A Secret Life" is a very important record for you.

A: Having done the book means that I can put down the past and move beyond it; this album has a very strong sense of putting my burden down.

In 2002, while Marianne was touring the U.S. to promote her new CD, "Kissin Time" [*sic*], I called her New York hotel to talk to her again, for *HITS* magazine. During our telephone conversation, Marianne, supportive as always, wanted to know about my book, and we discussed some of the characters to be found within these pages.

Q: Andrew Loog Oldham, who produced and managed the Stones 1964 to 1967, has included both of us in his 2*Stoned* autobiography, and you were included in his *Stoned* effort. I talked to him for this book. A fascinating character and writer who discovered and launched you.

A: Andrew reads so well in print, Harvey. He's a genius and a really, really good writer. *Stoned* was very well written. I wasn't surprised by his ability on the printed page. Not at all. He was always good with words and slogans and that's why he was such a genius. Imaginative press releases when I first broke. He was one of the people who made up my book. I loved my bit in *Stoned* of course, but what I really loved, and I told him this, he knows, I loved all the detail. "I was wearing a green jacket with a check button-down shirt . . ." I just loved that. Because it's just something I don't have. Andrew really does remember.

Q: Jack Nitzsche, whom you knew for decades and did some recording with in the 1960s, is in *This Is Rebel Music.* I used to see him at your live gigs when you played Hollywood.

A: Jack went to all my live shows . . . Brilliant man. My greatest feeling is incredible regret that we never made a record together. I'm sorry to be like that. I can't help it. It wasn't all his fault. I mean, the moment when he really wanted to make a record, after "Broken English," I was high, and he was clean. And then, when I came back to him, he was high and I was clean [Laughs]. It just went on and on like that, ya know. We could never quite get it together. Yet, it's the greatest regret of my life that Jack and I . . . We do have "Sister Morphine," but what we were going to do . . . I have a tape of Jack's ideas for songs for my record, and it's so wonderful.

Q: For this book, I've also included an interview I conducted with Berry Gordy, Jr., around the publication of his autobiography, *To Be Loved.* His book describes British music fans, and people in and around bands, like you, around 1964, '65, '66, really being hit hard by the music of his Motown Records label.

A: I was just talking to my manager last night about Motown! I told him, and I can tell you, that while Andrew turned me on to Phil Spector and Jack Nitzsche, Bob Crewe and the Four Seasons, the Mamas & the Papas, and a lot of things, the person who really educated me on the Motown level was Mick. I would have never really gone that deeply into Motown without Mick. We just played the songs at home constantly. It must have been great fun for him. There I am at nineteen and I've never listened to the Miracles before. "The Tracks of My Tears . . ." Mick would run down bass lines, song constructions on the label, and actually act out the songs in front of me! [Chuckles] And to this day I'm sure some Motown songs are in the Stones' live repertoire. It was really an amazing education. And of course, when I wanted another type of thing, I'd go see Keith and then it was all blues. It all kind of fitted in somehow.

Mick and I wore out the grooves on the records so much that we would have to buy them again. For a long time it was Vivaldi and Marvin Gaye in the morning. That's how we lived. Which is so wonderful. And I had Mick telling me everything. He knew everything. He knew the names of the session musicians at a snap. So did Jack Nitzsche.

Q: I just did a series of interviews with the Funk Brothers, the surviving Motown session men who are featured in the documentary film, "Standing in the Shadows of Motown."

A: Oh God . . . I'm dying to see that movie. Oh man . . . Oh man . . . Nice to see the players get some attention. I like the idea that Berry Gordy still cares that much. He cares about the Motown legacy and we're not just talking about money. There's something he did there that he cares very much about. It's incredible. Obviously, he knows what he did, but for me, it changed my life.

Hmmm. Mick knew the Motown records already, but they knocked me for six. That's why I know about the Four Tops doing "Walk Away Renee." I spent years listening to Motown. Smokey Robinson . . . His voice . . . The most beautiful stuff I've ever heard . . . "The Love I Saw in You Was Just a Mirage." [Sings the first two lines.]

I found Stax Records myself. I was very lucky.

Q: And your mate Keith Richards was a fan of Stax and Motown as well. Well, maybe more into the vulva of Chess Records 45s. I write to his "Wingless Angels" album.

A: I really liked that record, too. I loved it. It's just lovely. I put it on when I want to relax, chill and smoke a spliff. I've actually sat with Keith in Redlands listening to the Wingless Angels.

Keith Richards:

Papa Is a Rolling Stone

I did this interview with Keith Richards in San Diego while the Rolling Stones were concluding the second leg of their 1997–1998 American tour. The band had just released "Bridges to Babylon" (Virgin Records), their latest full length recording, and it was just before another tune from the CD, "Saint of Me," was issued as a single. The video was already airing on MTV.

Sunset Boulevard has geo-piety for the Rolling Stones. Much of their most classic and exciting music has been recorded on Sunset at RCA Studios, Sunset Sound, and at Ocean Way Studios, where both "Voodoo Lounge" and "Bridges to Babylon" were cut. Keith Richards and Mick Jagger, d.b.a. The Glimmer Twins, along with Don Was, are the executive producers on "Babylon."

A year before this interview, during a session one evening at Ocean Way, Keith Richards, the Stones' guitarist/singer/band leader, explained to me a new recording project he had just done with Rob Fraboni in Jamaica, "Wingless Angels," a collection of six Nyabinghi Rastafarian drummers and Sister Maureen in a drum, chant, and vocal forum. Richards also serves as executive producer on the just-released "Wingless Angels" offering, and it appears on his own Mindless Records label. "I'll talk to you 'bout it when we (Stones) tour," he promised.

The first time I really met the Rolling Stones was through drummer Charlie Watts, who invited me to their 1997 "Babylon" sessions. We talked a lot during breaks and meals with another visiting drummer, Jim Keltner, about L.A. and Hollywood's jazz history. A couple of years

Keith Richards during the Wingless Angels recording sessions.
Photo by Max Vadukul, courtesy of Raindrop Services.

earlier, Charlie had penned a liner note to an album audio biography I produced with Buddy Collette. I had a very long chat with Ron Wood one night, and he was very pleased to know that, yes, I did see his local 1979 New Barbarians show with Keith and friends at the L.A. Forum. I gave him the set list off the top of my head. Keith was immediately informed that I went to their gig, instead of my high school ten-year reunion that evening. "Come sit with us for dinner, mate," was the invite.

Keith really busted up when I reminded him that legend has it he once purchased an original copy of Albert King's LP "The Cool Sounds of Albert King," at the local Ash Grove music venue in 1968 for $75.00. That was news at my high school all semester. I then had to see King next time he played the Ash Grove.

During the week I was around "Babylon" tracking and mixing, Mick Jagger was very friendly, and most receptive to an instructional basketball narration album I produced on UCLA basketball coach John R. Wooden, that I gave him for his father, Joe Jagger. Mick was moved by the gesture. From my work and recording with Wooden, I learned that both Wooden and Joe Jagger, a physical education instructor and a former member of the British Sports Council, helped introduce the sport of basketball to Great Britain around the 1956 Olympic Games, held in that country. I later arranged for Wooden to send over a signed copy of one of his basketball coaching books for the elder Jagger that Mick requested be sent to his office in England.

If you know that Mick Jagger played basketball in school, and not soccer, you can further comprehend his stage moves and body dynamics when the Rolling Stones give a concert. One evening, Jagger, Bernard Fowler, a background singer with the Stones, and I watched the Chicago Bulls win an NBA playoff game on the lounge television set.

During a "Bridges to Babylon" tracking date one late evening, while Keith sang "How Can I Stop," producer Don Was and I talked about Keith's ability to deliver a tune. Between all the new and expanded education I had been receiving on classic rockers like Eddie Cochran and reggae music from Keith during small lounge chats and meals (he likes his steak—from the Pinot Hollywood restaurant—medium-well, sometimes with a vodka and cranberry juice), I mentioned to Don Was while Keith took a break from a take, what a wonderful singer he is, in addition to his writing and musical skills. "He's a great singer. He's a great singer, man," Was acknowledged. "He's like Willie Nelson, in the sense that Willie doesn't differentiate between his guitar playing and his singing. He just shifts his performance from one instrument to another. Obviously, anyone who can play like Keith can communicate on an intense level. I think Keith is a sensitive guy. He's tuned in to shit that most people miss. He hears. He's so quick and aware. He's plugged in to pain and he's plugged in to truth."

Often Keith would sing behind a music stand draped with images of Bob Marley and James Brown on display.

After "Bridges To Babylon" came out, I saw two marvelous L.A. Stones gigs at Dodger Stadium. At "Bar Babylon" before each concert, Keith greeted guests and friends and picked the CDs that played in the lounge area: "B.B. King Live at the Regal," and "The Ronettes' Greatest Hits"—that pleased producer Phil Spector, who was at one of the shows. Bob Marley and the Wailers were also in rotation.

A few months earlier, while mixing a reggae-type number for "Bridges to Babylon," "You Don't Have to Mean It," that Keith and Fraboni collaborated on, drummer and Stones musical pal, Jim Keltner, had remarked to me at a break in the action, "In every musician's life, there are hopefully people who point you in the right direction musically. I've been blessed to have had Keith Richards be one of those people in my life. He's one of the great late night DJs of all time." I second that emotion.

After witnessing a stellar Las Vegas Stones event at the MGM Grand Hotel in late November, still recovering from Charlie Watts' drumming all evening, I think it had something to do with the indoor arena venue and the best seats in the house we purchased, plans were made for a formal recorded interview with Keith backstage before their early February San Diego concert at Qualcomm Stadium.

Sagittarius, now 54, Keith Richards talks to you, not at you. Clad in jeans, open blue shirt, green scarf, black leather jacket, pants tucked inside his boots, hair a black-turned-to-gray color, beneath his lined face of experience is still the choirboy who performed for the Queen in the Royal Festival Hall and Westminster Abbey.

Keith greeted me holding a drink—what else, vodka and cranberry juice—and then asked, "How's Mr. Jack Nitzsche?"

"Saw him last Monday," I replied. "Jack remembered cruising with you in your car in England in the late '60s, listening to a tape loop of Lowell Fulson singing 'Tramp.'"

"[Laughs and nods] And did you see Marianne [Faithfull] when she did her last L.A. gig?"

"Yes I did."

"Heard from Jimmy Lee [Keltner]?"

"I talked to him yesterday."

Keith Richards is more telepathic than any of the X-Men characters.

Keith was delighted to have a half-hour to discuss "Wingless Angels" and also reflect on the current Rolling Stones U.S. tour. "Good one, lad," Richards grinned, acknowledging an extra cassette machine that I utilized for the dressing room taping, while smoking a Marlboro, and I again realized what a generous musician/person, rare combo, the Dartford, Kent-born Keith Richards is.

He is such a warm human being. As I unwrapped a top of the line Maxell 90 tape for our talk, it sort of hit me that I was going to have a cool hang and record Keith, someone I had seen on a concert stage many times since the late 1960s.

I was happy, a little nervous, but was ready to run the floor on the fast break. Keith had already vibed I had done my advance work digesting the tasty and beatific "Wingless Angels" CD his office had sent over a month ago to my front door.

I was going to be talking to someone I had made a connection with many times before. Besides, his music already defined him to me. He's not here to kibbitz; this is his life.

When you have a conversation with Keith Richards about music, or a specific album, tape, record, or CD, his unique insights and commentary about the environment and the process of that recorded document later make you investigate and hear and find further details about other tapes and vinyl in your own collection. The man really is his music. And he's totally open and cooperative when answering questions. Incense burned in the small room, with a couch and a chair as the only furniture.

Keith Richards with the Wingless Angels. (l to r) Richards, Bongo Locksley, Bongo Neville, Justin Hinds, Bongo Jackie, Warrin Williamson, and Sister Maureen. Photo by J. Bouquet, courtesy of Raindrop Services. (Tony is not pictured.)

During our very brief "sound check," before the *innerview* (not really an *interview*), I tossed out an opening remark about the smoke and the ashtray full of incense. As a

very young child in England around 1944 or '45, Keith had witnessed V1 raids and seen plenty of smoke, ruins, and rubble from World War II.

When we talked, he was eager to detail "Wingless Angels" to me, on February 3, 1998, 39 years to the day that Buddy Holly, the Big Bopper, and Ritchie Valens, and their pilot, died in an airplane crash.

Throughout our exchange, Keith would often lean forward to highlight a point about the "Angels" and their debut disc on his label.

Q: When I last saw you, during the Rolling Stones' recording sessions at Ocean Way in Hollywood, you mentioned you were co-producing with engineer Rob Fraboni a collection of six Nyabinghi Rastafarian drummers and Sister Maureen. Now "Wingless Angels," on which you served as executive producer for your own Mindless Records label, has just been released. It's a recording of Rastafarian drum and chant sessions.

A: They sing like angels, but they can't fly. I'm referred to as Brother Keith. The label emerged out of the recording. This started after the "Voodoo Lounge" tour. Recorded in my front room. It's evolved over the years, and each time I visited Jamaica I would drum and chant with the Rasta bred'ren. The recording was done on HDCD, with like four microphones, and you can hear frogs, crickets around the weed [Laughs]. Actually, the Wingless Angels come from Steer Town, and you might know the work of one of the members, ska legend Justin Hinds, who years ago had the Dominoes' "Carry Go Bring Come." A vocal harmony group. The drums are kept at my house (in Ocho Rios) in the hills of Jamaica. These are "healing meditations." They've been friends and family for over twenty-five years. They like to play, and are full of life and energy.

Q: I know a little bit about the Nyabinghi sect, which the Angels follow, and the Biblical dietary laws, and the one-drop drumbeat. And then there were the supplemental sessions you produced in New York with fiddle player Frankie Gavin, and bass added to the mix, as well as your own subtle guitar parts. Run down the healing and the soundwaves.

A: The healing aspects, yeah. I was always aware of it because I played with those guys for many years. That's what I do in Jamaica, apart from a few other things [Laughs]. And we gather around and play. And it always has that effect on us. They'll be the first ones to say why we do it. Because it heals us after the day, you know, the struggles of the day. In a way, I think it has something to do with the actual beat they play which is slightly under heart rate and it works on the human metabolism, even if you're not particularly listening to it or into it. If you're within earshot of it, it will affect you. It's soothing. It calms people down. It's good for the soul.

Q: During the recent Stones "Bridges to Babylon" tracking sessions, I remember you and Rob talking to Charlie in the studio about applying some of the drum set-ups you utilized during "Wingless Angels" to the "Bridges to Babylon" sessions. Like putting the front head back on the bass drum. Charlie Watts' drum head.

A: Yeah! I was working with Rob Fraboni, the same guy who recorded "Wingless Angels," which was primarily recording their drums and voices, and you become particularly intent on getting them right, ya know? And the fact is there's two heads on those drums and we figured out how to get a certain sound. Whereas in recording studios, ninety-nine and a half percent of the time, the engineer will have the front head of the bass drum taken off, and they stuff cushions in it and they ram microphones down it, and in actual fact, it deadens the drum. That's the easiest way to record a bass drum. And we wanted to record like a real bass drum. Charlie (during "Babylon") was very receptive. "Can you do that? It's been so many years since I've actually recorded with the skin on the front."

Q: Do you get a more natural drum sound? Like, can I hear it on the song, "You Don't Have to Mean It," from "Bridges to Babylon?"

A: There's no doubt that a drum is a cylinder with two skins, one on either side, and that's what really gives it a special sound. And I never realized that we were cutting drummers, especially Charlie, off from a whole half a drum. [Laughs]

Q: I have a friend, Chris Darrow, who used to be in the band, Kaleidoscope, and the Nitty Gritty Dirt Band, and twenty-five years ago did a solo album in the U.K. and put his Cajun fiddle on a song with a reggae group, the Greyhound. And, in a way, when I heard the Irish musician Frankie Gavin put fiddle in the Angels' chant, drum, African reggae thing you did, you know, it reminded me of what Chris did then, and I felt Gavin enriched the sound on your track. Afro-Celtic empathy. This stuff is pretty left-wing. But I also realized that the history of the music you are presenting as a producer and a label owner for this project goes way back.

A: Yeah. The melodies, the sounds, the Wesleyan hymns are from the British church and Scotland, then over to Africa. In a way this whole "Angels" thing is pretty left-wing. I didn't even intend to make the record. I got to Jamaica after the "Voodoo Lounge" tour just to kick back and write.

And some people came by from the Jamaican Film Board, and we were talking that night and they said, "You should record this." And in typical Jamaican fashion, with nobody saying anything, suddenly this truck arrives in my driveway. A recording truck from the Jamaican Film Board (grins). And I thought, "I've got the equipment. I've got the band. But, who's gonna punch the buttons?" These guys don't record just like that. Studios don't agree with 'em, because they're split up and you can't get the feel. Years ago we had a false start at a recording studio in Kingston, but tiny cubicles spread out. Then there's a knock on the door the next day, and Rob Fraboni turns up. He had just arrived in Jamaica to celebrate his wedding anniversary and I said, "Come here, you're working?" [Laughs.] And then, once we finished recording in Jamaica, I took it back to New York. I said, "I'm gonna try a few things on this. Experiment a little bit. I think, when we were recording, I heard other sounds. I'll play 'round with it." I get to New York, there's a knock on the door, and it's Frankie Gavin, who's the only guy. "I'm in town for two or three weeks. Got anything happening? Got any work?" So in a way, everything was thrown at me. I didn't plan this. Things started penetrating. I didn't intend to do it. But somehow it was occurring. So maybe, "Jah wonderful." Then Chris Blackwell came around one evening and heard what we had done, and said, "When you finish this, I'd like to put it out."

Q: How else did the "Wingless Angels" recording impact your recording activities as well as your work in the studio with the Stones?

A: With the Angels, I got very interested in ambient recording. The room is good if you know what you're doing. Use as few microphones as possible. All the tinkering, splitting things up can never achieve. The whole idea when you play music is to fill the room with sound. You don't have to pick up each individual instrument, particularly in order to do that. Because a band is several people playing something. And somewhere in the air of the room, that sound has to gather in one spot. And you have to find that spot (smiles).

Q: Are there advantages in knowing musicians who you know for twenty-five years and then record with them?

A: Yes. I've known them for a long time. That's the main answer. It was only years later that I was really filled in on the fact that they've never ever accepted anybody to play with them before. Black or white, or with an instrument. They were purely voice and drums. Over the years they invited me, and I don't know why.

They didn't know who I was when I first met them, if that means anything. The Rolling Stones meant nothing to them. They're fishermen divers who live in corrugated land-shacks and the Rolling Stones are not the first things on their menu, ya know.

Q: Do you like to write and record in Jamaica? I know the Stones' "Goat's Head Soup" was recorded in 1972 there. I totally dig the guitar in "Heartbreaker" by the way, even though it's out of tune with the electric piano. Maybe that's the idea.

A: [Laughs] Yeah. It's very easy to write in Jamaica. I don't find it difficult to write anywhere. But in Jamaica, it's particularly easy because they are so musically oriented, the Jamaicans. I mean, to be quite honest with you, the Jamaicans do nothing without music. Which for a musician is fantastic! Because, even if you're not playing music in your own house, you can hear half the town below in little villages and there's music playing. They do everything to music. It's an open environment when we record. You can hear the rain on the recording.

Q: A lot of trust in the scene?

A: Exactly.

Q: What did you gain from the initial recording of the "Angels" CD?

A: When you're recording something as seemingly simple as just drums and voices, for the first few days, microphone placement is very important. We're trying different angles. You never point the microphone actually at the instrument. You've got them in the corners pointing and once you've found those placements, you don't really change them. One of the joys of it was that you're not really aware that you're actually making a record. Yes, you are recording, but at the time I was recording it, I had no particular outlet for it. I mean, as I mentioned, Chris Blackwell came by that evening, "If you finish this, I'd love to put it out." You know, the whole thing was sort of handed to me mysteriously from above.

Q: For years I've been aware of Rob Fraboni's engineering and producing. I know he did a little bit of work on "Goat's Head Soup" in Los Angeles at Village Recorders. He also did Bob Dylan's "Planet Waves," and engineered and produced a lot of reggae. Twenty years ago I saw a Bob Marley Roxy gig with him and Blondie Chaplin, who was also there. He had produced Blondie's solo album and Blondie is on tour with you, while Rob did a lot of engineering and mixing as well on "Bridges to Babylon." What attracts you to his board work?

A: He knows an awful lot, man, about recording. He knows a lot about microphones and I've worked with him off and on for twenty-five years. Many years we didn't work together. Rob Fraboni is the only engineer I know, apart from, or maybe even including Jamaican ones, that knows these guys (Wingless Angels) for fifteen-odd years, ya know. The only guy who the Angels know, so there's no strangers in the room to inhibit the process. It has to have that feel. That's why we left on all the talk and some of the laughs.

Q: Have you, obviously of all people, noticed that time stands still when "Wingless Angels" is being played. Maybe it's the Jamaican location of the recording.

A: I think it's because it's timeless music. I mean, I've had African guys say, "This is more African than what is going on in Africa." I call it "marrow music." Not even bone music. It strikes to the marrow. It's like a faint echo . . . The body responds to it and I don't know why. You asked me earlier about "Goat's Head Soup." I was only really learning about Jamaica then, and when you're making records you're pretty much myopic. And it was only really after recording "Goat's Head Soup" and staying in Jamaica for several months, which was when I bumped into the Angels on the beach. And we got talking and playing. But in certain ways, Jamaica doesn't change that much. There's a very solid rhythm to life there, which they seem to be able to adapt even to incoming technologies that speed the rest of the world up. What I really love, I think, about Jamaica is that they have a rhythm all their own, and everybody, including yourself, after a few days you can't get out of step, man, you know?

Q: I know Sister Maureen co-wrote many of the chants and, I guess, joined, or was asked to join Wingless Angels during a gig at a Steer Town bar one night. I recall meeting Inner Circle, Jacob Miller, interviewing the Wailers, and I always noticed there were never any girls around in the studio. First you get on the team, then Sister Maureen. It's a heavy trip for a woman to be included, right?

A: Well, when I first met Wingless Angels, they wouldn't let women in the room while they were playing, let alone play with 'em. That's one of the changes, which is good.

Q: What did she bring into the recording?

A: She brought women into it. She stopped segregation. [Bongo] Locksley is the main man and he said, "You gotta hear what we're doing." O.K. "Sure, I'll pop up." Then he said, "We've got this chick in," and he started explaining it to me [Laughs]. "You guys?" You know, a woman in the band! Times change, you know what I mean. And she brought a lot of strength. A lot of new influences. And she brought the woman's touch in. That soft touch.

Q: What's it like, the mix, the recording? I noticed during the Stones' recording sessions it's very collaborative, lots of involvement in detail.
A: With the Angels, it's kinda like miking it. Once you've got the basics set up, the first two or three mixes are difficult because you're still searching, and then suddenly, it clicks. "We'll put the drum there," and then, "We'll hold that." After that, you can almost go through the rest of them and keep those same settings, because the music itself is not going to change.

Q: What's the best way or atmosphere to hear "Wingless Angels?"
A: Flat on your back, with some partners, rum, and weed [Laughs].

Q: Let's talk about the Rolling Stones.
A: Surely.

Q: I've seen both outdoor and indoor shows and the sound fills the stadium. I have a blast at the gigs. How has the tour been going?
A: Fantastic, man. The stadium parts have been great. I've never known a tour to go . . . You kind of accept usually when you start a tour for it to have its high points and low points and you start to go for a happy medium, and hope there's more high points than low. But this one is not like this. Very strange, but since Chicago, day one, the band and the sound, and the whole feel of it has gone on a steady upward plane. The graph looks amazing. As far as the band's feeling good, I think it's got a lot to do with the new sound system, and with Robbie McGrath, the mixer—he has really got our live thing down. I mean, we've got the guitars where we want them. But I think it's a mixture of that and also the experience of the band.

Q: Did the "Wingless Angels" experience have an impact on the way you play with the Stones now on this tour? You know what I'm trying to say. I think I can hear it in the live show, more holes, a little bit?
A: I'm playing a little different on this [new] tour. Yeah. I'm more conscious of dynamics. It's exactly what it's about. To make a record like the Wingless Angels, "Oh this is a great little pastime . . . a hobby" when you're doing it. You are not thinking in terms of that. But when you've finished it, you realize that you've learned a whole lot about

Mick Jagger and Keith Richards of the Rolling Stones at the Forum, Inglewood, California, November 1969. Photo by Kurt Ingham.

recording and music from like ten guys or so who live up in the hills in Jamaica, and they've taught me, or re-taught me, or reminded me of like the spaces that can be left, and that silence is your canvas, and never forget it.

Q: And what about playing on the second stage? A smaller place right in the middle of the stadium for a set of tunes that I know really involves the audience. Not that they haven't gotten their ass kicked from the gigantic full stage show they've also seen.

A: It's beautiful, great. It's another thing. Once you're on the stage, it's just some floorboards in spite of it. And you're not really aware of everything you are seeing. But what really keeps tours going and alive for the band, and therefore for the audience I think, is to change it and to play the smaller joints indoors. And the small stage with the show. It's necessary to change the scale sometimes. Otherwise you can really get used to the large thing. And you realize when you're playing a small gig that you get the dynamics back, and you can re-translate that back to the big stage.

Q: When you and the Stones were recording "Bridges to Babylon," did you know immediately that some of the songs would really work well in the live show? I'm so glad you're now singing "Thief in the Night" in the set. For weeks, everybody at Ocean Way in the hall would hum the melody to each other. And, I know that "Out of Control," which is sort of Mick's tune, really has become a show-stopper.

Keith Richards with Harvey Kubernik, backstage at Qualcomm Stadium, San Diego, California, during the "Bridges to Babylon" tour, 1998. Photo by Bob Sherman.

A: With these new Mick songs, like the things done with the Dust Brothers, I like to get my hands on them live. We've rehearsed "Too Tight" as well. In a way, maybe when you write songs without even knowing it, you're kinda saying, "Can I do this live?" And so in a way you add that in. You don't know if it's gonna work, but I guess what you keep in the

back of your mind is, "We're making a record here; what happens if they all like it and we gotta play it live?" So, in a way, maybe in the back of the mind that sets up the song to be playable on stage.

Keith and I then concluded our interview session, had a minute to talk briefly about Lenny Bruce as I packed up my equipment, and took a photograph together just before the show.

Epilogue:

Harvey Kubernik Visits Roger Steffens and His "World of Reggae Featuring Bob Marley"

Thousands of artifacts, album covers, photos, and the vast reggae archives and monumental Bob Marley collection of reggae activist/scholar, Roger Steffens, were displayed until September 30, 2001, in an exhibition housed in the English Village at the Queen Mary ship, docked in Long Beach, California. The exhibition is now touring globally.

Steffens, who has written dozens of liner notes for Bob Marley, Peter Tosh, and Bunny Wailer (and scores of others), is a world-renowned reggae music historian. From 1979–1987 he co-hosted the award-winning, internationally syndicated "Reggae Beat" radio program on L.A.'s NPR outlet, KCRW, and is also the founding editor of *The Beat* magazine, the premiere reggae and World Beat periodical, for which he edits an annual Bob Marley collectors' edition. He is co-author of *Bob Marley: Spirit Dancer*, and currently co-writing Bunny Wailer's autobiography, *Old Fire Sticks*, as well as *Bob Marley and the Wailers: The Definitive Discography; Bob Marley: An Oral History;* and a Vietnam memoir called *The Island of the Coconut Monk*. In 1995, Roger performed for me at a "Rock-'n'-Roll in Literature" Great Writers series that I curated and co-produced at the MET Theater in Los Angeles, reading from his "Nine Meditations on Jimi and 'Nam" chapter in the book, *Jimi Hendrix: The Ultimate Experience*. More recently, I produced a segment on Roger for a digital radio series for internet broadcast. In Spring 2002, Steffens served as a technical consultant, content provider, and on-camera featured interview subject in VH1 "Behind the Music" episodes on Bob Marley, Peter Tosh, the year 1970, and Alan Freed; "VH1 Confidential" programs on Tosh and Marley; and VH1's "Ultimate

**Roger Steffens in front of his archive, Echo Park, California.
Photo by Markus Cuff.**

Albums," which cited Marley's "Legend" album. Roger performed similar functions for "Soul Rebel" on PBS's "American Masters" series in 2001.

Steffens is also an accomplished actor and well-respected commercial voice-over artist, heard in films such as "Forrest Gump," "Wag the Dog," and "The American President," and is the narrator of an Oscar-winning documentary called "The Flight of the Gossamer Condor." And—check this—he is the corporate voice of Time Warner Audio Books, NARAS, the Museum of Tolerance, and the Seventh Day Adventist Church, and read Bill Gates' most recent book-on-tape, for which he was nominated for an Audie Award.

Goldmine magazine initially suggested that I file a story on my friend's Marley/reggae event. This is an expanded and unedited, full 2002 journal entry, not the word-restricted, condensed version that appeared in the magazine shortly after the 2001 opening.

"It's the great dream of my reggae life come true," exults Steffens, who was born June 17, 1942, one day before Paul McCartney, in Brooklyn, New York, at Israel Zion Hospital. "I tell my Rasta friends I was truly born in Zion," he beams.

"After almost thirty years, I've finally been able to open my collection to the public so that everyone can experience these amazing things that have been sitting in boxes in my basement." Steffens' house in Echo Park, California, has been the location of his personal reggae archives that were culled for this exhibit. His landmark collection contains 20,000 hours of tapes, 12,000 records and CDs, 10,000 flyers and posters, 3,000 hours of video, 25 four-drawer file cabinets of alphabetized clippings, plus uncounted thousands of reggae T-shirts, buttons, and other artifacts from the history of the music and the Rastafarian faith that animates it. Visitors to the Queen Mary only get a taste of his melodic obsession, selected from his three decades' accumulation of Jamaican music and memorabilia.

Now the whole world gets a chance to see, hear and feel what has literally until now only been available to Roger's friends and family.

Over the last twenty-five years, there have been some very interesting visitors and "lifers" to Roger's Echo Park home, just a mile or so from the Queen of Angels Hospital where I was born overlooking the 101 Freeway. Dig on the guest list: The Wailers band with six original members; British reporter/photographer Tim Page, who was Roger's roommate in Berkeley for two years in the 1970s, where writer Michael Herr would fall by when the ark-hives were just beginning to build; Richard Boyle; Toots Hibbert; Bunny Wailer; Ben Harper; Burning Spear; Danny Sims; Nina Simone; Remi Kabaka; Lee "Scratch" Perry; Richard Perry; Bob Marley's mother and most of his children; Robert Marley Jr. and Nzinga Garvey, granddaughter of Marcus Garvey; Oscar Janiger, the LSD researcher from the early 1950s at

UCLA; The Beastie Boys came in the mid-'80s; Phil Bunch; Paul Body; Michael Hacker; music journalist and film director Cameron Crowe, when he first came to Hollywood; Matt Groening—before "The Simpsons"—and many times since; actors John Ritter and Sinbad; the Minister of Finance of Jamaica; The Firesign Theater (member Peter Bergman is godfather to Kate, daughter of Roger and his wife Mary. They also have a son, Devon). My brother Ken definitely had his mind blown as well when he took the personal tour. Hundreds of reggae's top names have paid their respects along the way and had an engaging time.

It was also Steffens who recommended Ladysmith Black Mambazo to Jennifer Warnes (another visitor), six months before he told Paul Simon about them, but her record company wouldn't let her use them. One lazy

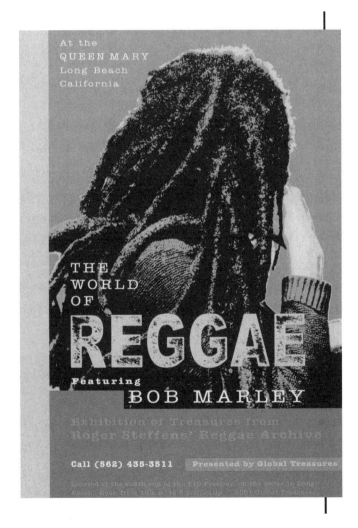

Courtesy of the Roger Steffens Archives.

Sunday afternoon, sometime in the 1990s, I bumped right into Carlos Santana at Roger's front door. I was happy learning what a hardcore record and tape collector he was as well.

In the late 1970s I had interviewed Carlos, along with Jerry Garcia, at Bill Graham's house for a *Melody Maker* collaborative story. I still carry something from that first conversation with him all those years ago: "I'm a vessel and a messenger for the music. And sometimes the bandleader."

A few years ago, *High Times* magazine brought Steffens over to Amsterdam, with Mountain Girl and Paul Krassner, for Bob Marley's induction as the first member of the Cannabis Hall of Fame. He lectured for three nights, while presenting and displaying some items from these archives at the Melkweg (Milky Way). He was then brought to the Hemp Fest sponsored by *High Times* in Oregon in July 1998, where he followed Ken Kesey and the Merry Pranksters on stage.

As I wrote portions of *This Is Rebel Music* and compiled and transcribed several of the texts and interviews over the last couple of years, I'd sometimes have Bob Marley's music playing within earshot. I'm also happy to confess that access to some of Steffens' rare Bob Marley and reggae tapes on a regular basis might have slightly impacted the results you read. Roger inspired me, too, letting me know that many of my own original long-form audio conversations and the subsequent interviews could translate into book form.

Today, I am now confronted and comforted by seeing some of Roger's collection inside the Queen Mary with a paid admission audience. "Curatorial Assistance," continues Steffens, "the Pasadena design firm that built the exhibition, took seven vanloads out of the house—and it didn't even make a dent. But there are still over 6,000 items on display. The catalog for it is a foot-square, 100-page full-color book with approximately 1,600 illustrations—and that's only about twenty-five percent of the actual stuff on display. And the exhibition is only one percent of my total collection. It's a great start though. I look at the Queen Mary show as a sketch for what will come as we begin to tour the world with it, doubling and tripling it in size."

The museum covers more than forty years of Jamaican music and art. This installation is not something put together by some academic, or geared solely for art students. The "sound" and images of reggae and Marley's impact and influence can be heard and felt by the serious reggae lovers, music fans, and anyone else who can feel the relationship that reggae has to doo-wop, rhythm and blues, and today's tunes on the airwaves. It is a reflection of Steffens' personal journey from the days of the birth of rock-'n'-roll, through the hippie consciousness of the '60s to the eruption of reggae into the world's ears from the early '70s forward.

"I'm a guy who saw Buddy Holly in person," says Steffens with evident pride, in his baritone broadcaster's voice. "I was lucky enough to be raised in

North Jersey, just across the river from New York City, at the birth of rock-'n'-roll, and I listened religiously to Alan Freed every night. I used to hang out at his radio station, WINS, and go to those wonderful huge stage shows of his in Times Square and in Brooklyn. I saw Frankie Lymon and the Teenagers, Chuck Berry, Bo Diddley, Jackie Wilson, Fats Domino, and even—prophetically perhaps—a group called the Dubs! One of the things I love about reggae is that it takes the best of the vocal harmonies of the '50s, marries them to the political commitments of the '60s finest music, and welds them to the beat of the healthy human heart at rest. It's irresistible and universal. There's nowhere today that you don't find reggae."

Beginning with the birth of Ska in the early 1960s and moving through the eras of Rock Steady, Reggae, Toasting (rap), Lovers' Rock, Two-tone and Ska Revival, Dub Poetry and through the present ascendancy of Dancehall and Raggamuffin, "The World of Reggae Featuring Bob Marley" is a sense-tingling experience. It's educational, entertaining, and rocks your eyes and ears. "We have a constant soundtrack in the exhibit," explains Steffens. "You can trace the whole history from the Folkes Brothers' 1959 'Oh Carolina,' which was the first real Jamaican record of locally created proto-reggae music, right through the end of the twentieth century. As each song plays, a spotlight falls on a record by that artist, so you can tell who you're hearing and what era it's from." The largest single display, of course, deals with the ice-breaking might and muscle of Robert Nesta Marley.

Before the opening-night reception, I went over to absorb the "World of Reggae Featuring Bob Marley" exhibition on the Queen Mary. I grabbed one of the striking event catalogs, with fantastic full-scale reproductions, and sent a signed book to Keith Richards as a birthday present last December. Paul McCartney also had his 1976 end-of-tour party for Wings on the ship. It's actually my third viewing. I've been hanging with Roger a lot this year as he prepared the display, and monitored things as they developed over the last few months with him.

Today, Harvey Robert Kubernik definitely needed another taste of Dub, Two-tone, Dancehall, Dennis Brown, Jacob Miller, Peter Tosh, Bunny Wailer, and Robert Nesta Marley.

I attended an Inner Circle recording session with Jacob Miller at the Record Plant, and interviewed the Wailers once at the old Island Records office on Sunset Blvd. in West Hollywood for *Melody Maker*. Let's just say that there was so much smoke in the room that I couldn't really see which Wailer I was speaking to, or at. I got so absorbed in the environment I forgot to turn on my tape recorder for the encounter! That's one of the reasons I now bring two cassette machines with me for field work.

I stood on the side of the stage in the wings with Peter Tosh and Mick Jagger, daughter Jade in his arms, and later brushed by Bob Marley when

Tosh joined him on stage for the legendary encore at the Burbank Starlight Amphitheater concert in 1978. Peter and Bob met backstage after Peter's surprise appearance in the middle of "Get Up, Stand Up." Tosh told Roger, "Mi slap Bob's hand and him say, "Bwoi, de Pope feel dat one." And three days later the Pope died."

Fred Shuster, music editor for the *Daily News* said it best when he cruised Roger's Queen Mary installation with me. "It may be the first museum exhibit you can dance to." The last time I talked to John Lennon was after a Wailers Roxy Theater show. I wish he could have seen and heard the reggae here.

"*The New York Times* called Marley 'the most influential musician of the second half of the twentieth century'," notes Steffens later, sitting in that Echo Park home. "Marley is still responsible for fifty percent of all the reggae sold in the world today, more than twenty years after his passing. That's unprecedented in any form of music. His sound is truly timeless—and most of all, his lyrics mean something. These are songs of solace, salvation, joy and healing. Not long ago, his rarest record, 'Selassie Is the Chapel' received a bid of $3,800. There are any number of $500-plus sides in his discography. Leroy Jodie Pierson, a writing partner of mine, and I have been working with Bunny Wailer and many others for the past ten years, compiling the definitive Wailers discography, and work continues through this day as new information comes to light. It's the never-ending Wailers, just as one of Bunny's albums was titled.

"I'm also about to publish another book with W. W. Norton in New York, a kind of follow-up to the *Spirit Dancer* book that Bruce Talamon and I did in 1994. Bruce and I met while touring with Marley in 1979, and he shot some of the most amazing pictures ever of Bob, both in the States and in Gabon, West Africa. The new book is a collaboration too, with Lee Jaffe, who in early 1973 was a precocious American filmmaker who ended up living with Marley and the Wailers for the next couple of years, playing harmonica on the 'Natty Dread' album, and producing Peter Tosh's debut, 'Legalize It.' It'll have hundreds of photographs from '73 to '76, plus fascinating accounts of Marley's first forays 'into foreign' as the Jamaicans say. It's called *One Love: My Life with Bob Marley and the Wailers*, and will be published on Bob's birthday, February 6, 2003."

To celebrate the world's first "reggae museum," the Queen Mary and sponsor Global Treasures held a grand opening gala in February 2002, with entertainment by Judy Mowatt, Marcia Griffiths, and Bob's son Ky-mani Marley, plus Bunny Wailer's Reggaestra orchestra and Psalms, Bunny's backing trio. They played to a standing-room-only, invited audience, studded with actors Bill Bellamy, Mario Van Peebles, Emilio Estevez, and Phil Proctor of the Firesign Theater, Sheila E., Ziggy and Rita Marley, and dozens more from the reggae firmament. The following day, Judy, Marcia and Ky-mani all toured the exhibit, fascinated by what they discovered. "There are so many things, you just can't see it all at once," said Judy. Marcia found covers on her albums that she had never seen before, and Ky-mani was deeply touched by a polaroid photo of his father, taken during his secret trip to Ethiopia in 1978. Ziggy and Rita Marley have also come by for a viewing, and left filled with enthusiasm, describing the exhibition as "amazing."

Other keen visitors have been Bunny Wailer, who brought his own film crew to shoot the exhibits for stills and video; Ras Michael; Santa Davis, Fully Fullwood and Tony Chin from the Soul Syndicate; Tippa Irie, the Britain-based toaster; Nigeria's Majek Fashek; Mikey Dread; Sugar Minott; Eek-A-Mouse; and members of the Twinkle Brothers, the Skatalites, Roots Radics, and Chalice, all delighted to find images of themselves on the walls of the sprawling exhibition. Favorite items included Joe Higgs' famous red beret; a drum head signed by crucial members of the Skatalites; and a poster signed by Marley and twenty-eight of the people closest to him in his life. Musicians could be seen throughout the recent Bob Marley Day weekend in Long Beach, bending down low to inspect the many columns of singles, nearly all of which are signed by the artists.

There is a film running in the introductory area, depicting the mini-history of the various styles of Jamaican rhythms. In the second, larger structure, a display brings viewers a film on the life story of Bob Marley, whose "Exodus" was recently chosen by *Time* magazine as "The Best Album of the Twentieth Century." There are 144 albums and twelve-inch sleeves, filling a double-sided wall, that show the wide range of images that have been used to market Marley's music. Three tall columns are filled with more than 300 seven-inch singles by Marley and his former partners in the Wailers—Peter Tosh and Bunny Wailer. There are also plaques and wall text materials, written by Steffens, that acknowledge Johnny Nash, Lee "Scratch" Perry, Coxson Dodd, and more than seventy other "featured artists."

Another major area is known as Haile Selassie Hall, where near-priceless objects from the life and palace of Selassie are on display. "One of my dearest friends is a white Rasta with a fourteen-pound clump of dreadlocks that hang to his knees, named Jim Marshall. Like his more famous namesake from San Francisco, this Jim 'Reggae' Marshall is a photographer, but, more importantly, a trained historian who has a world-class collection of Rastafarian artifacts that he has shared with us in the show. There's an autograph of Ras Tafari, before he became Emperor, and another of Haile Selassie on an envelope, postmarked at the United Nations the day he gave the 'War' speech that Marley set so memorably to music on the 'Rastaman

Vibration' album. There's a sword from 1800 that Selassie gave an American airman in 1943, and Coptic crosses dating back to the 1600s.

"You see, once you get into reggae, it leads to so many other things, because reggae is a music that you have to meet halfway. You must learn about the *patois* language spoken by most of the musicians, and about Jamaican folklore and history and politics, and especially Rastafari, the way of life that underpins the best of Jamaica's music. This leads to a study of Ethiopia and Africa and the Bible. After thirty years, I feel as if I'm just beginning to penetrate," Roger admits.

Over the years, Steffens has become a prime apostle of reggae's message. "It's all about peace and love, embodied in the Amharic (Ethiopian) word *wadada*. It's about non-violence, a resistance to aggression. But that doesn't mean that Rasta doesn't defend itself—it does. It's also about respect for the earth, and listening to its rhythms." Since 1984, Steffens has been lecturing around the world on "The Life of Bob Marley."

"It happened as a fluke. I got invited to participate in the National Video Festival, held in L.A. in 1984 at the American Film Institute. Bob Wisdom, one of the curators, asked me to show some of the 'unofficial' stuff I had in my archives of unreleased Marley material. It got such a great response that I started getting requests from local colleges to show these films and videos there, and eventually in nightclubs. I've even presented them at the bottom of the Grand Canyon for the Havasupai Indians, who regard Marley as the fulfillment of some of their ancient prophecies, and on the Hopi reservation in northeastern Arizona, where there is a huge community of Rasta-loving Indians. They all tell me that, because Bob was so tuned in to the planet, being a farmer himself, he understood their way of life. He's also revered by the Aboriginal people of Australia, the Maori in New Zealand, and 'first nations' everywhere.

"I'm not trying to make him out to be a saint," says Steffens, somewhat defensively, "because he was not. But the overwhelming majority of the actions he took in his life were, in fact, saintly. His business manager, Colin Leslie, confirmed to me that he was responsible for the direct support of some 6,000 people. Each month! He was like some medieval liege, from whom people regularly sought beneficence. And he helped virtually everyone who came to him. Jack Healey of Amnesty International says, 'Everywhere I go in the world today, Bob Marley is the symbol of freedom.' His legend is so incredible—and continues to grow every year. His greatest hits album, 'Legend,' has been number one cumulatively on the *Billboard* catalog chart longer than any album in the history of popular music. At the turn of this century, the BBC's 24-hour coverage used Bob's 'One Love' as the anthem of the millennium.

"The following year, he got a star on Hollywood Boulevard and the

Bob Marley in the Sports Arena dressing room, San Diego, California,
November 24, 1979. Photo by Roger Steffens.

Lifetime Achievement Award from the Grammys. But perhaps the most lasting honor came from the *New York Times*, whose millennial commemorations included the construction of a time capsule to be opened in the year 3000. They wanted to pick one video that would epitomize the best musical work of the twentieth century, so that people a thousand years into the future could experience that too. And the one they picked was 'Bob Marley Live at the Rainbow, London, 1977'!"

Steffens, who turned sixty in 2002, shakes his head as he reviews the course his life has taken. "It's totally unexpected, certainly nothing I ever thought I'd end up doing. I was a rock-'n'-roller, spent fifteen years in Catholic schools, was New Jersey State Champion in the American Legion National Oratory Contest, voted for Barry Goldwater, served twenty-six months in Vietnam working with refugees, came home and lectured against the war all during 1970 and then lived in Marrakech for a year when I didn't want to be an American anymore.

"By the early '70s, the music business had been usurped, taken over by the lawyers and accountants, and rock had died for lots of us '50s folks. But hearing Marley in '73 changed my life forever, and my life has gone on a far different path since that first moment of listening to 'Catch a Fire.' I've been able to bring that hope-filled message of redemption and love that Bob preached to the Rock and Roll Hall of Fame, to the Schomburg Center for Research in Black Culture of the New York Public Library, where I spoke alongside a hundred-year-old Black Cross Nurse, who had marched in Harlem in the '20s with Marcus Garvey. I've been brought to Paris, Japan, Amsterdam, Martinique, Hawaii, and Calgary to talk about Bob. And the few times I've tried to step away from this world through frustration or disillusionment, I've been snapped back into it so strongly that I know deep down that this is where my path must be."

The path finally brought Steffens to Kingston in July of 2001, to perform his Marley show for a hometown crowd of initially skeptical people that included many who had worked for Bob, grown up with him and otherwise felt they knew everything there was to know about him already. "Before the program at the University of Technology," Roger recalls, "the reviewer for the *Jamaica Gleaner* newspaper came up to me and asked me what I hoped to accomplish there that night. 'Well,' I said, 'I'd like to be able to leave the building alive.' He didn't even laugh, and then challenged me to tell him what I planned to do. 'I'm going to tell the half that's never been told.' 'What does *that* mean?' he snarled. I told him to just watch the show and if he still had questions, come back when I'm finished and I'd try to answer them. Well, that night was the first night since childhood in which I was actually nervous on stage. My wife remarked that she had never seen me that way before. But I ended up getting a one-minute standing ovation and the first guy up afterwards to shake my hand was the *Gleaner* writer. He wrote the most incredible review I've ever had, said, 'people's hands got sore from clapping.' A month later he was killed in a car crash in Kingston."

Steffens returned three months later. "In October of 2001, my wife and I were brought back to Kingston by the Jamaican government for two weeks of talks with a whole bunch of high muckety-mucks like the Minister of Finance, the rector of the University of the West Indies, the head of their Commerce Department, and the director of the Institute of Jamaica, which is like their Smithsonian. The outcome of all that was their commitment to purchase my archives—all six rooms floor-to-ceiling of our house in L.A.— and make them the National Museum of Jamaican Music.

"They want me to be their curator emeritus and come down for a couple of months every year to direct them as they build a home for my Queen Mary exhibition in one of their main tourist areas, perhaps Ocho Rios on the north coast. The more academic materials, the books, clippings and music, will be housed at the Reggae Studies Department of the University and at the Institute. They have agreed to my bottom lines—that the collection be kept intact forever and that it be made available to anyone who wants to use it. Imagine that—a white kid from Jersey who was able to give Jamaica back its own musical history, on which it had turned its back for the past forty years. What more could any collector hope for?"

"The World of Reggae Featuring Bob Marley" is an inspiring visitation. Steffens will be proudly schlepping his exhibit globally for the next ten years. It's the educational field trip that we never got in grade school. "This is a long way from the places they took us as kids from A.E. Wright Junior High in Calabasas," mused my pal Bob Sherman, on a visit to the installation at the Queen Mary in Long Beach.

After a recent birthday celebration at Roger's place in summer of 2002, I came home and programmed the Bob Marley and the Wailers "Babylon by Bus" CD as I sequenced my artist chapters to *This Is Rebel Music*. This just had to be the album to play as I crossed the victory line. How perfect it all felt as hundreds of pages of text on my office desk spilled over to a nearby carpet, while my speakers blared "Jamming" from the disc. Funnily enough, it was just released today in an expanded edition from the Universal Music Group, a record label I once worked for as West Coast Director of A&R. How precise and accurate the album's graphics and the recorded live Wailers' repertoire seemed to be at the moment to support, add depth, and enhance the choices and order of selections for my documented trek.

My book gig was now done. Tonight I was going over to a yearly bowling party record producer Phil Spector was having. It was a room packed with Phil's closest friends and his family, jazz-heads, recording studio veterans, label owners, my Rolodex®, music collectors, writers and authors and record geeks, all sharing an environment of confirmation and renewal. Honestly, even on the drive to the gathering, my own physical and emotional survival to arrival seemed to be marked by a "Glendale 2 North Freeway—Harvey Dr." exit sign.

Later at the party I told Roger Steffens that I had passionately sequenced *This Is Rebel Music* together, earlier in the afternoon, as the Bob Marley and the Wailers "Babylon by Bus" CD tracked for a few hours. The original LP had been culled from a series of concerts in Europe. I had luckily seen some of the regional live shows on the California leg of the same tour and told Roger that this recording served as a position rhythm to where I wanted my dialogues to be placed in the collection, akin to the map of California depicted on the "Babylon" package. "Well, you know," Roger explained, "they made a mistake on that map and placed the city of Santa Cruz above Berkeley!"

Whaat?!

"You shouldn't use that album as a compass," insisted the former Berkeley resident.

Then I confessed to Roger that when I was listening to "Kinky Reggae" and the rest of that newly re-mastered live album, it seemed rushed, loud, and hectic from the initial studio versions and other live renditions that I had previously heard many times of these same songs. "You should have told me that in the bottom of the ninth inning of *Rebel Music* you were assembling your book to 'Babylon by Bus,'" he stressed. "That really wasn't the album to play. It's not representative of the Wailers at *all*. In fact, it was a brief experiment in arena rock, and Marley told his two lead guitarists after the live recordings were completed, 'We don't do that no more!'"

Acknowledgments

For soul and inspiration, literary support, and sending me good vibes: Marshall and Hilda Kubernik, Ken Kubernik, Aunt Ray, Bob Sherman, Waldo, Johnny at Pink's, Michael Hacker, Denny Bruce, Dr. Jamie Azdair and China Kantner, Robert Marchese, Paul Body, Dan Kessel, David and Jan Kessel, Casey Kramer, Denny Rosencrantz, Freddie Gruber, Jim and Cynthia Keltner, Charlie Watts, Patti Drew, Stan Levey, Eric Burdon, Paul Jones, Ray Davies, David Carr, Ahmet Ertegun, Jerry Wexler, Art Fleischer, Suzanne Childre, Shel Talmy, Phil A. Yeend, NSI Sound & Video, Inc., Ole and Jutta Georg, OGM Music, Ken Kaplan, Holly George-Warren, Curtis Hanson, Jane Garcia, Olive, Jessica Hundley, Nancy La Perch, Warren Moon, Keyshawn Johnson, Lauren Glassman, Jim Brosnan, George Clayton Johnson, Doris Kearns Goodwin, Karen Dusenbery, Sophie Auclair, Charles Lloyd, Brian Wilson, Richard Williams, Hal Blaine, Stan Ross, Dave Gold, Larry Levine, Don Randi and The Baked Potato, "Wrecking Crew" alums and anyone who played on the albums "Pet Sounds," "Surrealistic Pillow," "Forever Changes," and "Way Out West," Janis Zavala, Nicole Spector, Steve Nice, Gail, Stevie Wonder, Fats Domino, Sandie Shaw, Bob Hite, Mitchell and Jackie of Antenne, Al and Donna DeLory, Lynn Grossman, Dick Clark, Casey Kasem, The Premiers, Pat & Lolly Vegas, Famous Hooks, Roger Corman, Robert Weiss, Ice Cube, Elliot Kendall, David and Eva Leaf, Les McCann, Gene Harris, Marty Balin, Paul Kantner, Grace Slick, Mick Farren, Bunny Wailer, Roger Steffens and your family, Dan Bourgoise, Gypsy Boots, Gary Null, Gary Stewart, Cole Cartwright, Lenny Moore, Jim Brown, Shannon Sharpe, Jim Plunkett, Sherry Hendrick and Mick Vranich, Crow Indians, Edward Abbey.

KBCA, KGFJ, KMET, KFWB, KRLA, KPPC, KBLA, KUSC, KDAY, KLAC, XERB, John Koenig, Jenny Eliscu, George Varga, Blair Jackson, Ken Sharp,

Gordon Jee, Greg Loescher, Danny Sugerman, Ben Edmonds, Jaan Uhelszki, John Flocken, Patti and Gavin MacLeod, Stuart Williams, Stephen Parker, Dr. Gilbert, Dr. Steven Jacobson, the Kubernick family, Rita Moreno, Anne Bancroft, Michael MacDonald, Chris Darrow, Maya Rudolph, Scott Goddard, Chelsea Peretti, Sherry Daly, Roger Daltrey, Lauren Graham, Heather Harris and her dogs, Mr. Twister, Badly Drawn Boy, The Turtles, The Byrds, Morley Bartnoff, Miles Ciletti, Louie Lista, Paul Eggett, Harold Sherrick, Lana, Leslie, Robert, Johnny Rivers, Richard Bosworth, Andrew Loog Oldham, Gered Mankowitz, Henry Diltz, Jeff Beck, Christopher Hitchens, Susan Faludi, Amiri Baraka, David Dalton, Bobby "Blue" Bland, Michael Point, G. Brown, Marsha Hunt, Lee Grant, Bernard Gordon, Anne Francis, Ruta Lee, Robert Vaughn, Anton Kline, Al Hernandez, Terry Kirkman, Lou Rawls, Freddie Scott, Al Green, Mya, Beyonce Knowles.

Vin Scully, Rex Wilson, Dr. Robert Wolfe, Robert Leslie Dean, Bill Holdship, Richard Havers, Mick Brown, D.A. Pennebaker, Greg Reitman, Moby Disc, Mother Superior, Henry Rollins, William Claxton, Willie Mitchell, Cher, Bette Midler, Cheryl "Salt" James, Zanti Misfits, Toulouse and Sally Engelhardt and your "Twilight Zone" daughters, Jello Biafra, Al Kooper, Robbie Robertson, Ian Blair, Jane Rose, Bill Maher, Aime Joseph, Laura Cohen, Lee Joseph, Lenny Kaye, Bruce Springsteen, Little Steven and his "Underground Garage" radio show, Holly Cara Price, Denise, Gloria, Mark Felsot, Laurette, Carolyn Hughes, Audri, Eddie Call, Jr., Soupy Sales, White Fang, Black Tooth, Patti Smith, Walter Bernstein, Carl Foreman, Burt Lancaster, Tony Curtis, Shirley Manson, Oscar Garza, Jeff Garcia, Eric Karros, Richard Cromelin, Steve Hochman, Geoff Boucher, Lina Lecaro, Natalie Nichols, Steve Appleford, Chuck Crisafulli, Todd Everett, Tony Sheen, Ruth Price at The Jazz Bakery.

Sandy Koufax, Larry and Norm Sherry, Maury Wills, Tommy Davis, Lou Johnson, Willie Davis, Reggie Smith, Mike Scioscia, Mickey Hatcher, Domenic Priore, Mark London, David Kramer, Brian Chidester, Jim Ladd, Tom Leykis, Nelson and Lil Gary, Burton Cummings, Bob Dylan, Gena Rowlands, Kirk Douglas, Richard Pryor, Drew and Jill Steele, Insect Surfers, Hal Jepsen, Bobby Womack, Toni Basil, Dr. Robert Lorenz, Mitch Meyers, Michael Horowitz, Roy Carr, Barney Hoskyns, Thom Yorke, David Bowie, Quincy Jones, Billy May, Stan Freberg, James Worthy, Michael Cooper, Kurt Rambis, Robert Horry, Richard Schuman, Richard Kimble and Lt. Gerard, Art Aragon, The Destroyer, Brother Matt, Richard Derrick, Robert Hilburn, Justin Pierce, Lisa Derrick, Don Calfa, The Chambers Brothers, The Mamas & the Papas, Donovan, Kaleidoscope, Keven McAlester, Jeff Tamarkin, Ian Hunter, "Alice," Alyson Carter, Chris Carter, "The Howard Stern Show,"

"Nigella Bites," Frank Sontag, "Impact Program," Lee Klein, "Roy Of Hollywood," Dave Emory, The Rascals, Cosmo Topper, The Malibooz, Splat Winger, Sam, Mardi, Michael Des Barres, Elmer and Mario, John Walker, Scott Walker, Levi Stubbs, Ice-T, Gary Jackson, Geoff Emerick, Bill Russell, Larry Bird, Kareem Abdul-Jabbar, Magic Johnson, Byron Scott, Michael Jordan, Gary Williams, Juan Dixon, Phil Jackson, John R. Wooden, Bill Walton, Dean Smith, Rick Fox, Roy Williams, Mike Krzyzewski, Barry Miles, Paul McCartney, Steve Winwood, Remi Kabaka and his talking drum, John Feins, David M. Berger, Harry E. Northup, Holly Prado, Lisa Freeman, Eloise Klein Healy, Kathi Martin, Wanda Coleman, Marisela Norte, Linda J. Albertano, Luis Campos, Dr. Noah Young, Jerry West, Elgin Baylor, Pat Riley.

Sompun Thai Restaurant, Krispy Kreme Doughnuts, Paru's Indian Vegetarian Restaurant, Genmai Sushi, Airport Village, the Musso & Frank Grill, Taste of India, the Apple Pan, El Tepeyac, the Original Pantry, the Fish Shanty, Dr. Hogly Wogly's Tyler Texas BBQ, the Ravi Shankar Center, the Bodhi Tree, Peter Piper, Randy Haecker, Sheryl Farber, Bill Bentley, Liz Rosenberg, Jasmine Vega, Sujata Murthy, Todd Nakamine, Karen Weissen, Sharrin Summers, Diana Faust, Frank Orlando, Ray Charles, Julissa Marquez, Stan Chambers, Lauren Sanchez, Jennifer Sabih, Roy Firestone, Chris Berman, David Robinson, Tim Duncan, Suzy Kolber, George Putnam, Larry McCormick, Patricia Lopez and the TV show "Mex 2 the Max." In fact, Melissa, Tricia and all the hosts on LaTv; Theta Sound Studio, Radio Shack, Kevin Burns, Van Ness Films, Ernest Lehman, Paul Schrader, Diane Gamboa, Hunter Hancock, Jim Dunfrund, Dede Allen, Walter Murch; Gabrielle for the iced tea, Larry King, Steve Lieber, Dennis Hopper, Curtis Harrington, Monte Hellman, William DeVaughn, Barbara Lewis, Deon Jackson, Barbara Mason, Rick Henn, Lance Alworth, Arthur Herman, the Monkees, Brenton Wood, Shelley Winters, Johnny Otis, Brendan Mullen, Dick Gregory, Robert Forster, Dick Miller, Harvey Keitel, Miss Haney, Mrs. Neshat, Dave Kephart, Joel Engel, David A. Barmack, Vivian Sisskin, Nancy Retchin, Kathe Schreyer, Randy Wood, John Wood, Hell Bent for Leather, Flash Records, Dolphin's of Hollywood, Lewin's Record Paradise, The Frigate, Norty's, Hollywood Free Press Bookstore & Kazoo, Wallich's Music City, The Parisian Room, The Ash Grove, BeBop Records, Lanny Waggoner, Lou Adler, Bruce Gary, Arthur Lee, Andy Paley, Madonna, Liberty Records, World Pacific Records, Brian Auger, Georgie Fame, John Mayall, Jerry Butler, The Kinks, The Zombies, The Beatles, Manfred Mann, Sylvie Simmons, Dr. Helen Caldicott, Chuck Berry, The Who, Todd Rundgren, Buffalo Springfield, Dustin Hoffman, American Cinematheque, B.B. King, Jack Nicholson, Malcolm McDowell, Levon Helm, Stan Ridgway, Gore Vidal, Rodney Bingenheimer, Johnny Winter, Rosemarie Patronette, Sunglasses Danny, Johnny Legend, Russ Regan, Frank Wilson,

Kim Fowley, Ryan O'Neal, Rudy Ray Moore, Leon Russell, Elton John, Clem Burke, James Brown, Luther Ingram, Johnny Carson, Muhammad Ali, Don Snowden, Don Waller, Phast Phreddie, Jeff Morrison, Jeremy Gilien, Martin Roberts, Jack Nitzsche, Jr., Jill Fraser, Kobe Bryant, Shaquille O'Neal, Henry Bibby, Steve Lavin, Sir George Martin, Martin Banner, Pooch, Toni King, Shan, Deepak Chopra, Peter Gabriel, David Branfman, Marina and Mick, Caroline (Dark Horse), Lisa Mitchell Silverman, Shadow Morton, Larry Taylor, Tom Johnson, Ronnie Wood, Bill Wyman, Mick Jagger, Keith Richards, Bill Withers, Burt Bacharach, Hal David, Jimmy Webb, Jerry Leiber, Mike Stoller, The Olympics, The Funk Brothers, Hugh M. Hefner, Bob Lefsetz, Tex Winter, Jeff Ballenberg, Amanda Hallay, Brian Shaw, Mike Watt, Dean Dean the Taping Machine, Geoff Baker, Kelly Brooks, Amy Dean, Shellee, Andy Jackson, Grelun Landon, Michael Hartman, Steve and Phil, Jim Roup, Melissa Tandysh, Evelyn Schlatter, Glenda Madden, Tim Doherty, Eddie Murray, Gary Carter, Merry Clayton, Billy Hinsche, Jane Pryor St. Clair, and Dr. David B. Wolfe.

Special Thanks to:
The British David Carr: Thank you for your help in preparing this book. I appreciate your participation in the endeavour. All I can offer to you after our last holiday toxic obligation gig is something my father and Bill Walton's dad once said: "If you're working on Christmas, then you're doing something good . . ." Also for reminding me that I do indeed have "journalistic dual citizenship" and am allowed to utilize both American and British spellings of words. Pass the bangers and mash?

Andrew Loog Oldham, for the cuff links, your studio fondness for reverb and tape echo, pointing me to the film, "Expresso Bongo," as well as asking me to write and chronicle my Hollywood heritage for your own 2*Stoned* autobiography . . . I felt for a moment I was a Junior Writer on the lot at MGM in Culver City, and that assignment aided the original outline for *This Is Rebel Music.*

Chris "I need to Billy Strayhorn just the opening paragraph of your book introduction" Darrow. CD: I welcomed that gesture and relish all the other 3:00 A.M. phone calls. You know I'll always play percussion in your pit band. Healing instead of entertainment. Coolness for the bottle of MSM, by the way. Nice to be able to throw a spiral again.

Bennie Davenport, of Blazer Youth Community Services, sociologist, and basketball coach, who called at 4:22 A.M. on my last birthday and said, "I just read and loved something you wrote on Berry Gordy and Motown

Records. You can definitely distribute the rock, young man. You're now the two guard with the pill in the neighborhood." What an endorsement, when I know the players and young people you've mentored. Besides, I've always told you that you need some vanilla on your squad. Mr. Davenport, now can you tell me that story about seeing Sam Cooke, Johnnie Taylor, and Otis Redding sing in a tent show in Florida?

Jack Nitzsche, who saw Etta James at the California Club, among other things, and years later yelled at me over the telephone, "Stop producing records for a while—you're not writing enough, you little motherfucker!"

Denny Bruce, who left a voice-mail message after viewing portions of the first manuscript of this book. "I must say, like Curtis Mayfield, you believe in people and their music. You're Donovan McNabb, Roger Staubach, John Elway, and Dan Fouts in the huddle. You put together a strong set list of veterans and ran the west coast offense, brother. You took the ball to 'The House.'" DB: Glad you believed I could run the option play. I could hear John Facenda calling the drive. "Quit bending them wires . . ."

Matt Greenwald, who uttered the monumental suggestion, "Man, this is strong word and music information! When you take some time from saving the planet and everyone in the Southern California area, and the UCLA basketball team is gone from the NCAA Tournament, why don't you check this UNM editor David Farber out? I met him when I was with Michelle Phillips of the Mamas & the Papas at a Monterey International Pop Festival conference last week. He's got a 'Graham Nash Sixties vibe' and I know he's gonna dig on your book. It needs to get published on a 'PCL' level. Here's his e-mail . . ." Matt: In addition to being a tremendous good karma investment, your technical sensitivity to my individual artist introductions and interviews were totally in the pocket and very productive in the clutch this past season. You pulled out some close games, like L.A. Dodgers' relief pitcher Eric Gagne coming out of the bull pen in the ninth inning to earn a save.

Vivian Sisskin, from "Positively 4th Street": Don't worry, I'll never forget 5th Street, either. I'm so proud of your work in the field of communications.

Laura Nyro: I treasure our last phone call conversation. More than you'll ever know.

Ray Manzarek, total team player, for vision and involvement, and turning me on to the Jazz Crusaders, Charles Mingus, and Bobby Timmons. Ray, I think I got it locked. It's A minor against F# minor.

Robert Sherman: Kosher Puppy Award Winner. You keep scanning the Zohar.

Mr. Paul Body: "See? This is how they do us . . ." As you suggested, "I'm your whitey."

Donna DeLory: "bliss," expansion, rhythm & hues.

Ram Dass: For the signed copy of your book, "Be Here Now." "Love, Serve, Remember." Namaste, friend.

Confidential to Mary Weiss of the Shangri-Las: "Tell me more."

William "Smokey" Robinson.

Dan and David Kessel: Let me say it one more time to you characters, like officer Joe Friday (Jack Webb) on "Dragnet." I care as much about writing as your dad, guitarist Barney Kessel, did when he was booked to play and sight-read on those 7:30 A.M. Warner Bros. cartoon recording sessions. So, it's no Mose Allison late set at Shelly's Manne-Hole. You guys may be my favorite rhythm section, but can't you Kessel cats deal with the concept that some of us have to work the next morning! I don't care if you've got an 8-track cartridge of Patsy Cline for the ride home. I've got a book to produce, man . . .

Danny Weizmann, who dropped some iron, sent me a note applauding the real-to-reel L.A. flavor that permeates my work and life, and demanding that I stick with my question and answer format for potential book publication. Shredder, I got it covered: Allen Ginsberg taught me, "First thought, best thought." I will never forget that benefit reading we did at the Braille Institute on Vermont Ave. Regarding the Ravi Shankar and Grace Slick entries, maybe that's what you get when you mix Norm's Restaurant and the Self-Realization Fellowship on Sunset Boulevard with a Blue Note Ojai chaser.

Dennis Dragon, you said it many years ago, between a glossy set of short waves, body-surfing in Malibu: "We don't define it, we just do it." Please, no plastic tips on drum sticks when we're recording.

Kim Fowley, who ran down the entire Liberty Records catalog, along with the label's producers and engineers, beginning at 2:29 A.M. one morning: Roy, Paul, and I enjoyed your Sugar Pie Di Santo live in Stockton concert story, and the early Los Angeles music tales on Motown Records, Dee Clark, T-Bone Walker, and B.B. King. KF: You're totally tuneful!

Michael MacDonald in Australia, for comprehending my music journalism in *Goldmine*, and for your invitational missive, "My girl Linda would like to make you potato pancakes when you come to our country." Count me in. No Vegemite! Sour cream, applesauce, and horseradish mandatory.

Author Miss Pamela Des Barres: The advice you gave me in front of the Argyle Hotel following the screening and reception for "The Man From Elysian Fields" really registered.

Ian Copeland and your *Wild Thing* book, bleeding for punk rock, and telling me that you enjoyed my *Melody Maker* weekly music news column before anyone ever complimented me on it.

Nancy Retchin: Just the sound of your voice, nutrition advice, seaweed salad, the Effervescent Vitamin C 1000 mg tablets, being a critter, Mato & Cottea, the Jeff Beck and Elvis Costello concerts, your golf swing, constant concern, and calling from England one night asking me, "Are you working on your book?" "Trying. Definitely trying."

Joey Ramone: I miss our phone conferences with Rodney Bingenheimer. You were definitely right about television anchor Maria Bartiromo on CNBC. Have not seen TV eyes so piercing since actress Susan Oliver appeared on "The Fugitive."

Rosemarie Renee Patronette, who played the first Ice Cube CD eight times one night in front of me: You always dazzle me with your decorative style and devotion to real deal music. Like Stevie Wonder sings, "You got it bad girl." Rosemarie, you are a constant dance of courage. I dug hearing Mick tell you at the Staples Center gig, "Nice to see you again." My best to your Italian father, Sam, for going on faith and giving Dr. Stanley Baker an opportunity early in his career. His hands helped my hands . . . Hey Wyline— "Baby You Got It."

Ellen Berman, for your friendship, and for saying a long time ago, after seeing my high school and multiple college newspaper rejection slips, "How dare these people say you'll never be a writer and that you have no communication skills? I bet you'll outlast them all . . ." Ellen: I've always remembered your kind words of encouragement. Then again, that's what I would expect a compassionate white chick from Ladera Heights to say, whose father is named Harvey . . .

Kirk Silsbee, for being Kirk Silsbee and bringing over recordings by Lenny

Bruce and Lord Buckley, as this book became a reality. Kirk, you're the only person who believes me that I used to subscribe to *Playboy* magazine primarily for their editorial content and monthly question and answer feature interviews.

Ken Kubernik, "What does mom ever say about your Bill Evans LP collection?"

Phil Bunch, a terrific drummer who produces awesome music with Franck Balloffet, and even offered grammar correction one night, as we were about to watch Eddie Izzard at the Henry Fonda Theater in Hollywood: Your mother was an English teacher, wasn't she?

Roy Trakin, New York Knicks fan who gave me Yiddish lessons: Roy, you and your *HITS* staff were always helpful on some of the earlier first published interviews now fully realized in this book. You were often receptive to some "classic rock" artists being interviewed in a youth-driven periodical, and I appreciated the opportunity. That being noted, as a native Angeleno, I will never forget your (comical?) advice, when I first started on this book endeavor, to "tell literary agents, book publishers, and editors that you're from New York. Dude, you could pass." Hey, Mr. Columbia Film School graduate: This isn't a scene from Douglas Sirk's "Imitation of Life" movie . . .

Little Steven, for your vision of rock-'n'-roll, and re-connecting: SVZ, you make many of my musical associates still believe in destiny. Peace and solidarity. "Power to the People."

Buddy Collette: You've constantly demonstrated a commitment to community and unity, and performed multiple roles for decades, moving our melodic literature forward for so many others. I am so grateful that your existence and constant healing instrumental actions prove "Hollywood is not a town that runs on heat, but runs on beat." I've nicked a few of your riffs for this book and my journey.

Harry E. Northup, poet-actor, who saw my first theater reading, understood and totally enjoyed the Calicentric music rhythms in my writing abilities, when so many people at the time had "been mean to me." Harry, you are a friend of truth, creativity, discussion, and baseball.

Fred Shuster and Barone's Pizza.

Nancy Sinatra and her thin crust cheese Domino's Pizza tip.

Rodney Bingenheimer, of the "Rodney on the Roq" radio show: For friendship, access to your record collection, the chance to hear advance CDs, and especially your constant belief in rock-'n'-roll. Believe me, your mother Marian will know I got over. She's here in spirit.

And always, for Phil Spector: From one Harvey to another, it's been stated many times before: "To Know You Is to Love You." Your songwriting, record productions, postcards, letters, e-mails, jokes, home gatherings, studio invites, and support over the decades have made some real contributions to my world, and to *This Is Rebel Music*, and occasionally, as Anthony Fremont (Billy Mumy) said in the "Twilight Zone" episode "It's a Good Life," "put me in the cornfield." Back to Mono . . .

To David Farber and David Holtby at the University of New Mexico Press . . . "Obviously Two Believers."

David Farber was a pleasure to work with in our collaboration, and was always receptive to the artists I profiled and included, during the construction of this tome. He wanted to know initially about the geography I wanted to document, and now, with this book, we all get to investigate it together. Dr. Farber, your involvement and editing direction were extremely important in guiding *This Is Rebel Music: The Harvey Kubernik InnerViews*.

This is a short list of credits. Plenty of other people have helped "along the way," and many events made this book possible.

Dedications

Dedicated to those who came before, delivered and passed:

To the memory of: Ray Coleman, Derek Taylor, Jack Nitzsche, Sonny Bono, Allen Ginsberg, Dr. Stanley B. Baker, Shel Silverstein, D. Boon, James Coburn, John Cassavetes, Rupert Cross, Tom Dowd, Maurice Gibb, Penny Valentine, Ian McDonald, Lester Bangs, Marty Cerf, Redd Foxx, Mickey Katz, Spike Jones, Frank Zappa, Charlie Rich, Sterling Hayden, Lee Marvin, Marc Bolan, Doug Sahm, Marie Windsor, Tennessee Williams, Harvey Kurtzman, Dewey Weber, Con, Murray the K, Johnny Guitar Watson, Samuel Arkoff, Sam Fuller, John Frankenheimer, Chick Hearn, Jeff Corey, Bo Belinsky, Johnny Roseboro, Abraham Polonsky, Peter Tosh, Bob Marley, George Harrison, Ken Kesey, Dalton Trumbo, Carey McWilliams, Upton Sinclair, Will Thornbury, Charles Bukowski, Paul Jarrico, Waldo Salt, Ring W. Lardner, Jr., Aleksandr Pushkin, Kim Hunter, HUAC victims, Suzan Carson, Henry Mancini, Bobby Troup, Julie London, David Janssen, Percy Mayfield, Donny Hathaway, Duane Allman, Bobby Hatfield, Lenny Bruce, Lisle, Otto Friedrich, Terry Southern, Jack Kerouac, Albert King, Paul Butterfield, Michael Bloomfield, Janis Joplin, Jimi Hendrix, Velvert Turner, Brian Jones, Ian Stewart, Laurence Harvey, Major Lance, Bryan MacLean, Waylon Jennings, Ray Brown, Duke Ellington, Albert Stinson, Eric Dolphy, Billy Stewart, Marvin Gaye, David Ruffin, Eddie Kendricks, Curtis Mayfield, Muddy Waters, Eddie Cochran, Gene Vincent, Elvis Presley, Sam Cooke, Rufus Thomas, Pops Staples, Dennis Wilson, Carl Wilson, Kevin Bartnoff, Randy California, Ewart Abner, John Carpenter, Paul Picard, Peter Matz, Jerry Colonna, Mel Torme, James Wong Howe, Jackie Robinson, Campy, Don Drysdale, Jim Murray, Mud, Woody Stroode, Kenny Washington, Bob Waterfield, Norm Van Brocklin, Sid Gillman, Johnny Unitas, Wilt Chamberlain, Bob Hayes, Rick Griffin, Mickey Dora, Archie Moore, Tim Moore, Hoyt Wilhelm, Ted Williams, Dr.

Jonas Salk, Nadine Darrow, Donna Darrow, Johnny Mercer, John Allison ("Jack") Carr, Joan Muriel Carr, Harry Boersma, Verna ("Esmereldy") Boersma, Mr. and Mrs. William Retchin, Stanley Pierce, Buddy Baker, Art Pepper, Chet Baker, Shorty Rogers, Rene Hall, Rod Serling, Claudia Jennings, Sally Baker, Pacific Ocean Park, Mary Wells, Walter E. Hurst, Lawrence Tierney, Jane Greer, Robert Mitchum, Walter T. Lacey, Harry Nilsson, Joe Pyne, Dick Lane, Eric Gilbertson, Lowell George, Rick Nelson, Mel Taylor, Barry Pritchard, Ritchie Valens, Alan Freed, B. Mitchel Reed, Wolfman Jack, Tom Donahue, Jerry Garcia, Roger Miller, Stan Kenton, Miles Davis, Douglas Fowley, Floyd Cramer, Chet Atkins, Erma Franklin, Dusty Springfield, Steve Douglas, Ray Pohlman, Rick Danko, Richard Manuel, Billy Higgins, James Jamerson, William "Benny" Benjamin, Robert White, Earl Van Dyke, Willie Dixon, Jim Morrison, Carmen Dragon, Buddy Rich, Frank Sinatra, Jack Lemon, John Lennon, B.J. Baker, Dexter Gordon, Leroy Vinegar, Milt Hinton, Bobby Sheen, Curtis Amy, Brook Benton, Nicky Hopkins, Michele Myer, Richard Creamer, Joey Ramone, Dee Dee Ramone, Warren Oates, Katrin Cartlidge, Oliver Johnson, J.W. Alexander, Sammy Davis, Jr., Richard "Pistol" Allen, Johnny Griffith, Guy Stevens, Noel Redding, Badatunde Olatunji, John Phillips, Grandpa Jack, Grandma Mary, Candy Dog, Howie Epstein, Richard Bien, Gene Panzer, Keith Moon, Homer Banks, Robert Stack, Jeffrey Barnes, Don & Dewey, Nina Simone, Godfrey Cambridge, Jackie Gleason, Mr. Moto, Freddie Blassie, Lance Loud, June Carter Cash, Johnny Cash, Mickie Most, Larry Doby, Greg Dwinnell, Conway Twitty, John Schlesinger, Stirling Silliphant, Gene Page, Barry White, Ollie McLaughlin, Erik Braunn, Jack Elam, Elvira Turri Easton, Sam Phillips, and Ethan James.